The Living Letters of
Mother Mary

The Living Letters of
Mother Mary

*Love + Blessings
Barb Beach,
Scribe*

Mother Mary, Author

Barbara Beach, Scribe

Copyright © 2012 by Barbara Beach.

MILL CITY PRESS

Mill City Press, Inc.
212 3rd Avenue North, Suite 290
Minneapolis, MN 55401
612.455.2294
www.millcitypublishing.com

All rights reserved. No part of this publication may be reproduced, stored in a retrieval system, or transmitted, in any form or by any means, electronic, mechanical, photocopying, recording, or otherwise, without the prior written permission of the author.

ISBN-13: 978-1-938223-47-1
LCCN: 2012941571

Cover design by Lubosh Cech,
Oko Design Studio, Portland, Oregon,
www.okodesignstudio.com

Cover art by Ann Rothan, Sacred Artist
Water color "DIVINE INTERVENTION"
1.800.685.1895, email: annlee360@aol.com
Prints available: www.whereangelsdwellsacredart.com

Printed in the United States of America

IN ACKNOWLEDGEMENT AND APPRECIATION FOR THE GIFTS THEY SHARE WITH THE WORLD.

To: Lubosh Cech, Naked River Films

Thank you for the incredible video that you put together for, Mother Mary's Kickstarter Project. You are a gifted artist and filmmaker. Your talents continued one step further as you designed the cover of Mother Mary's book. Thank you for the kindness, patience, and understanding that you shared with me during this whole process. www.luboshcech.com, 503-780-6318

To: Diana Byrnes, Intuitive Spiritual Counselor

Thank you for all the energy clearing and grounding work that we did together over these last months. Your help in clearing old core issues that surfaced during the process of bringing this book to its publishing pathway has been invaluable. http://www.dianabyrnes.com, 503-866-5900

To: Ann Rothan, Artist

Thank you for allowing me to use your painting as the art work for the cover of Mother Mary's book. Your kindness and support is so very appreciated. http://www.whereangelsdwell.com, 1-800-685-1895

EARTH ANGEL SUPPORTERS OF THE BOOK CALLED "THE LIVING LETTERS OF MOTHER MARY"

"THANK YOU" to my daughter Laura Black for her constant everyday support of this work and me.

"THANK YOU" to all the Backers of Mother Mary's Kickstarter Project.

Larry Nordholm and Gayle Smelser
Josie Coleman
Micki Swenson
Reanaleia
Georgina Jones
Karla Jandle
Gary and Wanda Witherspoon
Pat Durkin
Elayne LeBarron
Deborah Albrecht and Patrick Hummel
Lisa Bossio
Doreen Pierson
Shirley Catanzaro
Victoria Mogilner
Liz Beckman
Carol Johnson
Carol Ann Ivey
Karen and Dave Curl
Peggy Black
Pennie and Tom McGee
Colleen Storey
Ginger Carter
Jane Harding
Jo Durkin
Sandy Cerelli
Terry Andrews
Laura Black

"THANK YOU" to all the people who helped to edit this book and these letters.

INTRODUCTION

TO THE READERS OF MY BOOK

Dearest Readers,

    I am thrilled and excited that I am writing this letter to you. Writing this letter now means that time is near for my book to be published and out into each of your hands. I have been waiting sometime for this to happen. I am most anxious for you to have these words and letters. It is beyond important for each of you to know how much you are loved and looked after by all the beings here in my world. There are millions of beings there on Mother Earth who do not know that they are loved and cherished. THIS IS WHAT MY BOOK IS ABOUT. THE WHOLE PURPOSE OF MY BOOK IS TO LET YOU KNOW THAT WE ARE HERE LOVING YOU AND WANTING TO HELP YOU. THERE ARE MANY CHANGES THAT ARE HAPPENING TO EACH OF YOU AND TO THE WHOLE OF YOUR WORLD.

    The world, as you know, is in the process of a great change. Your world is going from being what I call a 3D world to a 5D world. I will explain to you what I mean by a 3D world. A 3D world is one in which the beings who live there are most interested in power, money, greed, hate, violence, war and self. They are most interested in what they have, what they can get and how important they think they are. This has been going on for centuries on Mother Earth, getting more and more extreme and out of control. People are dying. People are starving. People are killing each other. People are losing their homes and jobs. People are hurting the ones they love out of frustration, pain, and despair. Your governments are non-functional and at war within themselves. THIS IS WHAT I CALL A 3D WORLD.

    Over the last few years have you noticed that your world is not working very well? Your old systems are breaking down and becoming non-functional. In different countries of your world, people are standing up and saying they will no longer be controlled, abused and beaten down. They are banding together and saying no to all the extremes and atrocities that are taking place. It is no longer OK for a few to live with the extreme excesses provided by the work and tears of the many. THIS IS PART OF THE PROCESS YOUR WORLD MUST GO THROUGH ON ITS WAY INTO THE 5D WORLD. Many of the people who are standing up and doing the fighting for the changes do not realize that they are indeed warriors for the coming 5D world. The warriors only know that the world has to change and their lives and their worlds have become unbearable.

There are many other beings in your world that are leading the way into the 5D world. I am calling those beings the Wayshowers and Keepers of the Light. Many of you know them by the fact of how different they are from the other people you know. In your world, you might refer to them by saying they walk to a different beat than the average guy. Well, you are right. They do walk to a different beat. These Wayshowers or Keepers of the Light are more aware of the people in my world. Often, they can hear our voices in their heads, or they will see shadows of us as we pass through your world. They are often intuitive and are aware of information that they have no logical way of knowing. Most often they are not logical people; they are more heart-centered. They also have a knowing that all the beings of your world are connected and make a circle of the whole. Their knowing includes the knowledge that each person is responsible for their own life, the energy they put into the world and what they take back from the world. Wayshowers and Keepers of the Light know without a doubt that LOVE is the purpose of your Mother Earth and the connecting rod between all people.

Now and in the days to come you will notice that the Wayshowers and Keepers of the Light are living in a much different way from many of the people in your world. They are on a purposeful journey into what I call the 5D world.

Let me tell you about the 5D world. The 5D world is about LOVE. In fact, that is the most important word in the 5D world. LOVE has reached such a place of importance because it is the source of light and life in the 5D. All beings that reside in this world live from what I call a heart-centered place. There are no struggles for who is better or who has more or who is more important. All beings of the 5D world are equally important. All are accepting of one another. All are reaching out in love and heart-felt connection. Judgments and right or wrong thinking have been left in the 3D world. There is no room here for such thoughts or actions. THERE IS NO MORE WAR, NO MORE VIOLENCE, NO MORE GREED, AND NO MORE POWER STRUGGLES. All of that is in the past and is no longer alive and living here in 5D. As you can see, this 5D world is the exact opposite of the world you are now living in. The Wayshowers and Keepers of the Light are and will continue to show you the pathway into this new way of living and being. I say to you, watch how they are living and what they are doing. They are here to help you make this journey. It is part of their purpose for being here on Earth at this time.

The very most important message of this letter is that I am here with you every step of the way and I will continue to be here for you always. Please come and visit me on my blog: http://lettersfrommothermary.blogspot.com or on my website: www.thelivinglettersofmothermary.com for on-going letters and happenings.

Know that there are hundreds of thousands of beings here with me in my world all waiting to provide you with love, help, and support. You only need to ask for help, and we will be there. You are each greatly loved and cherished beyond your wildest dreams. I LOVE YOU, I LOVE YOU, AND I LOVE YOU.

Know you only need call my name and I will be there.
In Love, Mother Mary
12/12/11

LETTER 1

Dear Ones,

I have been waiting many years to be able to share my thoughts through my friend Anna. Yes, I do know that her name is not Anna in this form she now uses. In the lifetime that we shared I knew her by the name of Anna. So I will continue to call her by that name at this time.

My only words to each and everyone one of you this day is that you are loved greatly, just as you are. You each think inside of your mind that you cannot be loved unless you change and become more perfect, better in every way. Then if you are very good, very right, and very perfect, then you might be lovable. There are some of you who believe in your hearts and minds that there is nothing you can do or change to make you lovable. My heart hurts for each of you that believe in this way. None of those thoughts are true.

I love each and everyone one of you just as you are. Most important that you know and remember there are no exceptions to my knowing.

My knowing is that each and every being is lovable, just as they are. Please allow the love to come into you and allow yourselves to know it in each and every cell and organ of your body.

As you read or hear of these words know at that moment my arms are around you and that I am here with you. Stop and close your eyes and allow me to be with you for just one moment. For I love you as you are. I ask nothing of you but to allow me to love you just as you are.

In Love, Mother Mary
10/1/10

LETTER 2

Dear Ones,

Join me in feeling JOY and HAPPINESS. In your minds eye simply take my hand and we will walk in the garden of JOY. It will only take a moment in time to come and be with me here in the garden, but it will feed you for weeks and weeks.

On your earth, you have not a spot where you can go to feel just JOY. Your days and weeks are about work and making money, finding a way to survive, and holding yourselves and your families together. You are in need of more than that to feed your HEART and SOUL.

So again I say, please come with me to the garden of JOY. Remember it will only take a moment of your time.

My hand is always there. You only have to think my name and I will come and walk with you in the garden. This is a gift that I give to you with love and joy. Allow yourselves to accept my gift. Know that you are worthy of having this gift and the many other gifts that will be coming your way.

Your earth is in a transition right now and each of you needs support, love, and encouragement on your journey. At this time, in your world, you are in need of joy and happiness more than any other time in your history. Know that I am here with you and there are many other helpers here to be with you. So stop now close your eyes and take my hand and walk with me in the garden of JOY.

In Love, Mother Mary
10/5/10

LETTER 3

Dear Ones,

    Yes, I am here and I will continue to be here every day. You and your world are in so much need of LOVE and ENCOURAGEMENT. I am always right here; you have only to call my name and I will make myself known to you. The knowing that I am here will come differently to each of you. Some will feel my presence very strongly; some will feel me very lightly. I will be that feeling of comfort that flows through your mind and heart.

    I ask that you trust and know that I am here for each and everyone of you. Some want so desperately to believe that I would come to them, but it is hard for you to imagine that I could care about you. Your feelings of unimportance and unworthiness are within in you. That is not the way I feel about you. Each and every one of you is important to me and to the world. Each person is radiant and magnificent in my eyes. Each is special, unique and precious within my heart.

    Take your hand and touch your heart, know that I am there waiting for you. Do not wait to do this later. Do it right now. Simply put your hand on your heart for just a moment and allow yourself to feel my presence. It does not matter where you are or what you are doing. I will always be there for you. Allow me to walk with you this day.

In Love, Mother Mary
10/06/10

LETTER 4

Dear Ones,

You are going into the time of contemplation and separation. As fall and winter is here or getting ready to be here, there is more time to exam yourselves and your lives. Each year you find yourself lacking in your thoughts of who you are and the place you occupy in your world. All of this falls back into feelings of unworthiness and being unlovable.

Each of you is unable to see what or how you affect the people you connect with each day. Words of love, respect and appreciation are not shared with others. Those words are kept inside and hidden away in your hearts and minds. It is time to share those thoughts and feelings with the ones you connect with. Let others know how much you appreciate them or love them. And in your sharing of your love, respect, and appreciation, your hearts will open and allow you to rejoice and shine in your light.

As I share my heart thoughts with you, allow yourselves to bask in the light and love that I am sending your way. Know that there is great love, respect and appreciation being sent from my heart to yours. Be aware of how your heart swells and grows as you accept and allow the feelings inside of you. Know that you also can pass that light on to others by sharing your heart thoughts with them. Allow the light to grow inside of you and then share it with others.

Allow my heart thoughts to surround you and become part of you as you walk your path each day. And remember that you only need say my name and I will be with you.

In Love, Mother Mary
10/07/10

LETTER 5

Dear Ones,

You are so much more than you know or recognize yourselves to be. You live in a universe that is so much more than you know or recognize. You are all a part of a huge framework of worlds or realities that you are not conscious of. Your world, the place you know is changing and emerging into other realities now. Do not be fearful and afraid. Your world is changing rapidly now and who you are as humans is changing rapidly also. Know and trust that we are all here with you to help you during these changes. All is as it is meant to be. You are growing and changing and will no longer be stagnant and accepting of whatever has been.

Your eyes, ears, mind and hearts are opening and expanding to reach out to the new ways that are coming. You each will accept these new changes at different times. Each being will grow and change at their own speed. And that is as it should be.

Do not judge each other by the speed of your changes. Each being must find his or her own way in their own time. Each of you is unique and travels in your own way. There is no right or wrong way to make these changes. Open your hearts and minds to one another and honor each other's journeys and time frames.

Love and honor yourself as you make your journey into the new ways. Love and honor those you see ahead of you on the path and those you see behind you on the path. You are all walking the same path going the same direction.

Know that I am walking beside each and everyone of you. Know that you only need say my name and I will be there. I will walk beside you. I will hold your hand. I will put my arms around you. I will touch your cheek. I will love and hold you in my heart as a precious and most dear gift.

In Love, Mother Mary
10/08/10

LETTER 6
WE ARE ALL ONE

Dear Ones,

You have all heard this many times and most often you agree and say yes we are all one. What does it really mean and do you believe it in your hearts? It would make such a huge difference in how you treat each other if it truly lived in your hearts.

How could there be wars and violence and hate if you truly believed We Are All One. If you are judging the person beside you, in front or in back, then you are judging yourself and saying those words to yourself.

If We Are All One, then you are saying it to me, to God, to Jesus, to Buddha, to your Mother and Father to your husband or wife, and to your children. You all want the same thing. Every single human wants to be loved and cared about. Everyone wants to be important to someone, somewhere. If you are loving and caring about the person next to you, they will pass it to the next person and it can flow around the world, touching each and every being everywhere.

If, for one moment in time, everyone everywhere would just send out love and caring, each of you would be so uplifted. I can see a soft warm cloud of love traveling to each being, surrounding them and holding them in that love.

Take a moment right now as you read my letter to be part of this. Send out your love and feel it coming back to you. Allow your heart to become full to overflowing with love and caring.

Know that I am joining you and sending my love and caring to each of you. You have the power to change your everyday world and the whole world by just stopping for a moment each day to send out your love and caring and knowing it will be coming back to you.

Know that you only need call my name and I will be there.
In Love, Mother Mary
10/09/10

LETTER 7

Dear Ones,

    I am here; I am present in your world. You need only say my name and I will be with you. This is no trick or something that will fade away. This is now. I am real and I will be with you. I offer you love, support, comfort, and hope for a better tomorrow. I am here to remind you to love each other, to be supportive of each other, to reach out and allow yourselves to care, to feel, to hope, to know that your world is hurting and you are hurting, but it does not have to be this way. With very small steps, you and I can start to change the way beings see one another.

    It is time to bring unconditional love on a grand scale back into your world. It is time to allow beings to be who they are. There is no real freedom, unless there is unconditional love.

    As you walk down the street or into the grocery store, look at the people around you, open your hearts, recognize that they are just like you. Do not judge how big or small they are, do not judge how they are dressed, how they wear their hair or what religion they practice, or if they practice any at all. Look into their eyes, break down the barriers, smile and show them you care.

    For some of you, it will take great courage to break down the barriers and for others, it will simply take some of your time. What you receive back will be worth all your efforts. Know that everything starts with unconditional love. Miracles will happen when you reach out and care with open minds and hearts. Know that I love you just as you are. You are perfect.

Know that you only need call my name and I will be there.
In Love, Mother Mary
10/11/10

LETTER 8

Dear Ones,

Here we are again. I find much pleasure in coming every day to be with each and everyone of you. You are reaching out for love and connection from me and in turn you will be giving love and connection to each being that you meet in your daily life. You each are being filled with love and are then able to allow that love to spread and pass to someone else.

This is what your world needs, hand after hand touching, passing love and kindness. There is no time left where you can ignore each other and pretend that we are separate and not connected to each other. We are all connected and the energy you receive is what you will pass on to the next person.

So I am here to fill you with love and then you will be passing that along. So many of your world are desperate for a little kindness, a little caring. Some have gone past the point where they will be able to feel it when it comes their way, but if we keep a continuous flow of love passing out they will finally be able to come back and feel it.

Your lives were never meant to be lived in loneliness, separation, despair and fear. So this day I ask that you allow some amount of these feelings that you carry in your hearts to dissipate and to allow love and joy to fill this space within you.

Know that I am here with you and that I have more than enough love to fill all your hearts to overflowing. Allow the harsh and lonely feelings to dissipate and know that there is more than enough love and caring to fill you up. Know that we are on a journey and that I will be here to walk with you on this journey.

Know that you need only say my name and I will be there.
In Love, Mother Mary
10/12/10

LETTER 9

Dear Ones,

I am blessed that you allow me to speak to you through my letters. I am overjoyed that you are reading and hearing my words that you are feeling the love and energy that I am sending to you.

Know that there are many hundreds of thousands beings here with me offering their services, to you in any way that you might need them. Their only job is to be of service to each and every one of you. They wish nothing else but to help and guide you.

We wait for you to ask us for help, love, understanding, protection, guidance, knowledge and forgiveness. All of those things we are waiting to give to you. The most necessary of these is forgiveness, for each of you has long lists of things that you feel badly about, that you wish you had done differently and that you have great guilt about.

I say to you that you are forgiven, there is nothing that has been held against you or that you will need to pay for. All is forgiven now and forever. You each are held in love and joy. It is time to let go of all these things of your past that are keeping you from going forward and sharing the uniqueness and wonder of who you truly are with other beings of your world. So I ask you to go and share your love and light, to let go of the sorrows and guilts that you are holding in your hearts. They serve no purpose but to hold you back from receiving the love and light that you so deserve.

I am here and all the thousands of helpers are here to offer you only love and light. We wish to lighten up your lives and hearts with love, joy and peace. We wish for you to know that there are other ways to live and be. It is not necessary for you to carry such heavy burdens on your backs. So I say to you close your eyes, allow us to come, and take your heavy burdens away. Experience the lightness of your body without the guilts and sorrows that you have been carrying. Enjoy the ease, the lightness and love that are now able to fill your body. Allow yourself to walk through your days with only love and joy in your hearts and minds. Go out and share it with others.

Know that you only need call my name and I will be there.
In Love, Mother Mary
10/13/10

LETTER 10

Dear Ones,

Love is all there is. Without love, the world would cease to exist. Without love, you will cease to exist. The giving and receiving of love is what keeps you each moving and breathing. The opposite of love is fear. Fear has taken over a large portion of your every day lives. You see it in your friends' faces, in your neighbors' faces and in your family's faces. Fear is contagious and spreads from one person to the next with just a look. Stop for a moment and think about this and remember the last person you saw with fear on their face and in their eyes. It almost makes one-stop breathing for a second when you encounter it.

Know that love is also contagious in a strong and better way. Be conscious of what you are seeing and hearing. When you see and hear fear, stop and let your love replace it and vanish it from your being and your world. As I share my love with you, wear it as an outer set of clothes for others to see and feel. Love can be your protection from fear, for it cannot spread when you walk with love in your hearts and minds.

And when you see fear in your family's faces stop and take the time to see what you can do and how you can support them and ease their fear by passing on the love you are now wearing as your second set of clothes. Do this not just with your families but also with your friends, and neighbors and if you can reach out even further to the stranger standing next to you on the street.

It may be just smile or take a moment to speak to them to let them see your face and your second set of clothes. Slow down, take the time to see the people around you and to see the world around you. Each and every being is in need of love. Love will set you all free of the constant and every day fears that you carry with you just as you carry your wallet with you. Know that I am here with enough love to fill your world and erase all fear.

Know that you only need call my name and I will be there.
In Love, Mother Mary
10/14/10.

LETTER 11

Dear Ones,

It is time to wake up. It is time to pay attention to what is happening to the people of your world. I am not just talking about your families or your neighbors; I am talking about your whole world. People are starving, dying and wasting away from lack of love, care and concern. And I can hear you thinking what can I do. I am only one person.

All of the hurt, pain and abuse that has happened in your world can only be changed one person at a time. That change can start to happen by each of you sending loving thoughts to all the people of your world. Just as I am sending love and caring energy to you; you can also send it forward to all the people everywhere.

Some of you have time and energy to spare that you could help with one of the many volunteer programs and some of you have extra money to share that you could donate to help. People can help in their own way. Perhaps you are the one to send loving waves of energy out. Whatever is your way, please begin to share your resources and gifts with others. Know that in your sharing, it will return to you ten fold.

The expressing of love and caring is the most healing energy in the world. In sharing your love and caring you will help the healing process that your own being is going through right now. Everyone is on a healing journey right now healing old pains and hurts, regrets and sorrows. Each of you will heal faster when you reach out to help another. I will continue to be right here beside you during the healing process.

One of the reasons that my letters are being given to your world right now is that everyone is in need of more love, more caring, more support right now as they continue on their own healing journey and as they extend their hand and thoughts to support someone else on their journey. In the progress of your world, it has been forgotten by many that each human needs to be extending their hand in love and caring. That is how your world was meant to be. Each human helping the next human in whatever way they can. *Mutual aid*

Know that I am right beside you, that I am here extending my hand to each and everyone of you. To help and love you in whatever you may need. Know that you only need call my name and I will be there. Stop and close your eyes and say my name. Can you feel my presence? I am here.

Know that you only need call my name and I will be there.
In Love, Mother Mary
10/15/10

LETTER 12

Dear Ones,

I am here and I will continue to be here until the last person in your world feels loved and cared for. It does not matter how long it might take. I will be here. I have always been here waiting for you to feel my love. Know in your hearts and minds that I care and love each and every one of you exactly as you are.

You are all on a journey to find yourselves and your place in your world. For some this has been a most difficult journey with many challenges and rocky places. Some have learned from the challenges and others have not learned and have gone on to more difficult challenges. Your time here on your earth was not meant to be difficult and sorrow filled.

It was meant to be a time of love and sharing, to learn to be with other beings. A time of sharing and caring. A time to open your hearts to love yourselves and each other.

So today I ask you all to stop what it is you are doing, to check in your hearts and see what it has to tell you. Are you loving yourself, are you loving each other? For most the answer to one of those questions will be NO. It is time to change your answers so that both questions will be answered with a very loud YES.

Loving is not about who is right and who is wrong. It is about simply loving each other because you are here and you are in need of that love to exist. Love is like food. Your body needs nourishment or food to survive and your soul needs nourishment or love to survive. For too long your soul has gone without and it is shrinking and drawing up inside itself for lack of love.

So put aside your rights, wrongs and judgments. They serve no purpose but to harm you. So stop today and no longer see yourself or other beings with the eyes of right and wrong. Fill your hearts today with the love I am offering and see yourself and other beings through the eyes of love.

Does your world not look different now? You will need to practice this each day: stop and allow your heart to fill with love and then step out into your world and see it with eyes of love. Your lives will change quickly to one of loving and reaching out whether than one of sorrow and remorse for all that you are missing.

Know that you only need call my name and I will be there.
In Love, Mother Mary
10/16/10

LETTER 13

Dear Ones,

Where have you been? I am missing each and every one of you. There is a thread that connects each and every one of you to me. So many of you have turned away from yourselves and from love. I am love. That is my connection to you. I am unconditional love for I love you just as you are. There is nothing for you to do or to change. I know that I have spoken about this in previous letters, but it is necessary to speak of it again. It is not always believed that it is possible for me to love you just as you are. In your minds, you are set in believing that you are unworthy of love, you see no way for it to be true that I could love you as you are.

I say to you, STOP AND TELL ME, what good your harsh judgments and your thoughts of unworthiness have done for you. They have done nothing but beat you down. They have turned off your light; they have closed down your heart. Your heart is aching for love, caring, support, and unconditional love. Inside of your being you are crying out for what I offer.

I beg of you to let go of your resistance and your thoughts of unworthiness. Allow me to share my love with you for you are so worthy and so beautiful! You are a being of immense light and you have much work to do in your world!

Let of go of your fear and step into my light, and allow your light to turn on. Come and walk with me. Take my hand and join me. There is nothing to lose by joining me while there is much to lose by staying in the dark. Know that you have the courage to reach out and take my hand. Let us together begin to heal and then reach out to help others heal.

Know that you only need call me name and I will be there.
In Love, Mother Mary
10/18/10

LETTER 14

Dear Ones,

There is so much work to be done for the beings of your world. You have so many hurt and damaged souls who are suffering, wandering alone without hope. My heart weeps for the loneliness that I can feel coming from each of you.

Many years ago, your world took a turn towards the gathering of money, material possessions, and power over others. It is thought that the road to happiness is paved with gold, material possessions and how much more you have than your neighbors. It is thought that all of these things will make you a better and happier person.

You are so mistaken in your thoughts and beliefs. Money, power and material possessions say nothing about the kind of person that you are. Happiness, love, and joy speak to what is in your heart and how you choose to treat your neighbor. It does not speak to how much money you have in the bank or how nice your home is or which brand of clothes you choose to wear.

You can have all the money and material things you could ever want and you will still feel lonely and unloved. Love and caring does not come from objects or paper dollars. It comes from one person's heart to your heart. Love and happiness comes from looking into your heart and listening to what it is telling you. It comes from reaching out and sharing yourself with others. It comes from caring about your neighbors all over the world.

Being here on your earth was meant to be about learning how to live with all the other beings in the world, with love and caring, learning to appreciate the differences in other cultures, religions, and colors. Being here on your earth was never meant to be about who is better because of what religion you practice, the color of your skin or how you dress.

Today as you go about your lives and you see someone who looks different than yourself, open your eyes and really look, are they so different from you? Or do they just wear a different style of clothes? Or maybe their skin is a different color? But inside each of those beings is their heart not the same, are their bodily organs not the same?

YOU ARE ALL ONE ON THIS EARTH; the only differences are in your outward appearance. You all have the same need for love and caring. Buried in your hearts is the same need to reach out and help each other. I ask you today to open your hearts and reach out to help each other, to know that I am reaching out to each of you. Know that I love each and everyone of you just as you are. This journey here on earth is about learning to love yourselves and each other.

Know that you only need call my name and I will be there.
In Love, Mother Mary
10/19/10

LETTER 15

Dear Ones,

I am wishing you so much joy and happiness that your body and soul cannot hold it all. Your mind and heart is over flowing with these feelings of joy and happiness. Your heart is growing and opening. Your body and energetic field is expanding and allowing you the room to become more fully yourselves. Love, joy, and happiness needs room to grow and expand, so that it touches every person you see and connect with during the day.

As your body expands to hold all of these feelings, your light shines brighter and brighter. Soon you will be like one of the stars in the sky. People will see you and wonder what is happening in your life, as you glow and radiate warmth and love from your being. They will want to get closer to you and talk to you. They hunger for what you are offering. Your offering will be to pass on and share your love, joy, and happiness.

Soon you will look at the people around you and they will all have that glow, that look of warmth and loving. As they touch the people in their lives that glow and all the feelings that accompany it will be passed on. For love, joy, and happiness are contagious; they are able to travel anywhere in the world and touch anyone in the world.

This process starts with one person accepting my love and allowing it to grow and encompass all areas of their lives. Take the chance to believe that YOU are worthy of having love, joy, and happiness in YOUR lives.

ONE PERSON CAN CHANGE YOUR WORLD. YOU ARE THAT PERSON! Call my name and I will come and share my love, joy, and happiness with you. Allow my light to become one with you.

Stop what you are doing right now and close your eyes, say my name, I will come and we will begin the process of opening your heart. Each day I will return and your heart will open wider and wider until your heart is full to overflowing. Let us start today, right now! Allow me to love you.

Know that you need only call my name and I will be there.
In Love, Mother Mary
10/20/10

LETTER 16

Dear Ones,

In your world, you are being asked to go faster and faster, to do more and have more. I say to you slow down and enjoy your life, your family, your neighbors, and your world. Give yourselves room and time to take a breath and be at ease. Your hearts, minds, and bodies were not made to move through your life at the speed of sound. Yes! The energy on your planet and in the universe is speeding up and everything is going much faster.

Now is the time that it is even more important for you to reduce your personal speed, to appreciate and take care of yourselves, and your families. The faster your world goes the more important for you to not be caught up in the whirlwind. In the whirlwind, there is only time for doing and acquiring, there is not time for love and caring.

If you are living in the whirlwind day after day, what is happening when you return to your homes in the evening? Is there time to eat with your families? Is all your time spent getting ready to be in the whirlwind again tomorrow? Where is the time to love, time to care and time to listen? Where is your time to be with yourselves? Where is the time to appreciate all you have been given in this life? Where is the time for love, joy, and gratitude? There is no time left for the most important parts of your lives!

So I say to you SLOW DOWN NOW! Close your eyes and come with me on a journey. I want you to replay yesterday in your mind. Watch closely. Do you see yourself smiling, sharing a kind word? Did you take time to hug anyone? Was there time to take a deep breath and appreciate anything? Was there time for anything but going faster? Now replay your journey back to yesterday only turn down the speed to five instead of ten. Watch yourself, your family, your friends, and your whole world.

Do your eyes fill with tears to see what you have missed? There is no way to go back and re-live yesterday, but there is time to change today and tomorrow. I ASK YOU ONCE AGAIN TO SLOW DOWN! Do not miss your life, do not miss love, and do not miss what I am offering you. I will love you no matter how fast you travel through life, but if you live in the whirlwind world, you will never know that I am here loving you. You will never know that other people of your world are here loving you also. YOU WILL MISS IT ALL!

Take the time to slow down and know that I am here and I am loving you every day, every hour and every minute.

Know that you only need call my name and I will be there.
In Love, Mother Mary,
10/21/10

LETTER 17

Dear Ones,

Let today be a day of kind words and gentle thoughts and warm hearts. Today is the time to let worry, fear, and anger stay asleep. It is time for you to have a day of gentle thoughts and kind words. Allow yourself a day off from your worldly concerns and worries about money. Today see your concerns for your families in a gentle way, knowing that all is well. Just for today, you can give yourself permission to let your worried mind STOP!

Worry is a waste of precious time and energy. Worry does not help you to take care of your family, pay your bills, put food on the table, or keep your children safe. Worry makes all of the things that make up your everyday life more difficult. Worry fills your body with fear and anger. Worry causes stress and disease in your body and life.

Worry leaves little time for kind words and gentle thoughts and warm hearts. Worry does not live in the same house as joy, gratitude, and appreciation. There is not room in a home of worry for anything else. It erases the warmth and caring in your hearts and replaces it with fear, anger, doubts, and regrets. Worry steals your life from you without you even knowing it.

We think in our minds that we worry about the ones we love and care about. But the truth is there is no room for the love and caring because worry fills up all the spaces of your hearts and minds. Worry forms a vicious circle. When our loved ones are ok and safely back home after we have worried about them all day, is there not a small piece of you that is angry at them for causing you to worry all day for nothing? Do you not blame them for the bad day you had? It is not their fault that you used your day for worry, fear, and anger. Only you are responsible for the day you have chosen to have.

Each morning you get to choose what kind of a day you will have. Will it be a day of kind words, gentle hearts, and warm thoughts? Remember that a day used to worry is a waste of your time and energy. It serves no purpose in your life. It only causes you stress and disease.

If you have lived your life in the house of worry ask for help in letting it go. There are many thousand of helpers in my world waiting to be of service to each of you. They will help you to find ways to change your days from worry, fear, and anger to days of gentle hearts, warm thoughts, and kind words. It is always possible to change the things in your life that are not working for your best interest. Your lives are meant to be filled with thousands of days of love, joy, and kindness.

Know that you only need call my name and I will be there.
In Love, Mother Mary
10/22/10

LETTER 18

Dear Ones,

Your heart is the center point of your physical body, spiritual body, emotional body, and mental body. Most people have made the brain their center point and in doing so they have tried to make their life about logic and thought. Life is about LOVE. Life is about learning to share your love and yourselves with each other. Your physical body cannot live without your heart working and pumping life into your being. Your spiritual body cannot live and grow without love and the sharing of it. Your emotional body cannot live without the expression of that love from the heart. Your mental body cannot fully live unless it works in solid connection with your heart.

Yes! Some of you are saying right now. How can that be? Our minds can function without the heart. I say to you that nothing can function, as it was intended to function unless it is directed from the heart. Your hearts are the center point of all your bodies, your very existence. Your lives can turn into different degrees of disease, sorrow, regret, desperation, and aloneness when your heart is not the center point.

When you see your neighbors and people on the street, look into their eyes and what do you see? There is no spark, no life. Are not their eyes sad, alone, and empty of joy and love?

IT IS TIME RIGHT NOW TO STOP THE WAY YOU ARE LIVING! It is time right now to start to open your hearts and allow your heart to direct your life. CLOSE YOUR EYES go to your heart and allow it to show you how to live and be. Allow yourselves to open up to love and caring for yourselves and others. Know this will not happen in an instant. It is something you will need to work on daily. It will take time and energy on your part to make this huge change in your life. Then and only then will you truly start to have a life.

Ask for help in making these changes. There are thousands of helpers standing right here with me waiting to help you in whatever way you need and want. The journey of learning to live from your heart is not a journey that needs to be taken by yourself. There are helpers here with me to help you. There are also other beings on your planet that will be making this journey at the same time as you. So reach out for support, which is in the giving of support and also the receiving of support. Know that I am here and I will be loving you every step along the way. Know that I will love you even if you choose not to make the journey.

Know that you only need call my name and I will be there.
In Love, Mother Mary
10/25/10

LETTER 19

Dear Ones,

Let us talk about love today. Every human has the need to be loved and the need to be loving. Yes, these needs can be hidden and buried inside each of you. They are still there ever present, whether you bury them deep within you or wear them freely with your heart open for all to see. The needs of love that are hidden and buried can fester and turn into other emotions like anger, rage and hate.

Love is the most necessary and powerful thing on your earth. Babies can die and wither away from the lack of love and affection. Parents, friends, neighbors, and society can withhold their love if you choose not to act in a certain way. Love can be used as a powerful weapon to control and isolate other beings. Love was never meant to be used in that way. Love was and is needed for each being to grow and reach out to fulfill their potential. Each of you craves love and affection. If you are thinking right now, that is not so for me. I say to you stop and no longer lie to yourself. Each and every being on this earth needs love to sustain their existence.

Each of you needs to be loved for just who you are. Not for the things you do or how much money you may have. You each need to be loved because you are unique and beautiful just as you are. TODAY I ASK YOU TO STOP AND CLOSE YOUR EYES take some deep breaths and say my name. Allow me to put my arms around you and just hold you. Allow yourself to feel my love for you, just because you are YOU!

No one else need know what is happening to you, this is just between you and me. It is simply about me loving you and you allowing yourself to be loved. It is so necessary for your existence, for you cannot survive without it. We can talk to you about joy, happiness and gratitude and what those things can mean in your life, but if you cannot feel love, they have no meaning. First comes love, above all else. Learning, accepting, and practicing the giving and receiving of love comes first. If it is new for you to accept and give love, begin to practice it daily.

Begin each day by closing your eyes, allowing me to come and be with you. Let me put my arms around you and hold you for a moment. Then go out into your day with your heart filled with love. Pass along your love to the people that you see and keep in touch with. It is not necessary for you to put your arms around each person. Simply look at them with the eyes of love and not the eyes of judgment. In your heart wish them well. Wish for them that they might know simple loving warmth and kindness in their lives.

Know that you only need call my name and I will be there.
In Love, Mother Mary
10/26/10

LETTER 20

Dear Ones,

Today let us talk about hearts that have been closed down. This is a process that seems to happen to most beings. The closing down can best be described as if your heart were a vault with a huge security door with guards standing outside of the door at the ready to protect at all costs. The closed down heart happens at different times, depending on your own unique experience of life. The closing down happens, as you each perceive hurtful things happening to you. It depends on how you perceive the world in general, is it a friendly welcoming place or is it scary, are people being physically hurt every day? What do you see when you look out the windows of your eyes? What does the world look like to you? There are hundreds of thousands of reasons for one to close down their hearts.

NOW IS THE TIME TO START TO RE-OPEN YOUR HEART! It is almost impossible for my love to get through all the guards and the security door. I KNOW THAT YOU ARE HOPING AND MAYBE PRAYING THAT MY LOVE WILL GET PAST ALL THE SECURITY YOU HAVE AROUND YOUR HEART. I NEED YOUR HELP TO BE ABLE TO GET THROUGH ALL THE BARRIERS.

Starting to remove your barriers NEEDS to be a slow and gentle process. Take away one or two of the guards at a time. Slowly and gently loving yourself as you go through this process. Your eyes and mind can see what you have been missing because of the barriers. All the things you have been asking for are waiting for you. There are many angels and helpers here on this side to help in the process. We over here are aware of the great courage and strength that it will take for you to let down the barriers and ask the guards to leave.

I ASK YOU NOW TO CLOSE YOUR EYES, breathe deeply, call my name. I will come and be with you. Hold my hand as you ask your first guards to leave. Can you now start to feel my love, is there a soft warm gentle feeling coming over you, are there tears in your eyes? May I put my arms around you and just hold you. You are strong and courageous. There is so much waiting for you and my heart sings with joy that you are letting me in. Know that there will be many others who you will want to let in, all bringing love, joy, and kindness into your life.

Know that you only need call my name and I will be there.
In Love, Mother Mary
10/27/10

LETTER 21

Dear Ones,

Today let us talk about fear. FEAR is the opposite of LOVE. Where fear lives there is no room for LOVE. Fear overrides all other feelings and emotions. Think about the places or rooms that you walk into and they feel warm, welcoming, light, and airy. You know that love lives in this room. You can feel it. You know it in your heart. You feel good being there as if there were arms held out to embrace and welcome you.

Now stop and think about the other kinds of rooms you have walked into. They seem to not have much air in them; the air is heavy and the lighting is not good. It is dim and you wonder why someone doesn't turn on the lights. There are no out stretched arms to welcome you; there is only isolation and desperation reaching out for you.

Both fear and love are contagious, which one would you choose. Which one do you choose? Which room do you live in? Which room do you want to live in? All beings, have some form of fear in their lives. For some beings, it has become all consuming, taking over every part of their lives. Right now in your world fear of lack has grown to overwhelming proportions. It continues to grow everyday becoming bigger and bigger.

You are meeting fear every day as you go out into your world. IT IS TIME TO STOP THE GROWTH OF FEAR IN YOUR DAILY LIVES. Yes, I know most of you are unaware of how to stop this growth. So stop what you are doing right now. Close your eyes. Take a deep breath. Put your hand over your heart and say my name. I will come and I will give you a spiritual bath. We will clean your energy field, asking and allowing the fear you have collected in your daily lives to dissipate and be transformed to love. As you take your spiritual bath, all of your bodies will be cleansed and transformed. Can you feel the difference? Can you see the difference? Notice how you feel and what is happening in your bodies. Become aware of what it feels like to be without fear. Now, it is time to cleanse your home, your cars, your workplace and your earth.

PRACTICE DAILY TAKING A SPIRITUAL BATH, IT WILL BENEFIT ALL BEINGS AND YOUR MOTHER EARTH. I AM ASKING

FOR YOUR HELP. I AM ASKING YOU TO HELP YOURSELF AND YOUR MOTHER EARTH.

I will be here to help you as you practice this daily. There are thousands of helpers here to assist you also. Call on your angels and guides, we are all waiting to help you transform fear into LOVE.

Know you only need call my name and I will be there.
In Love, Mother Mary
10/28/10

LETTER 22

Dear Ones,

Let us talk about JOY today. Joy is the least felt emotion on your Mother Earth. Joy is the one emotion that beings feel they are the least deserving of. In some parts of your Mother Earth Joy is unknown and not believed to exist.

So I say to you today, JOY is real it lives in your world. Most often Joy is thought of coupled with other emotions, Joy and Love, Joy and Happiness. Today is about pure overflowing JOY.

Joy will come in different forms to different beings. Joy may come as you see a beautiful tree changing the color of its leaves in the fall. Joy may come as you see your child's face for the first time. Joy may come as you realize for the first time that you are a worthy and important being on your planet. Joy may come when you feel unconditional love for the first time.

There are beings on your planet that have never experienced joy in any of its forms. There are also those who have glimpsed it for just a second in time. Today I want you to feel Joy in all its power and wonder.

CLOSE YOUR EYES, TAKE A DEEP BREATH, PUT YOUR HAND OVER YOUR HEART AND SAY MY NAME. I AM HERE WITH YOU RIGHT NOW. MY HANDS ARE FILLED WITH JOY AND I AM PASSING IT TO YOU. It is like no feeling you have ever had before. Are you feeling like the sun lives inside your body? Is your body vibrating with the wonder of it? Do you feel like you are floating and your feet are no longer on the ground? Are you laughing for no reason, but that it feels wonderful to laugh out loud with pure joy?

I so wish that each of you could and would allow yourselves to feel JOY at least once each day. It only takes a moment to stop, close your eyes, speak my name, and ask for JOY. I will be there with JOY in my hands.

This is a gift that only you can give yourselves. Will you take that moment to allow yourself to feel the wonder that is waiting for you? Will you allow yourself to feel the Love that I am offering to you? I am here and I am waiting for each of you. Know that you each are loved and cared for beyond your wildest dreams.

Know that you only need call my name and I will be there.
In Love, Mother Mary
10/29/10

LETTER 23

Dear Ones,

Today let us talk about Personal Integrity. I am talking about having Integrity with yourself. Are you following your own belief system, your own values? Are you being true to yourselves? Are you listening to your heart? Are you following where it leads you?

What pain and agony comes from being untrue to yourselves. Let us look at what would cause you to be untrue to yourselves. Fear is the biggest culprit in stopping you from going where you want and need to go. What will others think? How will they feel about it? Will they stand by you? Fear will give you a hundred unanswered questions. Those questions will stop you and fill you with fear, which will bind your body and paralyze you.

The worst thing that will happen is that all yourself doubts, all your thoughts of unworthiness will rise up. They will come up from the depths of your soul and will stop you in your tracks. This will happen if it is a large thing that you need to do or a small thing. You are untrusting of yourselves and feel unworthy of even the smallest thing that your heart would desire.

I BEG OF YOU, STOP AND HEAR WHAT I AM SAYING. You each are worthy of all that your heart desires. You each are priceless beyond compare. What your heart truly desires is what you need and where you must go. THERE IS NOTHING MORE IMPORTANT IN YOUR LIVES THAN YOUR PERSONAL INTEGRITY. FOR IF YOU HAVE NO PERSONAL INTEGRITY, THERE IS NO LOVE. WITHOUT LOVE THERE IS ONLY EXISTENCE FILLED WITH DESPAIR AND HOPELESSNESS.

YOU EACH ARE WORTH MORE THAN EXISTENCE. Your lives are meant to be about love, integrity, hope and joy. We are all here waiting to help you in whatever way you need and want. Call for us and allow us to come and help. The road of love and personal integrity will not happen for most of you overnight. So start out with the small things and work your way towards the large ones. There are life altering and life changing decisions that are waiting to happen. They will allow your heart to be filled with love beyond what you can imagine.

STOP RIGHT NOW AND CLOSE YOUR EYES. TAKE A DEEP BREATH. PUT YOUR HAND ON YOUR HEART AND CALL MY NAME. Pick your one thing today that will honor you and your personal integrity. Allow yourself to see where it will take you? What is happening in your life? Are you following your heart? Where is your fear level? Is the fear stopping you or are you walking passed it? Hold true to yourself. We are here to help. We are standing right here beside you. Feel us and know that we are walking with you.

Know you only need call my name and I will be there.
In Love, Mother Mary,
11/01/10

LETTER 24

Dear Ones,

Let us today talk about Respect. As I am sure, you have noticed many of the things we talk about always go right back to you. How you think of yourselves. How you care for yourselves. How you love yourselves. Most of you throughout your lives have learned how not to care for yourselves, but how you most care for others first! How it is more important to think well of others, whether than thinking well of yourself. You have all been taught to love others before you love yourself. Or maybe you don't even think in terms of loving yourself. Respect is all swirled in with caring, loving and thinking well of yourselves. Respecting yourself is about honoring you. Honoring who you are as a man, woman or child. Most often we think of respect in terms of respecting other people for how they think, act, and treat others.

So stop for a moment and think about yourself. How do you think, act and treat yourselves? Inside your head how do you talk to yourself? What is the tone of voice that you use, what kind of words do you use? Is there kindness, support, understanding, and compassion in your inner voice? Take the time now to listen to the inner voice that continually talks to you. Is it uplifting you or is it beating you down?

Learning to respect yourself can start by changing the inner voice. If we were to meet on the street in your town, what tone of voice would you use in speaking to me? What kind of words would you speak to me? That tone of voice, those words that you would speak to me is how I want your inner voice to speak to you.

I WANT YOU TO STOP RIGHT NOW, TAKE A DEEP BREATH, PUT YOUR HAND ON YOUR HEART, CALL MY NAME AND IN YOUR MIND PICTURE, MY FACE. Can you feel the respect, love, and caring coming from your heart? Your eyes are looking at me with gentleness, and love. In your mind can you feel and see all that is happening?

LOOK ONCE MORE AT MY FACE, IT IS A MIRROR AND THE FACE YOU ARE SEEING IS YOURSELF. ALLOW ALL THAT RESPECT, LOVE, AND CARING INTO YOUR MIND AND BODY. ALLOW YOUR BODY TO ABSORB ALL THAT HAS HAPPENED HERE

TODAY. Each day look into a mirror, see your face; see my face inside your face. WE ARE ALL ONE.

We are all here to help you make these changes in how you see yourself, how you talk to yourself, and what you think about yourself. Know that you are loved beyond all that you can imagine. Allow us to assist you in whatever way you need.

Know that you only need call my name and I will be there.
In love, Mother Mary,
11/02/10

LETTER 25

Dear Ones,

Let us talk about Hope today. All beings think in terms of their worlds getting better, life being better in the future. That is called Hope. Hoping for more money, more love, a bigger house, and a better life for your children, are all things people hope for and the list goes on and on.

But, is that what hope is really about. Hope is what makes you get up in the morning and move out into your world. Hope is fuel and motivation for all beings. If there is no hope, there are no dreams, no way in your mind to change what is to what you want it to be. When there isn't hope in your heart and mind, then stress and disease steps in to take its place. Without hope, life becomes a downward spiral, where all color disappears and everything turns dark gray traveling into all black.

Hope is made up of colors; it comes in every color you can think of. Hope comes in the deepest blue, to the darkest pink, and the most vibrant yellow. Color is like nourishment to your minds and bodies. All systems of your being require color or hope to keep working in a healthy wholesome way.

Allow your mind to tell you about the colors in your life. What do the different colors mean to you? How do you feel about the colors? What is your mind and body telling you about how it feels, as you see the different colors? Notice where your emotions go depending on the color, you see.

RIGHT NOW STOP, TAKE A DEEP BREATH, PUT YOUR HAND ON YOUR HEART AND CALL MY NAME. LISTEN TO MY VOICE AND TELL ME WHAT COLORS COME TO YOU. You are loved beyond your wildest imagination. What color do you see? All things are possible in your life. What color do you see? Your life is filled with joy, happiness and love. What color do you see? Fear no longer lives in your mind and body. What color do you see?

Practice daily in your mind until you know and learn the colors that you need in your life. Always carry with you something in the color of Hope and Love. Something you can touch, be it a small piece of paper or a piece of clothe. Remember that hope is fuel and motivation for your mind and body.

Love is fuel and motivation for your very existence. Know that I am loving you and sending you lights of many colors to surround you and hold you.

Know that you only need call my name and I will be there.
In love, Mother Mary
11/03/10

LETTER 26

Dear Ones,

Today let us talk about making life decisions. Each being has their own particular process for making life decisions. There are some that make you stop and think, others you may not even think about. You just go ahead and do whatever seems right at the moment. Often times what seems right at the moment turns out to be wrong for you. It doesn't feel right or look right in your life pattern. The life pattern goes completely out of balance, which means you are out of balance.

Having your life pattern out of balance is like being on a steep road that is covered with black ice. You keep slipping and falling, trying to get your footing. There is nothing to grab hold of and no way to stop yourselves.

SO CLOSE YOUR EYES, TAKE A DEEP BREATH, PUT YOUR HAND ON YOUR HEART AND CALL MY NAME. GRAB MY HAND AND I WILL HELP YOU TO STOP. CHECK YOURSELVES ARE YOU STOPPED OR DO YOU NEED BOTH MY HANDS TO STOP YOU? I want you to just stand right here with me right now. Let your mind slow down for just a moment, be right here right now with me. Nothing else matters right now but just being here with me. RIGHT HERE AND RIGHT NOW YOU CAN BREATHE AND JUST KEEP BREATHING. It has been a while since you have been able to take a deep breath.

Fear, desperation and hopelessness can rob you of your breath, and the ability to make good life decisions for yourselves and your families. Life decisions are not about what goes on in your head and what it tells you to do. LIFE DECISIONS NEED TO COME FROM THE HEART AND THE HEAD. I AM TELLING YOU TO FIRST GO TO YOUR HEART, WHAT IS IT TELLING YOU? GOING TO YOUR HEART MEANS STOPPING, PUTTING YOUR HAND ON YOUR HEART, AND LET IT SPEAK TO YOU. IT WILL ALWAYS TELL YOU THE BEST DECISION FOR YOU. Now go to your head and let it show you how to make the heart decision work in your life. Good and balanced life decisions come from using both the heart and the head.

For all of you this is going to be a very different way to live your life. It is time for a new way to live your life. The old way is not working. Some of you want to say no, that is not true. I say to you open your eyes, look at what is happening, where are you going? It is time to live your life in a new way now.

Try it in small ways first and work your way up. We are here to help you, to hold your hand and walk you through these changes. You are not alone. There are thousands of angels and helpers here waiting for you. All you need do is think the word HELP and we will be there to help you in whatever way you need. You are all loved beyond your wildest dreams. Can you feel us? We are here holding your hand quietly saying your name? Can you feel us, can you hear us?

Know you only need call my name and I will be there.
In Love, Mother Mary,
11/04/10

LETTER 27

Dear Ones,

Let us talk about being in the present moment. About being in today, in this hour, and in this minute. Most beings spend 95% of their time in the past or in the future. Living in the past, remembering it, suffering through it time after time is a painful waste of your energy. You learn from your past so that you do not need to repeat patterns in your life over and over. You learn from the past so that your future will be different.

Suffering through your past and causing yourselves pain time after time is not what I am talking about. Causing yourselves continual pain over a past incident is of little use to you or to your families. It causes you not to live your life; you are only living that moment over and over. You are missing your life; you are missing your joy, happiness, and love.

Living constantly in the future, dreaming of how it will be and what you will be doing is of little use to you also. Dreams are good and all beings need to have dreams. If you are living in the future, once again you are missing your life. The only life you will have is your dreams. What is happening today, now in your world is what your life is about.

If you are living in the present, the now, you can start to work towards making your dreams happen. You can plan and work your way towards living your dreams in the real world. Do you see the difference between living in the now and living only in your dreams?

Living in the now working towards your dreams is your life. Life is about the journey of all that happens and the people that you touch with along the way. Life is about living in today with love in your hearts. Life is about going out into your world and sharing all that you are. Life is about sharing the love in your hearts with the world. As you share your love, it will be returned to you ten fold. Love is what your life and your world is all about.

SO CLOSE YOUR EYES, TAKE A DEEP BREATH, PUT YOUR HAND ON YOUR HEART AND CALL MY NAME. Come and walk with me through your past. Look at it with not the eyes of judgment but with the eyes of love. Look at it for the last time. Come and take my hand

and walk with me into the future. We are walking into your dream world, the world that you spend all your time thinking about. What do you see? There is nothing there to see, because all your time was used to dream instead of making it happen.

Now come with me to today. The past is gone; you no longer have to spend all your time thinking about it. You have your dreams and you know what you need to do to make them become reality. You are living your life. You are living it to the fullest. You are sharing, loving, and caring about yourselves and others.

It will take work to move from living in the past and the future to living in the now. Take the time daily to let us show you how to live in the now. Call upon us to show you each day how to accomplish this. Soon you will just be doing it. You will no longer even have the thoughts in your heads to live any other way. Ask us for help and we will be there. There are thousands of helpers here waiting to hear from you.

Know that you only need call my name and I will be there.
In Love, Mother Mary
11/05/10

LETTER 28

Dear Ones,

I am here whether you are thinking about me or not. As you go through your daily lives, I am right here beside you loving you and being with you. There are times when it seems to you that your days are getting longer and more difficult. Yes, what you are feeling and thinking is so. The times on your earth are becoming more challenging and chaotic.

It is important for you to know, that you do not have to fall into that wave of energy that is traveling far and wide on your earth. It is possible to step out of those waves of energy that are causing such frustration and havoc. You do not need to follow the other beings on your planet.

STEP AWAY AND STAND BY YOURSELF. Close your eyes right now and allow yourself to Stand-alone. PUT YOUR HAND ON YOUR HEART AND CALL MY NAME. Feel my hand on top of your head. Is the top of your head starting to tingle? I am sending the pure light of love down through the top of your head. The light will cleanse all your bodies, every cell and organ. Your mind will become clear and open. It will feel as if you are thinking clearly for the first time in months or perhaps years. Allow the light to travel down through your body back into Mother Earth.

At this time, on your earth, it is vital that you do not just follow what other beings are saying and doing. You must stand alone in your thinking and doing. We are right here to help you and be with you. YOUR WORLD IS CHANGING AND SHIFTING RAPIDLY AT THIS TIME. Standing with the whole at this time will fill your bodies and lives with FEAR, ANGER, and FRUSTRATION.

I AM HERE AND THERE ARE THOUSANDS OF HELPERS HERE WITH ME WAITING TO HELP YOU IN ALL THAT YOU DO. Take a moment many times during your days to close your eyes, feel my hand on your head. Allow the light of love to fill your body. It will only take 20 seconds. Your days and lives will change dramatically.

There will be a lightness and joy to your being and your days. Know that you are loved and cared for. We will always be here for you.

Know that you only need call my name and I will be there.
In Love, Mother Mary
11/08/10

LETTER 29

Dear Ones,

    I am sending you Joy, Laughter, Peace, and Love today. As you accept and rejoice in the receiving of these four energies, be aware of how your body is feeling. Does your physical body not respond in a positive way? Does it feel lighter and more easily able to move? Is there not less pain in your body?

    What you feel and what you think has a deep effect on your physical body. Disease can come from what you think, feel, eat, and do to your body. The cells and organs of your body are affected by every action. What you do, what you think, and how feel in your body. It does not matter the age of your body; it is always affected. As your body ages in your world it will begin to show the effects of all of the actions that have taken place over the years.

    It is possible to become aware of how the different actions affect your body. Once you are aware then it is possible for you to decide what you want to do. If you stay unaware, then you continue to harm your body. Knowing will allow you to change and perhaps repair some of the damage that has been done. I am not talking just of the kind of foods you eat or the exercise that you do. I am talking about the thoughts you have, the feelings you have about yourself and others. I am talking about the things that happen daily in your life that you hate, dislike, and feel so badly about. I am talking about the things you do that you feel you have to do, that you have no choice about.

    IT IS IMPORTANT RIGHT NOW TO STOP. PUT YOUR HAND ON YOUR HEART AND CALL MY NAME. Come and walk with me and let us watch a movie of your life. We will see the things that happen in your life that causes damage to your body. We will see ways that you can change your life. We will see the ways that it is possible for you to bring Joy, Laughter, Peace, and Love back into your lives. We will see ways for you to start healing the cells, organs, and the whole of your body.

    You will need to come and go to the movies with me many times so that we can change these things in your life that are not working, that are causing you damage. I am here and there are many thousands of helpers here waiting with me to come and go on a movie date with you. Will you bring the popcorn? Are you laughing? I hope so! I am here this day, touching you with Joy, Laughter, Peace, and Love. I may tickle your nose, touch your heart so that it is overflowing with love or fill your whole body with Joy and Peace.

Know you only need call my name and I will be there.
In Love, Mother Mary
11/09/10

LETTER 30

Dear Ones,

Allow me to love you. You read my letters and you like my words. Are you truly letting me into your hearts and minds? Are you believing that I love you? It is difficult for most of you to believe that I could love you. It is hard to believe that you could feel it in your physical world.

Would you like me to touch your cheek, hold your hand, kiss your forehead, or put my hand on your shoulder? All of these and more are possible. I can touch you and you will be able to feel it. I am here and I am loving you. Our energies are connected.

COME AND BE WITH ME RIGHT NOW. Put yourself in a quiet and separate place. CLOSE YOUR EYES, TAKE SEVERAL DEEP BREATHS, CALL MY NAME AND I WILL BE THERE. Know that I am here with you. Continue to take deep breaths allowing yourself to be here in this space only, letting go of your world. Think of your body and how it feels. Feel your own energy as it runs through your body. Being very quiet now and only focusing on your body and the energy running through it.

Where would you like me to touch with you? May I touch your cheek, or hold your hand. What will make you know that I am really here? Tell me what you need so that you will know for positive that I am here and I am loving you. You only need ask and I will come time after time to touch with you, to give you the love and support that you need. These are difficult and challenging times on your planet. I am here to help you travel through these times. There are thousands of others here to travel with you also. Every being on your planet is in need of love and support to travel through these times.

Your world is traveling so fast it feels like you are constantly running out of time. Are you feeling like it is difficult to keep up? Let us love you and support you as you make your way through your day.

Know that I am here and you only need call my name.
In Love, Mother Mary
11/10/10

LETTER 31

Dear Ones,

We have talked about Hope before and we will continue to talk about Hope from time to time. All beings need hope in their lives. Hope for a better life for your children, hope for a better life for yourself, and hope for your world.

Hope that the wars and the killing will come to an end. Hope that there will never be another reason to go to war. Hope that all the beings of the earth will finally come to realize that when you hurt someone else you are doing it to yourself.

All beings on your earth at one time or another has prayed for peace on your earth, peace for all the people of the world. You have heard this many times from many different people. Peace starts with you. Peace will only come to the world one person at a time. So my Hope today is that you will start to allow what you all have been HOPING for to begin. There will only be better lives for your children, yourself and your world when peace reigns.

SO TODAY STOP WHAT YOU ARE DOING OR THINKING RIGHT NOW. CLOSE YOUR EYES, PUT YOUR HAND ON YOUR HEART AND CALL MY NAME. In your head you are thinking I am a peaceful person; this is not about me. Stop and think back over the day. What do you see and what do you hear? Were you angry or resentful, at what happened when you watched your news? Everyday in every way there are small thoughts and actions that take away from the peacefulness of the world.

This is not something that you even know or that you are aware of doing. It is a way of life. Not only is it taking away from the peace of the whole it is taking away your peace, your hope. The anger and resentfulness will not change the things in the world that you don't like and don't want. It only adds to the hopelessness and the desperation. Sending out thoughts of love and support will be what begins to change your world. Giving yourself thoughts of love and support will begin to change your personal life.

Knowing and believing that I am here with thousands of others and we are sending you hope, support, and love. It will begin to change your lives.

Once you begin to practice sending out love and support you will notice a change will begin to take place inside of you. Anger and resentment will begin to vanish and be replaced with Hope. Hope for yourselves, your families, and your world.

Call on us. We are waiting here to help you make the changes that will make your life more peaceful and hopeful. Please let us help.

Know you only need call my name and I will be there.
In Love, Mother Mary
11/12/10

LETTER 32

Dear Ones,

Where in your body do you store the hurts and memories from long ago? So long ago that you aren't even sure they are still there. You no longer think of them except on rare occasions. However, they are still there in your cells and organs. They are what are causing disease, aches, and pains in your body.

It is time to let go of the hurts and memories of long ago. They are no longer needed in your life. I am here today to tell you I will take them away for you. You only need to agree that you would like me to take them. You need to agree to allow forgiveness to come into your heart, forgiveness for yourself and others.

We will make a trade; I will show you how to release those old hurts and memories. You in turn will give the hurts and memories to me. With the releasing, forgiveness will follow. BE WITH YOURSELF FOR A MOMENT AND THINK ABOUT THIS. IS THIS WHAT YOU WANT TO DO? CAN YOU ALLOW YOURSELF TO DO THIS? ARE YOU TIRED OF THE WAY YOUR BODY FEELS? WHAT ABOUT YOUR HEART, HOW DOES IT FEEL? ARE YOU NOT TIRED OF THE HEAVINESS OF IT ALL?

If you do not wish to join us today, then we will again visit tomorrow. I say to you go and have a day of joy, love, and happiness. I am here and I will be loving you today and every day.

For those of you who want to join with me today, NOW IS THE TIME TO CLOSE YOUR EYES, PUT YOUR HAND ON YOUR HEART AND CALL MY NAME. ALLOW MY ENERGY TO FILL YOUR BEING. THERE WILL BE A SOFT GENTLE FLOW OF ENERGY COMING FROM YOUR HEART AND FILLING UP YOUR ENTIRE BODY. Can you feel it now? Warm and gentle. I am here with each of you. You decide what it is you wish for me to take and it will be released from your body. Just with the releasing of it, you have planted the seed of forgiveness in your heart.

That seed of forgiveness will grow as you go through your days. Love and gentleness for yourself will be like sun and water for that seed. If there are others you are forgiving, your thoughts will travel through the energy waves to allow the forgiveness to happen. If you wish to do the forgiveness in person listen to your heart and what it tells you to do. Know that I will be with you if you choose to do it in your physical world also.

Know that I am here to help you with this and there are thousands of helpers here to travel with you each day in whatever you choose to do. Know that you are loved and cared for more than you can imagine. Please allow us to help you.

Know that you only need call my name and I will be there.
In love, Mother Mary
11/12/10

LETTER 33

Dear Ones,

What shall we talk about today? What if we talk about love, hope, caring, families, joy, and connection? It all comes down to connecting with others. That is what life is about; the connection and the sharing of love. THIS IS YOUR PURPOSE. THIS IS WHY YOU ARE HERE.

You connect with your partners, your families, and friends. There is a whole world out there that you are connected to without realizing it. Connection works in STEPS. You are connected to every being on your Mother Earth. You don't think about it or even allow yourself to consciously think about it. BUT, THE CONNECTION IS THERE. IT IS DEEP, ALIVE AND PERSONAL TO EACH AND EVERY ONE OF YOU.

If you were to acknowledge and take that information into your bodies and hearts, how could you live here on your Mother Earth? Stop and think about this for a moment. YOU ARE ALL ONE. WE ARE ALL ONE. The people who are killing each other, the people who are starving and dying of neglect, THEY ARE ALL ONE WITH YOU.

YOU ARE ALL CONNECTED TO EACH OTHER. COLOR, RACE, RELIGION, LANGUAGE, AND COUNTRY DOES NOT MATTER. You are all connected and one with each other.

So today let us begin to change those thoughts of separation. Today turn your thoughts to connection and love. TAKE THE TIME RIGHT NOW TO CLOSE YOUR EYES. BREATHE DEEPLY, PLACE YOUR HAND ON YOUR HEART AND CALL MY NAME. Take my hand and come with me to the Circles of Connection. Circles of beings holding hands with each other. There are thousands of circles entwined with each other. Every color, race, religion, and country is represented in each circle. The circle is opening for you. Step into the circle and join hands with all the different forms of yourself. There is a wave of love and connection traveling from hand to hand. You sending out love and receiving it back. A constant never-ending flow of love and connection.

It is possible for you to change what is happening on your Mother Earth. It is possible for you to make a difference. YOU ARE ONE PERSON AND IT ONLY TAKES ONE PERSON TO START THE CHANGE. Come and meet with me daily at the Circle of Connections and you will see that you are one person in a hundred thousand. All of you are wanting the same thing.

The waves of love and connection can and will travel over all of your Mother Earth, bringing you back to your beginnings and your purpose for being here.

REMEMBER! Your purpose here was to grow and learn about love and connection. This is STEP 1; we will talk about the other steps in the days and months ahead. Know that we are here to be with you as you learn and grow. We are here to help you in whatever way you may need. There are thousands of us here waiting for you. We are loving you and connecting with you.

Know you only need call my name and I will be there.
In Love, Mother Mary
11/15/10

LETTER 34

Dear Ones,

Let us today talk about Faith. Faith in yourself, Faith in me, Faith in God, Faith in your partner, and Faith in your World. As you can see there are many levels of faith and they all come directly back to you. For it begins inside of you. What do you believe? I am talking about the belief that is rock hard inside of you. The ones that are written in stone.

I am not talking about the one you think about in your head. I am talking about the one that comes from your core or center. That core faith is life sustaining. Whatever your core faith or belief is, it provides you fuel to keep on living and being. It gives you purpose and reason to participate in life.

There are many people who do not know or even think about what their core beliefs might be. As you grow as children, you may accept and file away what you see as your parent's core beliefs. That does not mean they are your core beliefs today.

Let us today question what your core beliefs are. How solid are they and how strong are they? Do they provide nourishment for your body and soul? Are they life giving or life damaging? Are your core beliefs true for who you are today?

LET US TAKE A MOMENT RIGHT NOW. CLOSE YOUR EYES, TAKE A DEEP BREATH, TOUCH YOUR HEART AND CALL MY NAME. Place one hand on your stomach and one hand on your heart. Just be with yourself for a moment. Allow your mind to clear and be right here with me. What are your core beliefs? Look at them one at a time. What do they mean to you? How does each one affect your life and how you live it? Do they match with who you are right now today?

This will be a process for each of you to discover what your core centered beliefs are. It will mean weeding out some old beliefs that are no longer truth for you and planting the seeds or shoots of new beliefs that you want to try out. There will be other new beliefs that you will want to plant full grown, with no waiting to see if they fit. You already know they are right, for those beliefs are instantly in your core.

Finding what your core beliefs are today will cause the inner chatter of your being to cease. It will bring you back to inner harmony and peace. Some of you might be saying, "but I know exactly what my core beliefs are." That may be true for some of you. Most people will find some changes have taken place in their core beliefs. Come and walk with the helpers and me on this side. Let us help you to discover what your core beliefs are today. Allow peace and harmony to be your way of life. Know that you are greatly loved.

Know you only need call my name and I will be there.
In Love, Mother Mary
11/16/10

LETTER 35
(What would you like to talk about?)

Dear Ones,

As Anna (Barbara) and I come together today to write this letter, I am wondering what you would like for me to write about. Are there things I have not mentioned in my letters that you wish to speak of? Let Anna or me know of these things and I will talk of them in my letters to you. If there are personal things that you are wanting to ask about, there will be time in the months ahead to do that also.

Allow me to say once again that you only need call my name and I will come and be with you. We can have a conversation. You and I, One on One. It is possible. First allow yourself to believe that it is possible. Second allow yourself to trust what you are hearing and seeing in your mind when we talk. It is not your imagination. In the words of your world let me say, "no you are not CRAZY"!

It is important for you to know that the energy and vibration of your planet has changed. Change will continue to happen. The vibration of your planet is becoming higher and higher. As this happens, the veil between our worlds is becoming thinner and thinner. Access to others and me on this side is becoming easier.

WE HAVE BEEN WAITING FOR THIS TIME! TUCKED FAR BACK IN YOUR MINDS, YOU HAVE ALSO BEEN WAITING! We are aware that the changes taking place on your planet have caused you some difficulties. All of your bodies have been affected. Time on your planet has increased; your body speed has increased. All things on your planet are moving faster and faster.

AS ALL OF THIS IS TAKING PLACE, IT IS NECESSARY FOR YOU TO BECOME MORE PURPOSEFUL. Make each and every action and thought count. Keep reminding yourself to stay balanced and in the present time. During this increase of speed, your minds are unfocused and jumping from thought to thought. Remember to bring yourself back to now and what is needed now. Thoughts of yesterday and tomorrow are causing more confusion and feelings of being unfocused.

IT IS IMPORTANT TO REMEMBER THAT WE ARE HERE. WE ARE WAITING TO HELP YOU. IT IS EASIER TO WALK THROUGH THESE CHANGES IF YOU ARE NOT FEELING ALONE. WE ARE HERE WITH LOVE AND SUPPORT TO HOLD YOUR HAND. WE ARE HERE AND READY TO TALK WITH YOU. WE ARE HERE LOVING AND CARING, WHETHER YOU REACH OUT FOR US OR NOT.

Know you only need call my name and I will be there.
In Love, Mother Mary
11/17/10

LETTER 36

Dear Ones,

Today let us talk about Letting Go. Letting Go of all the things in your lives that you have no control over. Letting Go of people who no longer fit with who you have become. Letting Go of all the old feelings of resentment, guilt, and anger. Letting Go of all the old images in your mind about who you could or should be.

The holding on of all these things fills you up and leaves no room for the new things coming into your lives. All of the old feelings and images about how your life should have turned out will stop you and hold you in stagnation. Stagnation or non-movement of energy will turn to disease. Letting Go of people, is often more difficult than the letting go of feelings or memories.

As you change and grow the people in your lives will change, some moving out to continue on with their lives or passing over on to my side of the veil. Their moving on is not because of you. It is because of where their journey is taking them, just as your journey is taking you on a different road. People come into your lives for what you need or want at the moment. There are precious few who have contracted to stay through the years. You can count on your fingers the ones you know who have a contract with you for all the years.

Treasure those few people who will be staying over the years. Allow the ones who need to move on to go in love and peace knowing that you each have fulfilled your contract with the other.

Let us practice Letting Go. CLOSE YOUR EYES, TAKE A DEEP BREATH, PUT YOUR HAND ON YOUR HEART AND CALL MY NAME. Come and be with me; hold my hand and let us walk in the meadow. We have blue sky; the meadow is green and lush with wild flowers. The air is clean and fresh allowing us to breathe gently and easily. Allow your mind to open and let go of all the resentments, anger and guilt. Watch them tumble out into the meadow and be absorbed back into universal energy. Allow your mind to clear out those spaces so long filled with stagnation. Fill up those spaces with the blue sky, the meadow, the wild flowers, and the clean fresh air.

Now, allow the people who you have been holding in your hearts, the ones who need to go or have gone, let them one by one stand in the meadow. Experience the joy and love they have brought into your lives. Carry this joy in your heart as you allow them to leave and go their way. Hold on to the joy and fill all the spaces in your being where they lived with joy. Allow the joy to come into your minds when you think of them. Honor and celebrate that joy, letting go of their leaving by honoring and celebrating the joy. Joy, appreciation and gratitude is the direction in which your world is traveling. Step into joy, appreciation and gratitude and allow your soul to soar.

Call my name and I will come and be with you as you go to the meadow. Call on the thousands of other helpers here on this side that are waiting to help. Going to the meadow is not something to do by yourself. BE gentle and kind to yourself, accept the support and love we offer.

Know you only need call my name and I will be there.
In Love, Mother Mary
11/18/10

LETTER 37

Dear Ones,

Today let us talk again about Love. You cannot talk too much about Love. Love is why you are here on your earth. Love is why I am here writing letters to you. Love is not about what you look like, or how you talk, or the clothes you wear.

Love is pure and simple. Loving yourself or someone else is about simply cherishing that being for who they are. It is about what is inside of that person. I can see what is inside each of you. I love you dearly, each and every one of you. Each and every being is beautiful and unique. There is no one like you in the whole of the universe.

I ask only that you allow me to walk with you and love you. There is nothing you need do or say to receive my love and support. It is just here, waiting for you. There is no need to think in terms of I will be a better person, I will do this or that. It is not necessary to earn this love, or to receive it as a reward.

It is given freely without attachments or requirements. Love is the purpose for you being here on your earth. Learning to love without attachments or requirements is the purpose. Learning to share your love and to receive love is your purpose.

You each have taken different paths to find your purpose and fulfill it. Some will succeed and others will not fulfill their purpose in this lifetime. The energies on your earth are pushing and shoving you forward to succeed. Your world is changing and your energy vibration is being lifted, all working towards the fulfillment of your purpose, learning to love yourself and all other beings of the universe unconditionally.

I am here showing you what it means and how it feels to be loved unconditionally. I am here to give to you what each of you needs. Love with out strings or attachments. Just love standing all by its self.

RIGHT NOW CLOSE YOUR EYES, PUT YOUR HAND ON YOUR HEART AND CALL MY NAME. QUIET YOUR MIND AND BE RIGHT HERE WITH ME. I am putting my arms around you. Can you feel the warmth? There is a softness that comes and surrounds you. I am right here just being with you. Allow yourself to stay right here for a few more minutes. Allow yourself to soak up this warmth and fill your body up, so there is no room for anything but LOVE. Know that I am here with thousands of others waiting to help you and love you.

Know you only need call my name and I will be there.
In Love, Mother Mary
11/19/10

LETTER 38
HOME

Dear Ones,

Let us today talk about Home. There are three kinds of Home. The home or house where you live on your Mother Earth. Home meaning your physical body, where your heart and soul lives. Finally, there is home where I live, where you go when you pass over.

All three of the homes are important for your well being. Home is where you go to feel safe. Home is where you go to be nurtured and revitalized. Home is where you go to find truth and balance. Home is where you go to be loved and comforted.

Let us speak of each home separately. Your home or house where you live in your world needs to be a place of joy and comfort. I am not speaking of money value, size, or elegance. I am speaking of what you feel in your heart when you walk in the door. Is there a sigh that escapes your lips when you walk in the door? Is your house warm and welcoming to you? Do you feel safe? Are you knowing that you can be who you are without judgment or worry? Do you feel loved and comforted?

Let us speak of your physical body, the home of your heart and soul. Look within yourself. How do you feel about your body? Are you continually judging it for being too big, too small, too short, or too tall? Is your hair not right or perhaps your eyes? All of that has little meaning. Your outside appearance is no different than the outside appearance of your house. Once again it is not about what others see or judge either of your homes to be. It is all about how you judge and see your homes to be. How do you feel when you think about them? How do you feel inside of your homes? How do you feel in your body? Is it comfortable, is it crowded, have you allowed others to live in your body with you? Remember your body is only home for you. Many of you have allowed others to live inside your body, in your mind. Their voices tell you what to do, how to live, and whom you can or can't be.

IT IS TIME TO CLEAN OUT BOTH OF YOUR HOMES. YOU KNOW ABOUT SPRING CLEANING, BUT WE ARE GOING TO DO HEART CLEANING TODAY. WE ARE GOING TO CLEAN OUT

YOUR PHYSICAL BODY HOME AND THE HOUSE YOU LIVE IN.

CLOSE YOUR EYES, TAKE A DEEP BREATH, PUT YOUR HAND ON YOUR HEART AND CALL MY NAME. Just be right here with me, right now. I am standing by your side. Can you feel me here with you? Take a deep breath and let us together look inside your mind. Who lives there besides you? Can you and do you want to ask them to leave? IT IS TIME NOW TO ASK THEM TO LEAVE. Remember you will never be alone. I am here with thousands of others to help you and to be with you.

We will not live in your mind, but you only need think of us and we will come to help you; to offer you love, comfort, and support. Take a deep breath. Allow yourself to relax. Your body is yours as it was meant to be. As they lived in your mind they also lived in your house. There is no longer room for their judgments and opinions. There is only room for love, comfort, and support.

Step outside take a deep breath, how does it feel to breathe with no voices in your head? How does your body feel? When you step back into your house how does it feel? Now there is more room, now you can relax. NOW YOU CAN BE.

It is vital for you to be able to JUST BE. When it is time to come to your third home, where I live you will find it is all about being. Being who you are. For you are one of a kind. There is no other being like you. You will find that you are welcomed for the exquisite, precious and beautiful being that you are. Being here will be all about JUST BEING YOU. Know that we are here waiting to help you. Know that we come with love, support, and kindness.

Know you only need call my name and I will be there.
In Love, Mother Mary
11/20/10

LETTER 39

Dear Ones,

Who of you have not had your heart broken? There is no being on your Mother Earth who has not had their heart broken at sometime during their life. Some of you picked up the pieces of your hearts and allowed it to mend part way, and then went on with what life had to offer. There is a large number of you who wrapped up the broken pieces of their hearts, but never allowed it to mend.

Those hearts are still broken and have never been mended or repaired. You have left the heart broken as a reminder of what you should never do or feel again. You thought to keep yourself safe and to never be hurt like that again. What has happened is that you have not kept yourself safe. You have kept yourself isolated and alone. Is that what you really want? You have never allowed yourselves to be loved or to love someone with your whole heart. This someone could be a spouse, a partner, a friend, or a child.

The broken heart is a closed and shut off heart. Your mind and body will follow your heart and become closed off and shut off. Stagnation takes place without the flow of energy. Disease replaces stagnation. This cycle repeats itself over and over. It is time to let your heart heal and be whole. It is time to let your body heal and be whole. It is time to reclaim your life.

STOP NOW AND COME WITH ME, TAKE A DEEP BREATH, TOUCH YOUR HEART AND CALL MY NAME. For a moment let us be quiet; quieting your mind and your racing heart. We are just being here together. Can you feel me? I am touching your hair? Now, put your hand on your heart. IN your mind can you see your heart? Can you see the pieces, can you see who and what caused the heart to break? Will you allow there to be forgiveness? Can there be forgiveness for who and what caused the breaking. Can there be forgiveness for yourself. Allow my hand to touch what you are seeing, hearing, and feeling in your heart. Allow me to join the pieces of your heart back together. Love and forgiveness is the glue and the mending tool to repair broken hearts. My love and your forgiveness joining together to repair the damage.

With your heart mended and whole once again there will be many changes coming into your lives. Many of the dreams and wants that you have for your life were impossible to have with a broken heart. Your heart needs to be whole and filled with love and caring to fulfill your dreams. We are here hoping that you will allow us to help you repair your hearts, so all that you ask and pray for can come into your life.

WE are here willing and waiting for your call. We will bring our love and you bring your forgiveness and we can repair and mend your heart TOTALLY.

REMEMBERING IN THIS PROCESS THAT YOUR PURPOSE FOR BEING HERE ON YOUR EARTH IS TO LOVE. IT IS NOT POSSIBLE TO TOTALLY LOVE WITH A BROKEN HEART. LOVE IS ABOUT LOVING YOURSELF, AND OTHERS, AND RECEIVING LOVE BACK. LOVE GOES AROUND AND AROUND IN AN UNENDING CIRCLE. We are here loving you and asking you to join us in our circle.

Know you only need call my name and I will be there.
In Love, Mother Mary
11/22/10

LETTER 40

Dear Ones,

What if you lived in a world filled with JOY. What if you could only see with the eyes of JOY? What if you could only hear with ears filled with JOY? Is that something you could even imagine happening to you? A world filled with JOY, which so fills you up you can only laugh with the wonder of it all. Your heart is full to overflowing and feels as if it could burst right out of your body. Your mind is full of a rainbow of colors. It overflows with love, warmth and the amazement of all you see, hear, touch, think, and feel.

It is not the world you know today, but it can be. You can be that person who lives in a world of Joy. It is not something that you have been taught how to be or do. You have been taught exactly the opposite. You have been taught to worry, to struggle, to be angry, to be frustrated, and to live in desperation and aloneness.

Your world and the universe are changing. The world is shedding its coat of negativity and turning back to love and joy. As your world changes so must you change. Each and every being of your planet must also shed their coats. It will of course be harder for some. Some have a coat that is thicker and heavier than yours perhaps. Some will choose not to shed their coats and in doing so will not be able to stay on your Mother Earth. Be at peace with their decisions. Know that for some the struggle to shed their coats is too difficult.

For each of you who are in the process right now of shedding your coats, I SAY WELCOME TO MY WORLD. I live in a world of Joy. I am constantly being amazed every day, every hour by the wonder of you and all that you say and do. The love in each of your hearts is amazing to see. Watching you learn to share it with others without conditions and rules is a Joy to me. Seeing you reaching for and accepting the love I am offering you is a Joy. Your acceptance of the help and love from the helpers here with me brings Joy to all our worlds.

TAKE THE TIME RIGHT NOW TO STOP, PUT YOUR HAND ON YOUR HEART AND CALL MY NAME. Quiet your mind and allow me to come and touch with you. My hand touching your heart; filling it with JOY. Rainbow colors of warmth and love will fill your heart to overflowing. Each day come and touch with me. Learn to know what Joy feels like. Notice how your world looks differently for a few moments after experiencing JOY. The Joy inside of you will grow as you experience it more and more. We are planting a seed. It will grow with wondrous speed and to fullness, if you feed it daily with love and joy. WE are here waiting to share our love and joy with you.

Know you only need call my name and I will be there.
In Love, Mother Mary
11/23/10

LETTER 41
GAMES

Dear Ones,

GAMES!!! Let us talk today of the games that you play with yourself. You all know that there are games played between humans. MORE IMPORTANTLY, THE GAMES YOU PLAY WITH YOURSELVES ARE DAMAGING BEYOND MEASURE. You have your most precious dreams and wishes. These things you have thought about sometimes for years. They are what you are asking for and wanting desperately.

The only thing keeping you from having your dreams and wants is yourself. Are you wanting to scream at me and say no it is not me stopping all of this? It just can't be. I say to you yes it is you stopping the dreams and wants before they can even get to you. And you are thinking in your head, how, when, what, and why. How is this possible? I can hear your cries of utter desperation and unhappiness.

In most cases what you dream of and want are what you are most afraid of. You think in your head, is it right, am I handsome enough, or pretty enough to do this or that? Am I smart enough? And the questions go on and on in your head. Those questions are about fear. Fear you can't do what you dream of, fear you aren't worthy enough, fear you aren't smart enough.

RIGHT NOW LOOK! WHERE HAVE THE DREAMS AND WANTS GONE? THEY HAVE ALL BEEN PUSHED AWAY, ERASED BY THE FEAR AND QUESTIONING.

LISTEN TO ME CAREFULLY, YOU ARE SMART ENOUGH, AND YOU ARE WORTHY OF ANYTHING IN THE WHOLE OF YOUR UNIVERSE. YOU ARE PERFECT AND YOU CAN DO ANYTHING THAT YOU DREAM OF DOING. YOU CAN HAVE ANYTHING YOU ARE DREAMING OF HAVING. THERE IS NOTHING STOPPING THE DREAMS BUT YOU!

TODAY CAN YOU STEP BACK AND WALK AWAY FROM THE FEAR. I ASK YOU TO WALK TOWARDS ME! I ASK YOU TO BELIEVE IN ME! I ASK YOU TO TRUST ME! I ASK YOU TO HEAR ME!

I ASK YOU TO LET GO OF THE HAND OF FEAR AND TO CHOOSE MY HAND! I ASK YOU TO COME AND WALK WITH ME!

Just hold on to my hand. You and I will walk and talk. We will talk of your dreams and your fears. We will talk of the games you play with yourself. We will talk of how to stop the games. We will talk of how you can make your dreams come true.

I beg of you to please allow me to help you make your dreams come true. What we here on this side wish for you is that all your dreams and wants will come true. Allow us to help you. Allow us to love you. We are here waiting to walk and talk with you.

Know you only need call my name and I will be there.
In Love, Mother Mary
11/24/10

LETTER 42

Dear Ones,

Let us talk of HEARTS today. Let us talk of the giving and receiving of Love, remembering that Love is the purpose for being here on your Mother Earth. Learning to love each other without rules or expectations.

Loving each other simply because you are exquisite wonderful beings. Loving without reasons or qualifications. Loving and appreciating each other as you would a 100-year-old beautiful tree. Loving each other for no reason except that you are here and you are alive. That in its self makes you deserving of love.

I love you simply because you are here, not because of who you are, or what you have done or will do. There is nothing you must do to deserve my love. You only need be here on this earth and I will love you, just as you love that brand-new baby. The feelings of awe and wonder as you look at that baby. Your heart fills with joy and love, simply because he or she is a part of you. Let us now remember that each and every one of you are part of each other. You are all one; you are all joined and connected.

COME WITH ME NOW, CLOSE YOUR EYES, TAKE A DEEP BREATH, PUT YOUR HAND ON YOUR HEART AND CALL MY NAME. Remember now that you are all made up of energy. Everything in the universe is made up of energy. Look around you; see the energy, see the small dots of light. Are they not all mixing and connecting with each other. Are they not all the same? Can you see any difference in any of the small dots of light? Each one is the same as the others. This is where you all come from. This is how you all start out, a small dot of light. This is your beginning. This is your essence. You are all stars in the night sky.

Can you not open your hearts and welcome all of these dots of light? Can you not love them and treasure them? Look how they glow, and shine. They are simply flowing, moving together in the dance of life. You each are loved and treasured by me and by the thousands of helpers here with me. We are embracing you and joining you in the dance of life. We each are glowing and shining right here beside you. Open your hearts and allow the love inside of you to flow out and encompass the whole of the universe loving and treasuring each and every small dot of life and energy.

We over here are loving and treasuring each of you. We are waiting to help with whatever you may need. Let us help you to open your hearts and your arms to love yourself and the universe.

Know you only need call my name and I will be there.
In Love, Mother Mary
11/25/10

LETTER 43

Dear Ones,

Today let us talk of yesterday's letter. Did you notice a difference in the letter or how it felt to each of you? Stop for a moment or even go back and read the letter again. My words are the same and the writing style is the same. What about the energy that comes with each of my letters?

Each of my letters comes with an energy that is supportive, loving, and nurturing. Many of you physically felt the energy when you first started reading The Letters. It is powerful and uplifting. The energy urges you to go forward and reach for more in your lives. It urges you to open your heart and begin to live your purpose here on your Mother Earth.

The energy that accompanied the letter yesterday was a small sample of the energy on your earth right now, a sample of the energy of your collective consciousness. It was not supportive or encouraging. Did you feel any urges to open your heart even though this is what we were speaking of yesterday?

The sample of energy was just a mild form of the energy that is on your planet right now. The energy was sad, depressed, hopeless, alone, and desperate. The feelings that accompanied the energy yesterday were in the mildest forms, compared to what is happening on your Mother Earth.

THE LETTER YESTERDAY WAS A WAKE UP A CALL FOR ALL OF YOU! YOU WHO KNOW WHAT IS HAPPENING. YOU WHO CAN CHANGE WHAT IS HAPPENING! I wanted you to be able to feel exactly what is happening. I wanted you to feel the difference in how the energy is affecting each one of you. Think about how your day was yesterday. Were you comfortable and at ease in your daily business. Did you feel the urge to reach out to others? Was your heart closed and locked down tight?

You have the power to change what is happening on your Mother Earth. This energy of your Mother Earth has been building for a long time and it is time to change. I AM ASKING EACH OF YOU AS YOU READ MY LETTERS TO OPEN YOUR HEARTS. THE ENERGY WILL BE THERE WITH THE LETTERS TO HELP YOU DO THIS. ALLOW YOUR LOVE TO POUR OUT AND ENCOMPASS YOURSELF, YOUR FAMILIES, YOUR FRIENDS, AND EACH AND EVERY BE-

ING ON YOUR EARTH. ALLOW IT TO SURROUND AND HOLD YOUR MOTHER EARTH IN LOVE AND GRATITUDE.

Each time you allow your heart to open in universal love the energy on your earth will shift and rise up. If you are a being who says they cannot feel the energy, trust me when I say some place in your body you are feeling the energy. The energy of each and every being on your planet is important and can help in the uplifting that needs to happen.

Let us all join together to lift up the energy of your Mother Earth. Let us join together to uplift each and every being so all beings can feel loved, supported, nurtured, and cared for. Help your world to start living the purpose that was intended learning to live with open hearts. Living joyfully and abundantly in the giving and receiving of love.

WE are all here sending you love, support, and great huge energetic bundles of encouragement and hope. There are thousands of us here waiting to help you.

Know you only need call my name and I will be there.
In Love, Mother Mary
11/26/10

LETTER 44

Dear Ones,

In our previous letter, we talked about energy and the raising of the energy vibration of your world. We talked of doing that by encompassing the world and its people in love and joy. There is another step you need to take in changing the energy vibration of the world. It is more personal to each of you.

It is one more step in taking care of yourself. You each in your own way attempt to take care of your body in healthy ways. That could be with exercise or healthy foods. A healthy body requires healthy energy. It is necessary to cleanse your energy, just as it is necessary to cleanse your physical body.

Cleansing your energy needs to be a daily practice. For some it will mean more than twice a day. You each will need to go within yourselves and decide what your energy practice will need to be. Later in this letter I will show you what it feels like to have healthy, clean energy. Healthy and clean energy meaning that there is only your energy in your body. All energy from the collective consciousness has been transformed and released from your body. All energy from family, friends, work and the grocery store has been released and transformed.

It is important for you to know exactly what your own energy feels like. What your body feels like with only your energy flowing through it. What your brain feels like with just your own energy whirling through.

It is also as important that your homes are clear of the other energies of the world. So in your daily practice, be cleansing your homes as you are cleansing yourselves. For those of you who have more than yourselves living in your homes, ask others in the home to participate in the clearing. If that is not possible then proceed with the cleansing of yourself and your home. At all entrances to your homes place cleansing shields that you and each person entering your home will need to walk through. This will allow all worldly debris to be released and transformed. You and your home will appreciate and enjoy being free of the energy of the collective consciousness.

Once you start to partake of these daily practices you will notice a big change in your attitudes and moods. You will find that many of your perceptions will change and that living on your Mother Earth will become easier. EACH OF THESE PRACTICES WILL HELP IN CHANGING

THE ENERGY THAT IS RUNNING RAMPANT ON YOUR MOTHER EARTH RIGHT NOW.

RIGHT NOW COME WITH ME, CLOSE YOUR EYES, TAKE A DEEP BREATH, PUT YOUR HAND ON YOUR HEART AND CALL MY NAME. Take my hand and walk with me. We will walk into the field up ahead. As you reach the edge of the field, there will be a large bubble waiting for you. The bubble is large enough for you to sit in. Walk into the bubble and make yourself comfortable on the pillows. It is warm and cozy inside. This bubble is going to cleanse and transform all energy that is in and around your body. Allow yourself to enjoy a few quiet moments being with yourself. Be aware of how your body is feeling. Can you feel the lightness and the flow of your energy? Pay attention to emotions, are you not happier, more at peace, is your heart starting to open and expand. All of these things are possible when your body is processing and holding only your own personal energy.

We are here to help you in this process. Come back to the bubble as many times as you need. Call on us to help you find your way there. Call on us to help you in anyway. We are here waiting and wanting to be of service to you. We are loving each and every one of you. THE PROCESS OF CHANGING THE ENERGY LEVEL ON YOUR PLANET IS SO IMPORTANT TO THE PURPOSE OF YOUR WORLD AND EACH OF YOU. PLEASE ALLOW US TO HELP YOU IN THIS PROCESS.

Know you only need call my name and I will be there.
In Love, Mother Mary
11/29/10

LETTER 45

Dear Ones,

Today I invite you to come and spend time with me. I ask you to come and sit beside me, allow me to put my arms around you and just hold you. For some of you, it has been forever since you have allowed yourself such comfort. Just for a moment let all things in your world take care of themselves and let us focus just on you.

You, who support, nurture, and take care of others. I say to you who nurtures, supports, and takes care of you? Each and every being on your planet needs love and support. I will call it a Mother's Love. Then again, maybe I should call it Mother Mary's Love. There are some beings on your planet that have never experienced what it feels like to have a Mother's Love. Perhaps their mothers were not physically warm and touching.

There are some of you who will back away and say no I don't want you to put your arms around me or stroke my hair. It would be too painful for them to allow that to happen. So I say to each of you, no matter where you fit in the circle of Mother's Love, IT IS TIME! Time to allow yourselves to experience what that is like. If it is painful, then it is time to let go of the pain. If it is scary, then it is time to let go of the fear. If it is joyful, then it is time to feel the joy and bring your memories back into your mind. If you do not allow time in your life for this kind of thing, then it is time to make time to feel loved.

SO RIGHT NOW TODAY, PUT YOUR HAND ON YOUR HEART AND CALL MY NAME. I am here with you in your home, your car, or wherever you are. I am right there with you. Come and sit with me, sit right up close next to me. Can I put my arms around you, can I hold you close? Let me touch your hair and stroke it gently. Can you feel me kissing your hair? Can you feel me rubbing your arms? If it is painful, allow the pain to flow out of your body, let the tears wash it away. If it is scary, allow the fear to move down and out your feet. Just hold tight to my hand until the fear moves out and away forever. If you are thinking there is not time, then put the clock away. Know when it is all said and done only a few moments will have passed. There is always time for Love and Comfort.

AND NOW I SAY TO YOU "THANK YOU" FOR LETTING ME SHARE MY LOVE WITH YOU. THANK YOU FOR SHARING YOUR LOVE WITH ME. IT IS ALL ABOUT THE GIVING AND RECEIVING OF LOVE. From me to you and you to me.

Know that we are here loving you always. We are here to help and be of service to you in whatever way you may need. We are waiting for your call.

Know you only need call my name and I will be there.
In Love, Mother Mary
11/30/10

LETTER 46

Dear Ones,

Come and sit with me again today. Let us take a journey into your heart. We will look at all the different pieces that make up your heart. Imagine your heart is a puzzle and today we are on a journey to discover and put all the pieces in order.

Some of the pieces you know so well. There is your family, even if you have harsh feelings about your family and things of the past. They still hold a place in your heart. Above all other things of the past, there is love. If you look and think, the answer is there is no love, I ask you to look deeper into the darkest corners. Everyone has deep dark corners in their hearts. For most that is the spot where they have hidden the sorrows.

Sorrow for the disappointments or not being loved the way they wanted to be loved. Is it now time to empty out those dark corners? Is it time to let go of the sorrows? Is it now time to recognize that before there were sorrows there was love? The love did not go away or get replaced with the sorrow. It is as if sorrow has taken a nap on top of the love.

Sorrows can be in the dark corners of your heart for hundreds of reasons. The reasons all come back to love; your not being worthy of love, or not being loved the way you wanted. In the wanting you have lost the knowing that every being on your planet is different. They look different; they act, talk, think and love differently. They each express love in a different way.

In your great need to be loved it is forgotten that each being loves in a different way. They express it in a different way. In your sorrows of not being loved the way you need to be, the differences are forgotten. Only the sorrow of the not being loved is remembered.

SO RIGHT NOW TODAY LET US TAKE A SMALL JOURNEY TO THE SORROWS BURIED DEEP WITHIN YOUR HEART. CLOSE YOUR EYES, PUT YOUR HAND ON YOUR HEART AND CALL MY NAME. I am right here with you. Hold my hand, I will take this journey with you. You know the way to your sorrows. They are always right there on the outskirts of your mind. Today just pick one sorrow to look at. Is it possible that there was love there? Look deeply into all that comes to your mind about love and sorrow. Allow your mind and heart to blend and see the truth. Allow yourself to release the sorrows. Allow the pieces of your hearts to come together and fit in a new way.

Is your heart not lighter now that there is less pain and sorrow? As you go through your days ahead allow yourself the space to clean out the dark corners. Allow your heart to become filled with gratitude and appreciation for all things that have come and gone in your lives.

Allow us to help you with this clearing and cleaning of your heart. We are always here to be with you. We will walk this journey with you, holding your hand, and supporting you in all ways. For we love you greatly. We are here waiting for your call.

Know you only need call my name and I will be there.
In Love, Mother Mary
12/02/10

LETTER 47

Dear Ones,

Oh, my children, I only wish to love you and help you to find an easier way to live on your Mother Earth. Life on your Mother Earth has become so difficult. It is so challenging, cold, cruel, and un-forgiving. It is as if love, generosity, support, nurturing, and comfort have been lost.

Your world is coming into a new time where you will see that love is the all-important thing in the whole of time and universe. That is as it was always meant to be. Your world was never meant to be this off course. It was never meant to go the extremes of greed, violence, and hate that it has gone to.

Your hearts, minds, and bodies were not made to with stand this kind of abuse. As disease, stress, violence, and emotional problems run rampant on your earth. This is all caused by the wrong turns that have been taken.

There are those of you who do not even know that there is love and comfort here waiting for them. They do not believe they are worthy of such things. There are those of you who are going so fast in your daily lives, you do not know that the things you need are waiting for you.

I say to all of you, come and stand with me. Stand with your hearts, minds, and arms open to all beings on your planet; remembering that you are all the same. You are all one. There are no differences in who you are. You are different colors, different religions, different cultures, different traditions, and you are from different countries. I WILL SAY TO YOU TODAY AND ALWAYS THAT THOSE THINGS ARE OF NO IMPORTANCE.

THE ONLY THING TO KNOW AND TO REMEMBER IS THAT YOUR HEARTS ARE ALL THE SAME. THEY ARE THE SAME COLOR, SAME TEXTURE, THEY ALL WORK THE SAME, AND THEY ARE ALL CAPABLE OF LOVE. You are all brothers and sisters.

We are all connected. We are all one. The purpose for your world is to learn to share love with all the beings on your Mother Earth. I AM ASKING YOU TODAY TO START REACHING OUT AND TOUCHING WITH YOUR BROTHERS AND SISTERS. LOVING AND HELPING ONE ANOTHER IN WHATEVER WAY YOU CAN.

Allowing us here on this side to help each one of you to begin reaching out, to begin to love each other without the lines of differences in your minds. Loving each other in the knowing that you are all the same. WE are here waiting to help you. WE are here loving you in all ways.

Know you only need call my name and I will be there.
In Love, Mother Mary
12/03/10

LETTER 48

Dear Ones,

Today let us talk about PEACE. Every being on your planet prays, wishes, and dreams of world peace. No more War, no more fighting, no more killing, and no more damaging beings for the rest of their lives.

World Peace will only happen when each and every being on your planet is at peace within themselves. Each and every one of you has a war raging inside of themselves. Each being's war is different and unique to them. I ask how would it ever be possible for your Mother Earth to be at peace, when there are hundreds of millions of little wars going on every day inside of you.

I know that you have heard it said before that peace starts with each one of you. Each of you thinks when you hear those words that they are meant for someone else. TODAY I MUST TELL YOU TO STOP AND TO KNOW THAT IT APPLIES TO EACH AND EVERYONE OF YOU ON YOUR PLANET. The war inside of you may be small and you think it has no meaning in the big picture, but it does.

The little wars inside each of you are exactly the same as the big wars between countries. It always comes back to one person or one group of people thinking that someone else should live in a different way, or be different. It is about everyone wanting the next person to be like them, so they will know they are on the right path, thinking the right way, and living the right way.

In your small wars, it usually goes back to your families and the children living and doing differently than the parents. SO TODAY I SAY TO YOU THERE IS NO RIGHT OR WRONG WAY TO DO ANY OF IT. THERE IS ONLY THE WAY THAT EACH OF YOU CHOOSES TO LIVE. The small wars also have to do with the war you fight with yourself about what you deserve or don't deserve. The war inside of yourself often comes down to, whether you like yourself or not.

SO I SAY TO YOU RIGHT NOW STOP THE WARS, WHETHER THEY ARE THE BIG ONES OR THE LITTLE ONES. PUT ASIDE YOUR JUDGMENTS OF YOURSELF AND EVERY OTHER BEING

ON YOUR PLANET. LET US ONLY WORRY ABOUT WHAT IS GOING ON INSIDE EACH OF YOU.

HOW CAN WE HELP YOU TO ALLOW THE WAR INSIDE OF YOU TO CEASE? I ASK YOU TO COME AND BE WITH ME RIGHT NOW. TAKE A DEEP BREATH, PLACE YOUR HAND ON YOUR HEART AND CALL MY NAME. I am here with you, and I want to show you who and what I see when I look at you.

I want you to see yourself through my eyes. I want you to see what I see. It is nowhere near the same as what you see when you are warring and fighting with yourself. This is who you truly are. You are a person of love, joy, compassion, and caring. It is time to un-bury these things and to allow them to come out and be with you. You are truly not the person who has been warring and fighting with yourself. That is the person who has taken on the collective consciousness of the world and is living it each and every moment of the day.

Today, right now, take off the coat and mask of negativity and allow the world to see you. Let the wars be gone and let yourself begin to live. It is time to live the life you were intended to live. Your purpose for being here on the planet is about love, loving yourself, loving each other, and loving your Mother Earth.

Do you see and do you understand what I am saying about peace starting with each individual? No more small wars will lead to no more big wars. COME AND WALK WITH ME AND ALL THE THOUSANDS OF OTHERS HERE WITH ME. WALK FREE OF THE WARS AND JUDGMENTS. COME AND WALK IN YOUR WORLD AS WHO YOU TRULY ARE.

Know that you are truly loved beyond what you can imagine. We know that you are working hard at washing away the negativity of your world. We are here waiting to help you in any way we can. We are here with open arms, waiting to hold you and love you.

Know you only need call my name and I will be there.
In Love, Mother Mary
12/06/10

LETTER 49

Dear Ones,

Today let us talk of Gratitude, my gratitude for who each of you are. Gratitude and Joy that you read my letters. That you come and be with me, that you allow me to share my love with you. I have great joy and appreciation for the love you share and give back to me.

Today I wish to honor your courage and your heart for all that it takes to live on your Mother Earth. These are the most challenging times on your planet and each of you has chosen to be here during this time. You each have said, let me go and be there to help others. Let me be the one to lead the way.

You are the Wayshowers and the Keepers of the Light. During these times on your Mother Earth, the dark is being brought out to face the light. The violence, greed, and hate are being brought out into the light of day so all can see what is happening. The governments of the world and the financial empires are all being exposed for what they are.

Your job or what is being asked of you is to simply stand and allow your light to shine out onto the world. You need only stand in love, love for yourself, and love for all other beings on your planet.

The dark and all that it brings with it will be washed clean and made new by the light. You need not worry about how all that will happen; you just need to know that it will. You need to know that it is already happening. This is not something that you can see with your human eye at this time. Trust in me and all the thousands on my side of the veil that it is happening now as we speak.

As more and more of you gather together, shining your light, all will be washed clean and new. You only need reach out in love and joy. So once again I say to you that I HONOR YOU THIS DAY FOR YOUR COURAGE AND YOUR HEART. FOR STEPPING INTO THE LIGHT AND BRINGING IT ON TO YOUR MOTHER EARTH FOR THE GOOD OF ALL.

Know that we are here waiting at the ready for your call. We are here loving you and honoring you this day. Call us and allow us to help you.

Know you only need call my name and I will be there.
In Love, Mother Mary
12/07/10

LETTER 50

Dear Ones,

I am feeling such sadness today. My sadness comes from the ways that I see you treat yourselves. The harshness in the way you talk to yourselves is hurtful. Hurtful to my ears and to your whole being.

There are many unkind words that you say to yourself. It is your way of trying to push yourselves to do the things that are uncomfortable for you. It is a way of making fun of yourselves for the fears and anxieties that you have. Do you not know that it is human to have fears and anxieties? Every being on your planet has some fears and anxieties hidden away inside of them.

There is no shame or need for embarrassment because you have these feelings. Let's take them out of hiding and let us look at them. Often when fears are brought out into the light, they change and become more manageable. Sometimes once they are in the light, they fade away. It is in the hiding that they become consuming and stop you from doing the things that you want.

Harsh words and ugly names do nothing to relieve the fears; they only make it harder for you to function and live the way you wish. Would you speak to me in that way, would you call me ugly names, and brow beat me? Would you do that to your neighbor or friend? In most cases, you would be appalled to think that you would act in such a way to someone else. So I will say to you the next time you start to talk to yourself in that manner, when you look in the mirror, it will be my face you see.

You are a person worthy of kindness, love, support, and caring. In the times that you are all living now it is more important than ever to be loving and supportive of yourself. The challenges in your world are greater now and it takes greater strength and courage to walk your paths. It also takes greater support and love to help you along your journey.

SO TODAY I ASK YOU TO CLOSE YOUR EYES, CALL MY NAME. Let us take the first step in loving yourself. It is time to let go of the old ways of abuse and harshness. Just stand right here with me. Look in the mirror and let us talk about who and what you see. I am standing right here beside you. Can you not see my face in the mirror also?

YOU ARE A UNIQUE AND SPECIAL CREATION, ONE WHO IS MEANT TO GROW AND THRIVE ON LOVE AND SUPPORT. THIS IS WHAT FEEDS YOUR HEART AND SOUL. You have been starving for years. You have not allowed yourself the love and support that is needed. Now is the time to accept and enjoy all that I am offering.

Now is the time for you to change your voice from harshness to love. Now is the time for you to recognize who and what you are. YOU ARE A BEING OF LIGHT WHO IS TO BE HONORED AND CHERISHED. I BOW TO YOU THIS DAY AND PAY HONOR TO WHO YOU ARE AS A BEING OF LIGHT. I SEND YOU MY LOVE AND GRATITUDE FOR WALKING ON YOUR PLANET AND SHARING YOUR LIGHT.

Know that we are here with you offering our love and help to assist you in making your life easier. We are loving you and honoring you in each moment and each day!

Know you only need call my name and I will be there.
In Love, Mother Mary
12/08/10

LETTER 51

Dear Ones,

Let us talk today of the illness and disease that is effecting so many beings on your Mother Earth. Disease is about energy. Energy that is stagnant and dead. The disease affects all of the bodies. Physical, emotional, spiritual, and mental can all be affected.

As you look around can you not see all the different beings on your planet that are suffering. Perhaps you are seeing yourself and where you are being affected by illness or disease.

If you do not have a daily practice of energy clearing or cleaning, then it is time to begin one. It is an easy and simple gift to give yourself. Are you thinking right now, we have talked of this before? The answer is yes! We have talked of this before and we will talk of it again. It is of the utmost importance to each being of your planet.

Keeping your energy field in a clear and crystalline condition is more important than how you take care of any of your other bodies. I am aware how many of you are working to improve the food you put in your physical body. But it is more important to remember that your energy field encompasses all of your other bodies and it has an affect on each of them.

So just as you wash your physical body and provide it with healthy food. It is time to take equal care of your energy field. Daily clearing and cleanings is mandatory. Releasing the energy that has accumulated from the collective consciousness is imperative. It is almost impossible for you to see and be aware of how the collective consciousness is affecting you. Your perceptions and moods are altered and changed. How you treat yourself and others comes into question.

Do you have sudden and unexplained flashes of depression? Are there times when you feel like you are going from one extreme to the other? You are lying on the floor in tears and an hour later you are laughing and feeling wonderful. This is just a small piece of how the collective consciousness affects you.

Call on us to come and help you clear your energy. There is no need for you to suffer in these ways. You only need ask us to come and clear your energy field and that of your home. We will be instantly there to help and assist you. We are waiting to be of service to you. Please allow us to help you and your world. For Mother Earth needs her energy field cleared as often as you do. She carries all the energy of all of the beings that live on her. So daily clear your energy field and also assist Mother Earth to clear hers.

Know you only need call my name and I will be there.
In Love, Mother Mary
12/09/10

LETTER 52

Dear Ones,

I would ask you over the next week to take the time to celebrate life. Starting with your own life. Celebrating who and what you are. Recognizing all that you have given this world. If your first thoughts are I haven't given this world anything. Please listen to me closely when I say that each and every one of you has given back to your world in some way.

Just the fact that you are living on your Mother Earth is one way to give back. You have added to the collective consciousness of your planet by being there. Have you not seen a beautiful sunset, a mountain range, or the ocean? In each case were you not in awe of the beauty and wonder of it. What energy was that you just added to the collective consciousness? Did your energy not enrich the collective? Did it not add to the joy and love that moves through and around your Mother Earth?

Giving back to your world most often does not happen in huge earth shattering ways. It is the hundreds of little ways that come together to make the whole. The little ways are almost more important than the giant huge ones that make a big splash. Each of those little ones is unique and adds a special flavor to your world.

Stop and think of the times that you have reached out to a friend, co-worker, neighbor, or family member. You have made a difference in your world. You think of that as a small thing, but you do not know or see what difference you have made in that person's life. Your eyes only see the outside and the real differences happen on the inside.

What of the children in your life? Grandchildren, nieces, nephews, and friends' children. You have made a difference in their lives by just being there. It may have been a smile, a hug, or an acknowledgement that they are here and you are listening.

All of these things are everyday things that you do not even think about doing, but they are all important and essential. These are the things that make up the energy of kindness, caring, support and love on your planet. The energy of your Mother Earth needs all of these things to thrive and survive.

Are those not reasons to celebrate? So take the time to honor, celebrate who and what you are, and what you offer daily to your Mother Earth. We here are daily celebrating and offering thanks for each and every one of you. We celebrate by sending love, joy, comfort, and support to your Mother Earth and each of you. Join us in our celebration of you. Know that we are here waiting to be of service to you.

Know you only need call my name and I will be there.
In Love, Mother Mary
12/10/10

LETTER 53

Dear Ones,

Are you loving yourself today? Just in case you're not, I want you to know that I AM LOVING YOU TODAY AND EVERYDAY. That I will not ever stop loving you. Each of you are a precious and unique gift. You are to be treasured and cherished. So I am here loving you, treasuring you, and cherishing you.

On your Mother Earth there has been no one to show you how to love yourself. It is not taught in your homes, your schools, or in your world at all. What the children of your world see are beings who believe they are not good enough, not smart enough, not pretty enough, not thin enough, and not worthy enough.

I want to know who made these rules. I want to know who set the scales to decide who is worthy and who is not. I want to expose their lies and untruths. Who is this God that you all believe? His name is negativity and he lives in his world governed by fear, rage, anger, and violence.

I am asking you today to step away from his influence and allow your eyes to clear so that you may see the truth. I AM HERE HOLDING A MIRROR FOR YOU. ALLOW YOURSELF TO SEE WITH THE EYES OF TRUTH. LOOK IN THE MIRROR AND TELL ME WHAT YOU SEE.

ARE YOU SEEING YOUR FACE AND MY FACE MIXING AND MINGLING? WHAT YOU SEE IN MY FACE IS THE SAME AS WHAT IS IN YOUR FACE. REMEMBER WE ARE ALL ONE! WE ARE THE SAME! I AM STANDING HERE LOVING YOU AND I AM STANDING HERE LOVING ME.

Will you not come and join me? As I am hugging and loving you, will you not hug and love me. In your loving and hugging me, you are loving and hugging yourself. STOP FOR A MOMENT AND LET YOURSELF KNOW WHAT THAT FEELS LIKE. Right at this moment there is nothing else but your face in the mirror and my face in the mirror. WE are looking at each other and flowing into and becoming each other. Can you feel the love? Will you allow it inside of you, around you, and encompassing every inch of your being?

    I will never stop loving you, for you are a precious gift to the universe. I am hoping that you will start now today loving yourself also, so we can stand together loving each other and loving ourselves. WE ARE ALL ONE!

Know you only need call my name and I will be there.
In Love, Mother Mary
12/11/10

LETTER 54

Dear Ones,

Today let us talk about Passion. What is Passion? What am I talking about and what does this mean? I am talking about your heart's desire. I am talking about the dreams that you have buried deep within yourself. The ones that you have not talked about forever, that you do not let yourself think about, and no longer allow yourself to dream about.

We are talking about the passions and dreams of your soul; the fulfillment of your purpose and destiny. The reason you each returned to your Mother Earth. NOW IS THE TIME TO LET GO OF YOUR FEARS. NOW IS THE TIME TO STEP OFF THE CLIFF AND EXPERIENCE ALL THAT WAS MEANT TO BE.

You each know in your heart and soul what it is that I am speaking of. You have had hints and flashes of insight about what it is that you are to be doing. During these times of your earth changes, it is the time to come forward and live the life that you dreamed of. It is time to take the first steps in allowing yourself to be who you truly are.

It is time to let your light shine. You are the Wayshowers and Keepers of the Light. Your light needs to be shining brightly and clearly, so that others may know to follow. You are the leaders of the coming days. For others to know the way, you must be willing to shine the light so that they may see the way.

You each have been given many gifts to share with the others of your world. NOW IS THE TIME TO SHARE THOSE GIFTS. YOU ARE GREATLY NEEDED AND WE ARE CALLING EACH OF YOU TO COME FORWARD. WE ARE CALLING EACH OF YOU TO COME AND STAND WITH US. AS WE COME TOGETHER THE LIGHT INCREASES AND SHINES BRIGHTER AND BRIGHTER. The brighter the light, the more people will see and come to stand with us. SOON THE LIGHT WILL BE SO BRIGHT ALL WILL COME AND ALL WILL BE STANDING WITH US.

LOVE AND LIGHT WILL SHINE AND SURROUND ALL. IT WILL BE AS IT WAS MEANT TO BE ON YOUR MOTHER EARTH.

EACH AND EVERY BEING GIVING AND RECEIVING LOVE WITHOUT RULES OR JUDGMENTS. EACH OF YOU JOINED AND CONNECTED TO THE OTHER IN LOVE.

   COME AND ALLOW YOURSELF TO BE WHO YOU ARE. LET GO OF THE FEAR AND ALLOW YOUR LIGHT TO TURN ON. We are here waiting to help you. Waiting to put our hand over yours to help in the turning on of the light. You were not meant to do this alone. We are here helping you and holding you. TURN ON YOUR LIGHT AND STAND WITH US.

Know you only need call my name and I will be there.
In Love, Mother Mary
12/13/10

LETTER 55

Dear Ones,

Today let us talk about your hearts. For many years on your planet, you have been taught to live with your heart closed. The teaching did not happen in the words that were spoken but by the actions of the people around you. Today on your planet that same tradition is still taking place. The children of your world are shown that the best way to live is with a closed heart.

There is a belief that the only way to survive life on Mother Earth is to live with your heart closed. It is believed that living with your heart closed is the only safe way to be. Living with your heart open is not about being hurt and being unsafe. It is about loving one another without judgments of right or wrong. It is about loving one another without seeing the color, religion, and cultures of others.

Living with an open heart is first about loving yourself. For the truth is that you each are only capable of loving others to the same degree that you love yourself. Everything in your world starts with each of you. War, Peace, Joy, Caring, Love, Hope, and Belief all starts within each of you. You are the beginning of all.

You are the beginning of all in each and every step of your universe. You each have the immense power to change your world simply by changing yourselves. What you do and how you do it washes out from you in waves changing each and every other wave it touches. Your wave or energy affects everything that it connects or touches with.

You often think that what you do and say has no matter in your world. How often have you heard it said? I am just one person, what difference could I make? I SAY TO YOU VERY LOUDLY THAT EVERYTHING YOU SAY AND DO MAKES A DIFFERENCE. BECAUSE YOU CANNOT SEE IT WITH YOUR EYES OR HEAR THE DIFFERENCE, IT DOES NOT MEAN IT HAS NOT CHANGED THE WORLD.

CLOSE YOUR EYES, TAKE A DEEP BREATH, PUT YOUR HAND ON YOUR HEART, AND CALL MY NAME. Clear your mind and be with me for a moment. I will show you what happens and the connections between what you say and do. Once again, we will watch a movie and you are the main actor in the movie. You are going about your daily routine. It is time to go to work. You're walking on the street, looking at the people who are passing you by; you are frowning. Watch your energy hit them, your anger, frustration, and sadness. Watch what happens as your energy connects with them. Their energy field changes and becomes darker, heavier, and denser. Their minds become slower; their heart shuts down tighter and their steps are slower.

I SAY TO YOU THAT YOU HAVE IMMENSE POWER TO CHANGE YOUR WORLD. Do you see what one person can do? Also remember that the people on the street are also looking back at you and passing their energy on to you. IF YOU ARE WALKING ON THE STREET WITH YOUR HEART OPEN SENDING LOVE AND JOY TO EVERYONE, WHAT A HUGE DIFFERENCE YOU WOULD MAKE IN YOUR WORLD.

DARE TO BE THE PERSON ON THE STREET WALKING WITH YOUR HEART OPEN AND KNOW THAT YOU WILL NOT BE WALKING ALONE. I WILL BE WALKING BY YOUR SIDE AND THERE WILL BE THOUSANDS AND THOUSANDS WALKING WITH US.

KNOW IN YOUR HEARTS AND MINDS THAT ANYTHING AND EVERYTHING IS POSSIBLE. YOU HAVE THE POWER TO CREATE AND BE WHO YOU DREAM OF BEING.

Know you only need call my name and I will be there.
In Love, Mother Mary
12/14/10

LETTER 56

Dear Ones,

In the craziness of your world right now, I am asking you to stop and take a breath. Your bodies and minds are running so fast you aren't seeing what is happening right in front of you.

SO I SAY TO YOU TODAY STOP! RIGHT NOW, JUST STOP! I KNOW THAT IT IS YOUR HOLIDAY SEASON AND THERE IS MUCH THAT YOU THINK YOU MUST AND SHOULD DO. I AM SAYING, STOP AND DO NOTHING RIGHT NOW.

Take a few minutes for doing nothing. Allow yourself to breathe. Allow your mind to slow down and come back to you. It is as if you are flying about in different directions. Yes, I know that this is how you have always been during your holiday season. But this year it needs to be different. The energy of your world is different now and your energy field is different also. What happens is that you become like a runaway train. Run away trains eventually crash and become non-functional.

There is no need for you to follow that path. There is no need for you to harm yourself in that way. This is all about learning a different way and recognizing that there have been changes to the energy of your world and yourself. SO ONCE AGAIN TAKE A DEEP BREATH AND JUST BE HERE WITH ME. WE ARE BOTH DOING NOTHING RIGHT NOW. BY DOING NOTHING RIGHT NOW YOU WILL BE ABLE TO BECOME MORE FOCUSED LATER.

NOW THAT WE HAVE STOPPED, I ASK YOU TO LOOK AT WHAT IT IS THAT YOU THINK YOU MUST AND SHOULD DO. MY QUESTION TO YOU IS WHAT DO YOU WANT TO DO? IT IS TIME TO LET GO OF ALL THE I MUST OR I SHOULD, IN YOUR LIFE. During your holiday season, this becomes a huge energy field encompassing everything you see and do.

This year it is time to honor yourself, your friends, and families by doing what it is your heart is telling you to do. This is a gift that only you can give to yourself and others. This is a gift made of love and is given in the valuing of yourself and others.

Let your mind free itself of the old ways that are of the past and have no place in the new world and life that you are creating. It is time to let go of the old ways. The letting go will be as if you have released a thousand pounds from your heart, mind, and body. The letting go of your old ways will allow you to celebrate your holiday season in the spirit of LOVE and JOY.

CALL ON US TO ASSIST YOU IN THE LETTING GO. We are here loving you and wanting to be of service to you. Come and walk with us.

Know you only need call my name and I will be there.
In Love, Mother Mary
12/15/10

LETTER 57

Dear Ones,

Today you are still in the build-up of your holiday season and STRESS is running rampant in your world. Yesterday I asked you to stop and take a breath. Today I am asking you to stop, SMILE, and remember, when was the last time you laughed right out loud? TAKE A MOMENT RIGHT NOW AND ALLOW THE MEMORY TO FLOAT BACK UP INTO YOUR PRESENT MIND. ENJOY THE WONDER OF THAT LAUGH AND HOW GOOD IT MAKES YOU FEEL.

LAUGHTER is the most natural medicine in your world. It lightens up your heart and soul. It expands your mind and releases the negative energy collected in your body. Your stress level plummets to zero. It is as if you are a new being. All the anxiety, fear, distrust, and loneliness disappear.

What an amazing gift that you could give yourself if you agreed to allow yourself to really laugh once a day. Would it be easy to do that for yourself? Do you have a favorite funny story, a joke, or picture that makes you laugh? Whatever it is that brings that response to you, let us find it and put it where you can see it daily.

Imagine starting your day with a wonderful laugh. Laughter, Love, and Joy walk hand in hand. What if you could start each day out walking hand in hand with Laughter, Love, and Joy? How would your world look if you chose to start each day in that way? How does your mind, body, and soul feel starting your day in that way? Imagine the wonder of that.

Imagine how you would change your personal world and the whole of the world. LET US STOP RIGHT NOW AND WATCH THAT MOVIE AGAIN WHERE YOU ARE WALKING DOWN THE STREET. DO YOU REMEMBER THE ONE I AM TALKING ABOUT FROM LETTER 52? Only this time as you look at the people you are passing on the street the energy you are sending out is Laughter, Love, and Joy. Watch their faces as it connects with each of them. Can you see the transformation that takes place? Their eyes light up, their faces relax and you can almost see the burdens lift off their shoulders. You are smiling and they are smiling back at you.

LOOK AT WHAT YOU HAVE DONE. BY ALLOWING YOURSELF THE PLEASURE OF STARTING YOUR DAY WITH LAUGHTER YOU HAVE CHANGED THE ENERGY OF YOUR PLANET. NOW IMAGINE IF 10 PEOPLE DID THAT. WHY NOT GO FOR 100 OR 1000 PEOPLE DOING THAT OR MAYBE EVEN 100 MILLION.

One person can make a huge difference in your world. Laughter is contagious and it is possible for it to become an epidemic and travel throughout your universe. An epidemic of Laughter, Love, and Joy. Allow me to come and walk with you and we will start this epidemic together.

Know you only need call my name and I will be there.
In Love, Mother Mary
12/16/10

LETTER 58

Dear Ones,

Let us talk again today about your holiday season. Many of the beings on your Mother Earth become generous and open hearted over the holidays. My question to you is why just at the holidays? For those of you who have the means to help in supporting others, it is needed for you to continue this throughout the year.

There are so many in your world who are in need right now. The numbers have grown to be in the millions. The difference between the people of your world who have and who do not have, has become immense. There is a sameness to the number of people who have closed their hearts down completely to those who have started to open their hearts.

It is as if your world has started to become divided in half. There seems to be no middle ground. Hearts are starting to open or hearts are closing up tighter. Some people are seeing the energetic changes to your world and then there are those who are still sound asleep. Your world was not meant to be black and white. It was meant to be a world of color. Look about in the nature of your world. There are thousands of different colors and shades of colors. There is no black and white; no rigid rules of how to live your life, and no need to be totally awake or totally asleep.

I am asking each of you to come to the middle ground in every area of your life. Taking the time to be generous all year around. Helping the people who do not have the means to feed themselves or even provide a place to sleep for their families. Helping the person beside you see the world in a different light, or maybe even a color.

Do not turn your back on someone because they think differently or see the world in a different way. Of course, all of this goes back to opening your hearts. During your holiday season, you each work very hard to have your hearts open. Many of you are afraid that by having your heart open just a little that someone will hurt you.

TODAY I AM ASKING YOU TO OPEN YOUR HEARTS WIDE AND TO LET YOURSELVES BE VULNERABLE TO LOVE AND CARING. Allow the joy of your holiday season to come and be with you in all ways. I am also asking that you keep that Joy and Holiday Season with you all year long. It is not necessary to feel it only once a year. If you wish, it can be there at all times.

The trick to keeping those feelings all year long is to keep your heart open and vulnerable to the love and caring of your world. It is time to step away from one side or the other. It is time to come and stand in the middle where the colors are. The colors are life in its best clothes. Come and join us in the colors, let there be no more one side or the other, no more black and white, and no more awake or asleep.

Come and live your life to the fullest. Loving and caring about others and loving and caring about yourself. We will walk with you and show you how to live your life to the fullest. We will sing and laugh with you as you find your way. We are waiting to hear from you.

Know you only need call my name and I will be there.
In Love, Mother Mary
12/17/10

LETTER 59

Dear Ones,

OH, MY DEAR CHILDREN. I can see that you are hurting. For some it is emotional pain from issues of the past or anxiety about today and the future. For others, it is physical pain from aging or disease. Just for today, can I carry that for you?

I am giving you each a backpack and in this backpack place whatever it is I can carry for you today. CLOSE YOUR EYES RIGHT NOW, TAKE A DEEP BREATH, PUT YOUR HAND ON YOUR HEART AND CALL MY NAME. I just want you to be right here with me. What pain are you carrying and what pain are you willing to let me help you with today? There are just a few who will put anything in your backpack. You have each learned to suffer and being in pain is part of suffering. You have been taught that pain and suffering is just part of life and the best you can do is to endure them.

That is not a truth, no matter who taught you that. Yes, it has been passed down through the generations, but still it is not truth. Pain and suffering was never meant to be part of your everyday life. They were meant to come and go with the flow of life. They do not need to stay and punish you for a lifetime.

We will go back and speak again of the new energy coming into your universe. There is no room in the new energy for continued and unnecessary pain and suffering. It is not something that you can bring with you into the new world. As you have learned over the past year, it has been necessary to let go of many things. Today I am calling you to let go of pain and suffering.

I am asking you to let me carry it for you today. I want you to allow yourself to see what your life would be like without the pain. For many of you this is the only way you have learned to live. Test the waters today and see what you feel like without it. For some it will feel like your safety net has been taken away. We are here and we can help with those feelings of fear. We are right here and will help you with the letting go and the learning to live with ease and gentleness. PAIN FREE. REMEMBER THAT IN THE NEW ENERGY THERE IS NO ROOM FOR OLD UNNECESSARY PAIN.

For those of you who are in body pain from illness or disease, please allow us to help you deal with that in your daily lives. Allow us to teach you new ways to deal with it. The new energy of your universe will also be working with you to lessen your burdens and to help you live your life with more ease and gentleness.

TAKE THE TIME RIGHT NOW TO FILL YOUR BACKPACKS WITH YOUR PAIN AND I WILL TAKE CARE OF IT FOR YOU TODAY AND FOREVER IF YOU WISH TO LET GO! We are here loving you and standing right beside you as you make these immense changes in your lives. We are honoring and appreciating your courage and strength. We are applauding your bravery in taking care of yourselves and how you are moving into the new energy of your world.

It is easy to see why you are the chosen ones. The WAYSHOWERS and KEEPERS OF THE LIGHT. FOR YOU HAVE GREAT STRENGTH, WISDOM, AND LOVE. YOU ARE FOREVER READY TO DO ALL THAT IS NECESSARY TO KEEP YOURSELF MOVING FORWARD AND SHOWING OTHERS THE WAY. WE THANK YOU AND HONOR YOU FOR WHO YOU ARE.

Know you only need call my name and I will be there.
In Love, Mother Mary
12/20/10

LETTER 60
DEPLETION

Dear Ones,

You each are so exhausted and depleted. Your holiday season is very hard on all your bodies. Pushing yourselves to your very limits seems to be part of your holiday season. The pushing is the only way you know to do the season. Shopping and running here and there and everywhere is considered normal in your world.

Perhaps, there is a different way to prepare and enjoy your holidays. LET US FOR A MOMENT STOP RIGHT HERE, RIGHT NOW. Yes, I can see the lists in your head and I do hear you thinking, there is no way I can stop right now. I AM SAYING TO YOU THAT YES YOU CAN STOP RIGHT NOW. IN FACT, YOU DESPERATELY NEED TO STOP RIGHT NOW. Your physical body is exhausted and depleted. Your emotional body is flying off in every direction. Are you not close to tears or ready to scream at the next sales clerk? Your spiritual body has a flat line. Do you know that term "flat line"? It is from your hospitals and it means your heart has stopped.

Are you shaking your head and saying what is she talking about? Your heart is the center of your spiritual body. It is the center of all. Right now, your SPIRITUAL BODY IS DYING FROM LACK OF CARE. In the energies of your changing world, your spiritual body is the most important. It is to be nurtured and taken care of above all else. You can only take care of it if you have taken care of your other bodies, meaning your physical and emotional bodies.

Your physical body has not been taken care of. In the new energies of your world, the taking care of yourself is most important. It is necessary now to take care of self first and others later. I know that this thinking is foreign to you. For you were taught and it has always been so on your

Mother Earth that you take care of others first. That is no longer a truth and in fact, was never a truth. You must come first. If you are not first how can you have the strength, courage, and love to share with others?

IT IS SO IMPORTANT FOR YOU TO UNDERSTAND WHAT I AM SAYING. THINK BACK TO BEING ON AN AIRPLANE AND THE ATTENDANT IS EXPLAINING ABOUT THE OXYGEN MASKS. HOW TO USE THE MASK AND WHAT TO DO IF NECESSARY. CAN YOU HEAR WHAT SHE IS SAYING TO THE PARENTS? The parent has been taught from the beginning that they take care of their child first, but the attendant is saying, take care of yourself first. Put the mask on your face first and then give it to the child. If you care for the child first and give them the mask, you may be dead or not have the strength left to take care of yourself. NOW WHERE IS THE CHILD? THERE IS NO ONE TO CARE FOR THEM.

Do you understand what I am saying to you? Taking care of yourself first is taking care of your spiritual body and then others in your life. Giving yourself the nourishment, sleep, care, and love needed is crucial to yourself and your world. What you give yourselves is what in turn is given to your universe or Mother Earth.

You and your Mother Earth cannot afford to be depleted any longer. YES, I KNOW THAT YOUR HOLIDAY SEASON IS IMPORTANT. SO, IT IS TIME TO LOOK AT HOW YOU DO HOLIDAYS. ALSO HOW YOU COULD CHANGE THEM FOR THE REST OF THIS SEASON AND ALL FUTURE SEASONS.

Is not the reason for the Holiday Season getting lost in all the craziness that happens? IT IS TIME TO STOP AND TAKE A LOOK AT WHAT IS IMPORTANT TO EACH OF YOU ABOUT THE HOLIDAYS. WHAT ARE YOU CELEBRATING AND HOW DO YOU WANT TO CELEBRATE? HOW CAN YOU CARE FOR YOURSELVES AND ALSO CARE FOR THE HOLIDAYS?

Yes, I know it would be difficult to change your ways overnight, right now. So, take the time to think about it. Perhaps making a small change heading in the direction of taking care of yourselves, as well as your holidays.

We are loving you and waiting to hear from you. We can help you decide which changes to make and how to make them gently and easily. Making these changes will be going against everything you have been taught and we are aware of that. Giving yourself support in doing this would be taking good care of yourself. So call for us and we will be there to help in whatever way you want. We are loving you beyond all measure.

Know you only need call my name and I will be there.
In Love, Mother Mary
12/19/10

LETTER 61
THE FINAL PHASE

Dear Ones,

Your Earth has just shifted into the final phase of the coming of your new energy transformation. Last night there was a powerful alignment of the Moon, Stars, and your Mother Earth. Now begins the final phase of coming together.

Now is the time of coming together in recognition of love and our ultimate oneness. There is no longer room on your Mother Earth for eyes of mistrust and separateness. You are beings of love and light. You have come to the place of stepping into all that your Mother Earth was meant to be.

There is no longer time or room for thoughts of unworthiness, guilt, shame, and the on- going list of words and feelings used to devalue yourselves. Now is the time to shed that coat of unworthiness and stand for who you truly are.

You have worked hard over the past months and years to bring yourselves to this place in your time. All of us are here now applauding all that you have accomplished. We are also here to let you know that we will continue to support and love you in the days ahead as you complete your journeys.

There is much left for you to learn and grow with. This final phase will be faster and more accelerated than what you have previously experienced. Once again, I say we are here and we will be helping even more during this final phase. Everything you have worked through thus far has led you to becoming awakened to the essence of pure love. Awakened to the oneness of all beings on your planet.

You will be coming together and accepting in the days ahead that love is all there is. Your whole purpose for being here on your planet was to learn about love. LOVING YOURSELVES, LOVING EACH OTHER, LOVING YOUR MOTHER EARTH, AND LOVING ALL OF US HERE STANDING AT THE READY TO HELP. YOU WILL BE TRULY RECOGNIZING YOUR BEAUTY AND LIGHT. YOU WILL BEGIN TO SEE YOURSELVES THROUGH OUR EYES. YOU WILL BEHOLD YOURSELVES THROUGH THE EYES OF PURE LOVE.

YOUR AMAZEMENT WHEN YOU RECOGNIZE WHO YOU TRULY ARE WILL BE BEAUTIFUL TO SEE. I AM LOOKING FORWARD TO THAT MOMENT AND ALL THAT WILL HAPPEN IN YOUR HEARTS AND MINDS AT THAT TIME.

Know that we are here helping you make these changes and that we will continue to be here during this final phase of changes. We are loving you, applauding you, and joining hands with you as you continue on your journey.

Know you only need call my name and I will be there.
In Love, Mother Mary
12/21/10

LETTER 62

Dear Ones,

I am holding you dearly today. I use the word DEARLY today meaning that I am holding you with reverence, love, respect, and with great honor for who you are. You all have worked so hard to prepare yourselves to be the Wayshowers and Keepers of the Light. Each of you has been working from the time of your birth preparing yourself for this time in your lives.

This is the time when all you have worked for is coming into being. There are some who are seeing their purpose and they are taking the risks to fulfill them. There are others of you who have not quite acknowledged your purpose for being here. You are so close and when you open your eyes all will be revealed and you will each step forward.

I know that I have said this many times, but it is necessary to say it again and again. WE ARE HERE FOR YOU, SUPPORTING YOU IN ALL WAYS. YOU MAY NOT SEE US OR HEAR US, BUT BELIEVE ME WHEN I SAY WE ARE HERE. YOU ARE ALL BEING GUIDED AND SHOWN THE PATH TO FOLLOW. You may not be conscious of these things, but they are happening anyway. When you are ready you each will start to see us and hear us.

You each are opening your hearts and minds to things beyond what your world knows of. There are times when you find yourself wondering why am I believing these things. You are believing because your soul and your heart knows the truth. This time on your planet is about believing in the things you cannot see, hear, or touch. This time is not about your 3D world. It is about learning what lies beyond what is known in the 3D world.

Now is about stretching out and finding all the things that have been just beyond your knowing. The things that have been just outside your everyday thinking. It is as if you have known that something was there waiting for you. You have never been sure how to reach out and claim these unknowns. You are awakening to your inner truths and the knowing of all that has been just beyond reach.

I WILL SAY AGAIN WE ARE HERE SUPPORTING YOU AND LOVING YOU. WE ARE ALWAYS RIGHT BESIDE YOU. IN THE

COMING DAYS OF YOUR FINAL PHASE WE WILL STAND AT THE READY FOR EACH OF YOU. WE ARE WORKING HERE ON THIS SIDE TO MAKE THE CHANGES ON YOUR PLANET AS GENTLE AND EASY AS POSSIBLE.

KNOW THAT WE ARE HERE APPLAUDING YOU FOR ALL YOUR HARD WORK AND YOUR IMMENSE COURAGE AND STRENGTH. WE ARE LOVING YOU.

Know you only need call my name and I will be there.
In Love, Mother Mary
12/22/10

LETTER 63
MERRY CHRISTMAS

Dear Ones,

This will be my last letter before your Christmas Day; the day where you will celebrate the birth of my son. I THANK YOU FOR PAYING HONOR TO HIM AND FOR YOUR BELIEF IN ALL OF US HERE ON THIS SIDE.

Many people go back and forth about what they believe and what they don't believe. It is always most important to question all things in your world. The questioning is what makes you each grow and stretch. I want to assure you that all of your answers will come back to one thing. LOVE AND ONLY LOVE.

YOUR EARTH WAS FORMED FROM LOVE AND MADE WITH THE INTENTION OF BEING A UNIVERSE OF LOVE. You each have chosen to come to this universe because of love. You came to learn about love. The whole and only purpose for each of you being here was to learn how much you are loved. Your journey is about learning to love yourselves as much as we love you.

WE ARE HERE LOVING YOU JUST AS YOU ARE. YOU STAND HERE BEFORE US IN PERFECTION, JUST AS YOU ARE. We know that in your minds, you find it hard to take in that you are in perfection just as you are. It is in your nature to strive and strive to be better in every way. You strive to reach what you call perfection. SO I WILL SAY AGAIN VERY LOUDLY. YOU ARE IN PERFECTION JUST AS YOU ARE. We love you greatly and applaud you hourly for your courage, strength, and determination to be better and better. We also say to you it is ok to slow down and stop pushing yourselves to be better and better.

You have recently stepped into the final changes of your universal energy transformation. Soon you will be able to see with your new energetic eyes your own perfection. You will see the rightness and brightness of all in your world. The rightness and brightness will be pure love in its original form. The form that your universe was created with and as each of you were created.

WE WILL CLOSE FOR NOW, SENDING YOU LOVE AND CARING FOR YOU AS YOU PARTAKE OF YOUR HOLIDAY CELEBRATIONS. WE ARE HONORING YOU AS YOU ARE HONORING MY SON. MAY YOU EACH BE FILLED WITH UNIMAGINABLE AMOUNTS OF LOVE, JOY, AND LAUGHTER?

Know you only need call my name and I will be there.
In Love, Mother Mary
12/23/10

LETTER 64
PREPARATION FOR 2011

Dear Ones,

Welcome back from the craziness of your Holidays. Yes, I know there is one more celebration, the celebration of your NEW YEAR. In a few days, we will be moving into the year 2011.

2011 will be a year beyond compare. It will be more challenging and eye opening than any year in your lifetime. You will meet your biggest challenges and move on to overcome those challenges with grace and love. WE WILL BE RIGHT HERE WALKING BESIDE YOU AS YOU FACE THOSE CHALLENGES AND AS YOU OVERCOME THEM.

It will be a year of learning and seeing wondrous things. As your eyes open during this year, you will find yourself seeing into the unseen worlds around you. You will become aware of all the help and helpers that are available for each and every being on your planet. Trusting yourself and knowing that you are exactly where you need and want to be.

It will be a time of great awakenings and joy. You will find that all those fleeting thoughts that you have been pushing away as imagination are really truth. The other realties of your world and other worlds will come into focus. You will rejoice in all the possibilities that you can see and take advantage of.

Let us now speak of preparing yourself for the beginning of your New Year. In the next few days before your New Year, start clearing and cleaning out your home. Moving out as much of the old as possible. If you are not finished before the New Year continue until all in your home is fresh and made new. Complete this as soon as possible after the New Year.

Between now and the New Year when you take showers ask that all the old energies be released and washed away. During the shower allow your mind to wander wherever it will go. As the bits and pieces of your life float up before your eyes allow your shower to wash them away. The goal is to take as little as possible with you into the New Year. Continue the washing away into the New Year until you have released as much as possible.

Cleaning and clearing your homes and your being will allow the New

Year to float in on a gentle and easier wave of light. All of the clearing and cleaning makes way for the new energy to come forward. If there is room for the new energy to come and be with you, there will be less of a struggle for it to find its place in your life.

There will be an immense flow of energy and light to your world as 2011 comes into being on your Mother Earth. Take the time to prepare yourself for a gentle entry into 2011. Remember that we are here waiting to help you. Please call on us over the next week as you are preparing for 2011. WE can be of much help in your clearing and cleaning.

WE ARE HERE LOVING YOU AND HONORING YOU FOR ALL YOU HAVE ACCOMPLISHED AND ALL YOU WILL ACCOMPLISH IN 2011.

REMEMBER THAT YOU ARE THE WAYSHOWERS AND THE KEEPERS OF THE LIGHT. SHARE WITH OTHERS YOUR WISDOM AND INSIGHTS. LET OTHERS KNOW WHAT YOU ARE DOING TO PREPARE YOURSELF FOR THE COMING OF 2011.

Know you only need call my name and I will be there.
In Love, Mother Mary
12/27/10

LETTER 65
MORE PREPARATION FOR 2011

Dear Ones,

Let us talk once again about the coming of your New Year, 2011. This New Year is one to be celebrated. Your world has been waiting a long time for what is to come. The New Year will be a time of opening hearts and minds. I am speaking of hearts wide open accepting and loving all beings, all worlds, all animals, and Mother Earth.

You each will see such a difference in yourselves and others as you travel through this year. The changes that will take place as you open yourselves up to who you really are will amaze you. You will find yourselves in gratitude saying over and over again, Thank You, Thank You, and Thank You.

You will recognize the glory of being part of this Universal Energy Transformation. Knowing that you are one of the Wayshowers and Keepers of the Light will bring appreciation and joy to your whole being. Sharing your wisdom and insights about how you arrived at this place will give you great pleasure and fulfill your obligation.

The OBLIGATION I speak of is a promise made before you returned to your earth this time. There were contracts made and agreed to by each of you. Contracts that your SOUL and HIGHER-SELVES ASKED FOR AND WERE HONORED TO BE A PART OF.

YOUR PART OF THE CONTRACT WAS THE AGREEMENT TO BE A WAYSHOWERS AND A KEEPER OF THE LIGHT. That included sharing your wisdom and insights with others. The contract included lighting the path ahead so that others could follow in your footsteps.

PLEASE KNOW THAT ALL IN MY WORLD ARE CHEERING AND CELEBRATING ALL THAT YOU HAVE DONE TO HONOR THIS CONTRACT. WE ARE ALSO CHEERING BECAUSE WE KNOW THAT YOU EACH WILL CONTINUE TO HONOR YOUR CONTRACTS. EACH OF YOU HAS DONE SO WITH LOVE, DIGNITY, TRUST, AND FAITH IN YOURSELVES AND IN US.

There is still much to be accomplished on your Mother Earth and all of that will happen in the days to come. Some beings of your planet will continue to sleep through the coming days. We here also honor those beings that are choosing to sleep. That is their choice and we will honor that. They will find that the earth is no longer a comfortable place to sleep and then they will have other choices to make.

AS YOUR NEW YEAR COMES INTO BEING WE ARE ASKING THE WAYSHOWERS AND KEEPERS OF THE LIGHT TO BE PRESENT. WE ARE ASKING THAT YOU BE PRESENT WITH YOUR MINDS AND HEARTS OPEN WIDE TO WELCOME IT AND BRING IT INTO BEING.

Once again, I will say that we are right here. We will be very present standing right beside you as your New Year comes into being. I say that there are always thousands and thousands of helpers on this side waiting to help you. As your New Year comes into being there will be hundreds of thousands waiting here to help. Remember that nothing is too small to ask for help with. We are here to help with the big things and the little things. We are always honored to help no matter what it is you need. We are loving you and holding you to our hearts.

Know you only need call my name and I will be there.
In Love, Mother Mary
12/28/10

LETTER 66
AGAIN MORE PREPARATION FOR 2011

Dear Ones,

Yesterday, we spoke of preparations for the coming New Year, 2011. I have been urging you to clear and clean your homes and your physical bodies. Letting go of old unused objects and clothing in your homes that you no longer need or want. In some cases, things you did not even remember owning or having in your home. It is also time to let go of any old feelings of unworthiness, guilt, disappointment, and anger.

Each item and each piece of unused clothing takes up space in your home. Old feelings and emotions also take up space in your mind and body. That space is energy filled and part of what you hold around you. Old stagnant energy drains you of your life force. Life force is what is required for you to travel through your today, tomorrow, and into 2011. I will say to you that the keeping of these items is a way of hanging on to the old way of life. It is time to let go of the old ways and step in the new energy. It is time to step into the universal energy transformation that is happening on your Mother Earth.

You each are part of that transformation. The universal energy transformation is your main purpose for being here on your planet. Yesterday, we spoke briefly of obligations and contracts. You each have come back to your Mother Earth with a contract signed by you to play a certain role in this transformation.

I can almost hear your voices saying what contract, what obligation? Each individual agreed to their own unique contract of what they needed and wanted to do and be during this transformation. Some of you have already remembered and have stepped into the becoming of who you truly are. I will say it is wondrous to behold. Others of you have only allowed yourselves a small glimpse of what it is that you are meant to do.

Most of you feel there is great fear and risk involved in stepping into being who you truly are. Look around you to the ones you know who have made that step. They have survived, and they are growing and shining brightly. You will arrive at that place also. Each of these beings that have taken the risks have not been alone. They each had great help and support from us here on this side. Just as we will be here to help you and support you.

NOW IS THE TIME TO CLOSE YOUR EYES AND BE HERE WITH ME. ALLOW YOUR MIND TO WANDER. ASK YOURSELF WHAT IT IS THAT YOU ARE MEANT TO BE DOING? WHAT DOES IT MEAN TO YOU TO STEP INTO BEING WHO YOU TRULY ARE. WHAT PART ARE YOU TO PLAY IN THE UNIVERSAL ENERGY TRANSFORMATION? THE ANSWERS WILL COME. THEY MAY COME IN SMALL PIECES AS IF YOU WERE PUTTING TOGETHER A PUZZLE.

COME EACH DAY AND ASK ME TO BE WITH YOU. TOGETHER WE WILL DISCOVER WHAT IT IS YOU AGREED TO IN YOUR CONTRACT. ONCE YOU HAVE THE KNOWING OF WHAT YOUR CONTRACT IS ABOUT, THEN YOU WILL KNOW WHICH ROAD YOU ARE TO TRAVEL.

REMEMBERING ALWAYS THAT YOU ARE THE WAYSHOWERS AND THE KEEPERS OF THE LIGHT. THAT IS THE TITLE OF THE CONTRACT YOU SIGNED. MAY I SAY ONLY THOSE WHO WERE BEING HONORED WERE GIVEN THE PRIVILEGE OF BEING HERE AT THIS TIME. IT IS A GREAT HONOR TO BE A WAYSHOWERS AND KEEPER OF THE LIGHT.

I will close for now knowing and trusting that you will indeed find the time to discover what your part of the journey is about. Also knowing and trusting that once you know your purpose you will step into it with courage and strength. DURING ALL OF THESE CHANGES, THERE IS ONE THING THAT WILL NEVER CHANGE AND THAT IS OUR LOVE AND SUPPORT OF YOU. OUR PART OF THE CONTRACT IS TO CONTINUE TO LOVE AND HONOR YOU FOREVER AND EVER. WE ARE HONORED TO BE ABLE TO SURROUND YOU WITH LOVE AND SUPPORT AS YOU FOLLOW YOUR CHOSEN PATHS.

Know you only need call my name and I will be there.
In Love, Mother Mary
12/29/10

LETTER 67
WE ARE ALMOST THERE

Dear Ones,

I have been giving you an immense amount to do before the New Year arrives. As always, it is about you doing exactly what you feel is right for you. The clearing and cleaning I have spoken about is to ease your journey into the new energy. The more clear space there is for the new energy the easier it will be to bring it into your body and life.

The energy will arrive no matter where you are in your clearing and cleaning. Your bodies and lives may begin to feel very crowded with old energy and the new energy pushing in. So continue your clearing and cleaning on into the New Year. Once you let go of the old, your body and life will begin to feel more comfortable.

As the remembering of your obligations and contracts starts to come into your consciousness, there will be more ease in your mind and body. Each day continue to call me and we will together find all the pieces of your puzzle and all will be made clear. REMEMBERING ALWAYS THAT FEAR AND RISK ARE ABOUT MAKING CHANGES ONLY. ONCE YOU HAVE TAKEN THE STEPS TO MAKE THE CHANGES, ALL WILL BE AS YOU WISHED.

Look for support in your world and in mine. Talk about your dreams and the strange fleeting thoughts that you might have. Do not dismiss any of your thoughts as being crazy or unrealistic. DO NOT HONOR ANY THOUGHTS OF "NO I CAN'T DO THAT." You are each capable of so much more than you realize. You are capable and able to do things beyond your wildest imagination. SO LET YOUR IMAGINATION GO AND ALLOW IT TO SHOW YOU WHAT IT IS YOU COULD BE DOING.

THERE ARE NO LIMITS TO WHO AND WHAT YOU ARE. THE ONLY LIMITS ARE IN YOUR MIND. THERE IS NO TRUTH IN THE LIMITS THAT YOU HAVE SET FOR YOURSELVES. WE ARE STANDING RIGHT HERE AT THE READY TO HELP YOU EXPLORE ALL THE WONDROUS POSSIBILITIES THAT ARE AWAITING YOU. YOU NEED ONLY TAKE OUR HANDS AND WE WILL

WALK YOU GENTLY THROUGH EACH AND EVERYONE OF THOSE POSSIBILITIES.

CAN YOU FEEL THE SPARKLE, SIZZLE AND EXCITEMENT AS YOU STEP INTO YOUR WORLD OF POSSIBILITIES? LET THERE BE A KNOWING AND BELIEF IN YOURSELF THAT YOU ARE CAPABLE OF DOING EACH OF THESE POSSIBILITIES. We are standing here ready to help you try each and every one of your possibilities. YOU WILL NEVER KNOW WHICH ARE RIGHT FOR YOU UNTIL YOU TRY THEM.

As the New Year comes into being, please join us and allow yourself to come into being. THERE IS A WHOLE NEW YEAR WAITING FOR YOU. A YEAR FILLED WITH POSSIBILITIES, LOVE, JOY, AND WONDER. COME AND JOIN US, WE ARE WAITING FOR YOU.

Know you only need call my name and I will be there.
In Love, Mother Mary
12/30/10

LETTER 68
HAPPY NEW YEAR

Dear Ones,

HAPPY NEW YEAR, HAPPY NEW YEAR, HAPPY NEW YEAR!

Can you feel the excitement and joy in the air? Every living breathing being on your planet is breathing a sigh of relief. You have made it. You have arrived to this special appointed time in your life.

Over the past year, you each have grown and stretched out to meet all that has been happening in your own personal lives and to the life of your planet. The energy changes you have grown and processed through have been immense. There has been energy change after energy change happening on your planet. You have walked through them. Sometimes I know that it seemed like you were crawling through them.

YOU EACH ARE TO BE APPLAUDED BECAUSE YOU MADE IT THROUGH WHETHER YOU WERE WALKING OR CRAWLING. YOU ARE HERE NOW ON THIS SIDE. WE ARE RIGHT HERE BESIDE YOU GIVING YOU LOVE, SUPPORT, AND APPRECIATION FOR ALL YOU HAVE ACCOMPLISHED.

NOW I SAY TO YOU VERY LOUDLY, TAKE A BREATH, AND TAKE A BREAK. Allow yourself some time to adjust to the energy shift that happened on your planet as 2011 arrived. The air is lighter and less intense. It will seem clearer and smoother to be out in the world. Reactions to the energy will be unique to each person. Some will be happy and almost giddy with excitement; others will just want to sleep and let the world go away. Still others will be in neutral, not seeming to be aware of anything or anyone around them. REMEMBER THAT THIS IS A TIME OF ADJUSTMENT. BE GENTLE WITH YOURSELVES AND OTHERS. TAKE GENTLE AND LOVING CARE OF YOURSELVES.

All will be changing shortly as more energy shifts arrive on your Mother Earth. Each of you will be taking steps out into the world to claim all that you are. You will start with small steps, working your way up to the large ones as you become comfortable. REMEMBERING ALWAYS THAT I AM RIGHT HERE BESIDE YOU. ALLOW ME TO HOLD YOUR

HAND AND BE WITH YOU EACH STEP OF THE WAY. WE, HERE ON THIS SIDE, ARE LOVING YOU DEARLY.

You each have worked so hard to get to this point. You each are absolutely perfect right where you are in your journey. You have done your very best throughout your lifetime to bring you to this point. Many of you have made your journeys without feeling or being unaware of any love or support. PLEASE KNOW THAT WE ARE HERE OFFERING YOU LOVE AND SUPPORT. PLEASE ALLOW US TO BE WITH YOU AND TO WALK HAND IN HAND WITH YOU AS YOU CONTINUE ON YOUR JOURNEY.

During the next weeks and months, I will be sending down sprinkles of love almost as if it were raining love. The sprinkles will arrive in unexpected moments and you will notice and remember that I am here with you. At those times allow yourself to take a breath and know without a doubt that you are not alone. We are doing life together. All becomes easier when there is love and support.

WE ARE RIGHT HERE LOVING AND SUPPORTING YOU. PLEASE ALLOW US TO HELP YOU.

Know you only need call my name and I will be there.
In Love, Mother Mary
1/2/11

LETTER 69

Dear Ones,

Are you being gentle with yourselves and taking a break? After your holiday season and the coming into 2011 it is necessary to take a breath. Most of you have stretched yourselves to the end of your rope.

Now is the time to sit back relax and once again come back to your center. During the last year, you have been pulled in a hundred different directions. Working with all the energy shifts and the chaos that they caused in your lives has depleted your systems. So now it is time to re-energize and rejuvenate your whole being and all of your bodies. Your minds and brains have worked over time trying to figure out all that has been happening in your world.

SO I WILL SAY TO YOU, COME AND BE WITH ME. CLOSE YOUR EYES, PUT YOUR HAND ON YOUR HEART AND CALL MY NAME. I am right here. Can you hear me breathing? Breathe with me very slowly in and out. Just stay right here with me, eyes closed, breathing slowly in and out. Hold my hand and in your mind come walk with me. Walking through fields of wild flowers, by the ocean, in the mountains, or by the slow-moving creek. Take me to your favorite place. Let us just be together. Allow the energy that you are feeling in my hand to move into your hand and travel through your body.

The energy is warm and fluid, calming your body, mind, and spirit. Each organ, each cell, every part of your body is absorbing and taking in all that I offer. Your body is becoming lighter and lighter. Colors and lights are swirling in your mind and body. You are being renewed, and re-energized. All the worries and stresses of 2010 are washing away, leaving your body and mind never to return. This is a New Year and a New world to come into. Stay in this place for a time, just being right here with me, eyes closed, breathing slowly in and out and holding onto my hand.

As you slowly return to your every day world know that this is a New Year, a new beginning, and you will be learning a new way of being. During this year, you will step into all that you are and can be. You will find yourselves and find your place in the world. You will find where you fit and what is right for you. Your hearts will continue to open and become connected to the universal heart of the whole.

REMEMBERING ALWAYS THAT YOU ARE HERE TO LOVE AND BE LOVED. THE PURPOSE OF YOUR WORLD IS ABOUT LOVING. OPEN HEARTS WITH ALL HEARTS CONNECTING IS THE GOAL AND FULFILLED PURPOSE OF YOUR WORLD. WE ARE STANDING RIGHT HERE WITH OUR HEARTS OPEN WAITING TO CONNECT WITH YOU, HEART TO HEART.

Know you only need call my name and I will be there.
In Love, Mother Mary
1/3/11

LETTER 70

Dear Ones,

Today let us talk about CHANGE. In this year of 2011 there will be many changes happening in your personal lives. There will also be many more changes happening on your Mother Earth. When this year is over you will wonder if there is anything that has not changed over the last year.

I WANT TO SAY VERY LOUDLY THAT CHANGE IS GOOD. CHANGE IS ABOUT LEARNING, GROWING, AND NEW BEGINNINGS. FOR THE UNIVERSAL ENERGY TRANSFORMATION TO HAPPEN AND BE COMPLETED ON YOUR MOTHER EARTH THERE NEEDS TO BE CHANGE. CHANGE IN ALMOST EVERY AREA OF YOUR WORLD.

NOW I COME TO WHAT I REALLY WANT TO TALK ABOUT TODAY AND THAT IS FEAR OF CHANGE. At least, 95% of the beings on your Mother Earth are afraid of change. The degree of fear varies from a small amount for some to paralyzing fear for others.

You are now in 2011, The Year of Change. My name for 2011 will be THE YEAR OF CHANGE! Today I am wanting you to start looking at the fear you carry in your minds and bodies about change. If you can look at it now and start to release it and let go of it, the days ahead will be easier and gentler for you.

There is no way to stop the changes that will be happening, so it is necessary for each of you to find the gentlest way to travel through them. The gentlest way will only happen if you are able to release and let go of the fear regarding changes.

I am asking each of you to come and spend some time with me each day and together we will work on releasing your fears. RIGHT NOW I ASK YOU TO CLOSE YOUR EYES. TAKE A DEEP BREATH, PUT YOUR HAND ON YOUR HEART AND CALL MY NAME. I am right here with you. Hold my hand, touch my arm do whatever you need to do to feel safe and comforted. Take me to your favorite most special place, the place where you feel safe and secure. If you do not have a place in your mind like that, take a moment and look about you and see if you can find such a place. Today we are only interested in finding a place where you each feel safe and secure. Just let yourselves be there, allowing all the worries, stresses, and fears to leave your minds and bodies. There is no place for them here in your special place. Find a place to send them to. If you need them back after you leave your safe place, then they will be waiting for you. I will hope that you will no longer need them with you.

All we are looking for today is a place where you feel safe, a place that you can go to when the changes start to cause fear in your world. Over the weeks and months ahead your safe place will become your safe haven in a changing world.

It will become a precious tool to use in taking care of yourselves. Your safe haven will become your most important tool in allowing your life to be gentler and more rewarding. Your safe haven will give you the power and the ability to make decisions in your life that are not fear-based. A whole new world of opportunities will become available once fear is not part of the decision process. FREEDOM AND CHOICES MADE FROM YOUR HEART RATHER THAN FROM YOUR FEAR. WHAT A HUGE CHANGE THAT WILL MAKE IN EACH OF YOUR LIVES AND IN YOUR MOTHER EARTH.

KNOW THAT WE ARE HERE READY AND WAITING TO HELP YOU FIND YOUR SAFE PLACE. WE ARE LOVING YOU AND WANTING TO BE WITH YOU.

Know you only need call my name and I will be there.
In Love, Mother Mary
1/4/11

LETTER 71

Dear Ones,

Again today I want to talk about FEAR. Yesterday we talked about change and how most beings on your planet step into fear as soon as change steps forward. We worked on finding a safe place to be when fear does come forward. A safe haven where you can go and not be so overwhelmed with fear. IT IS SO IMPORTANT THAT EVERYONE HAVE A SAFE HAVEN. A PLACE TO RETREAT TO AND TAKE CARE OF YOURSELF.

THERE ARE A HUNDRED DIFFERENT WAYS TO DEAL WITH FEAR. If you look around at the other beings that you spend time with you can see the many ways that others deal with fear.

Today we are going to try a new and unusual way to deal with fear. One that will be new and different for you. Does that cause more fear to come up? Today we are going to take fear out of the closet, from under the bed or any of the other places that it has been hidden away. Most especially we are going to take it out of your bodies.

I AM ASKING YOU TO BRING FEAR OUT INTO THE SUNLIGHT, INTO THE ROOM WHERE YOU ARE. I AM ASKING YOU TO START TALKING ABOUT IT. I AM ASKING YOU TO LISTEN TO OTHERS TALK ABOUT THEIR FEAR.

TODAY I AM ASKING YOU TO BRING FEAR OUT INTO THE OPEN, TO ROLL AROUND ON THE FLOOR WITH IT. TO REALLY GET TO KNOW FEAR AND START TO UNDERSTAND IT.

I AM ASKING YOU TO LET YOUR LIGHT SHINE UPON THE FEAR. For always and always fear has been kept hidden away in the dark places. Fear is something you don't talk about or admit to. It is believed that beings are not to admit to being afraid. I am wondering who made that rule? STOP AND THINK ABOUT THIS, WHAT IS WRONG WITH BEING AFRAID? SOMETIMES IT IS VERY WISE TO BE AFRAID. THERE ARE TIMES WHEN BEING AFRAID HAS KEPT YOU SAFE AND OUT OF HARM'S WAY. SO ONCE AGAIN I WILL SAY TO YOU, WHO MADE THE RULE THAT SAYS YOU CAN'T ADMIT TO BEING FEARFUL? WHO MADE THE RULE THAT IT IS NOT OK

TO TALK ABOUT YOUR FEARS OPENLY?

IT IS TIME TO BREAK THESE RULES. IT IS TIME TO BRING FEAR OUT INTO THE OPEN. IT IS TIME TO ROLL AROUND ON THE FLOOR WITH YOUR FEARS. IT IS TIME TO GET TO KNOW EVERY THING ABOUT EACH AND EVERYONE OF YOUR FEARS. IT IS TIME TO LET THE LIGHT OF DAY SHINE IN ALL THE DARK CORNERS.

Fears that are brought out into the light of day and talked about openly seem to disappear. It may seem as if they have magically vanished once they are standing in the light.

The energy surrounding fear is all consuming and takes over your physical body. Your bodies can become heavy and ill from carrying this type of energy. So I will say to you lighten your load, go out and play with your fears, bring them into the light, and allow them to magically vanish into the light.

We are right here ready and willing to roll around on the floor with you and your fears. We will listen to you as you talk about your fears and we will talk with you about them. We are loving you and wanting to help you. We are holding you in our hearts.

Know you only need call my name and I will be there.
In Love, Mother Mary
1/5/11

LETTER 72

Dear Ones,

Let us once again talk about FEAR today. Perhaps you are thinking I am a broken record. TALKING and TALKING about FEAR. In your world today FEAR is the strongest emotion traveling your planet. All other emotions pale compared to the scope and amount of fear that is running rampant on your planet.

WHAT I AM ASKING IS FOR YOU TO BECOME INTIMATELY ACQUAINTED WITH YOUR FEARS. IT IS TIME TO DIG INTO EVERY NOOK AND CORNER WHERE YOUR FEARS ARE HIDING. DIG THEM OUT; FIND OUT WHY THEY ARE THERE; WHAT ARE THEY REALLY ALL ABOUT? MOST IMPORTANTLY WHAT DO YOU WANT TO DO WITH THEM?

Are your fears necessary to keep you out of harms way? Are they needed to keep you alert and safe? These are the ones you will want to file away and keep; perhaps changing your perceptions of the fear and recognizing that fear can also be healthy and a helpful emotion to have.

Today I want to talk about the other fears, the ones that are keeping you from being the person you were meant to be. The fears that are stopping you from having the life that you want and pray for daily. Each of you came to be on your Mother Earth at this time with a special purpose. You each came with a gift to offer the world. FEAR IS STOPPING MANY OF YOU FROM BEING ABLE TO OFFER THIS GIFT.

Some of you know what your gifts are, but feel that the risks are too great too be able to step forward and say, this is me and this is what I have to offer you. Others of you have closed your minds and hearts to even letting yourselves take the first step to discover who you really are.

WHAT I AM WANTING EACH OF YOU TO KNOW IS THAT YOU ARE EACH VITALLY IMPORTANT TO YOUR WORLD. THE GIFTS THAT YOU HAVE COME TO OFFER THIS WORLD ARE SO IMPORTANT.

I AM ASKING YOU TO CONSIDER TAKING YOUR FEARS OUT OF THE DARK AND BRINGING THEM TO THE LIGHT. I

AM ASKING YOU TO LOOK AT YOUR FEARS. TO BRING FEAR OUT AND ROLL AROUND ON THE FLOOR WITH IT, TO PLAY WITH IT, TO TALK ABOUT IT, AND UNDERSTAND WHAT IT IS ALL ABOUT.

ONCE FEAR IS OUT IN THE OPEN, I WILL GUARANTEE YOU THAT YOUR WORLD WILL CHANGE FOR THE BETTER. There will be such a sense of FREEDOM and JOY in your mind and body. You will be amazed at the difference you will feel inside of yourself. Who and what you truly are will be able to come into the light of day.

Know that this is not something you have to do all by yourself. We are right here beside you waiting to help. We will roll around on the floor, play, talk, and help you to understand. WE ARE LOVING YOU AND CARING ABOUT YOU. KNOW THAT OUR HEARTS ARE REACHING OUT TO CONNECT WITH YOUR HEART.

Know you only need call my name and I will be there.
In Love, Mother Mary
1/6/11

LETTER 73

Dear Ones,

For one more day let us talk about CHANGE and FEAR. These two walk hand in hand. It is rare on your Mother Earth for there to be a being who does not see those two hand in hand. There are some of you who will say that's not me. I am not afraid of change and I say to you when was the last time you allowed change to happen in your life?

Being afraid or fearful is not something to be ashamed of and embarrassed by. It is simply part of who you are as human beings. Being fearful or afraid is no different than any other emotion. It is part of your emotional makeup. What you each decide to do with these emotions is the big question.

You can pretend those emotions don't exist and use much of your energy trying to keep them hidden away. Hiding your emotions away causes your energy to become stagnant and does not allow growth, progress or change in who you are as a human being. Your purpose and gifts for being here on Mother Earth at this time are lost and forgotten.

You can choose to become a victim and blame your fears on others and the universe, never seeing with your own eyes that it is your fear and something that is yours to work with. Once again, your purpose and gifts for being here on Mother Earth at this time are lost and forgotten.

There is a third option and one that more and more of you are starting to see and deciding to try. This option is to start working with your fears. Trying to understand where the fear comes from and why it is in your life at this time. Once again, I am saying that when fear is brought out into the light, it changes, decreases and sometimes vanishes as if by magic. Fear likes and loves being in the dark that is where it can grow and multiply.

Facing the fear will bring change to your lives. Change can bring wondrous things into your lives. Joy, Love, Appreciation, Gratitude and Fun are all emotions and feelings that can come into being with Change. LET GO OF THE ATTITUDE THAT SAYS CHANGE IS BAD, WHICH IN TURN TRIGGERS FEAR. AT THIS POINT, FEAR IS ONCE AGAIN RUNNING RAMPANT THROUGH YOUR MIND AND BODY.

IT IS TIME TO CHANGE THESE OLD PATTERNS AND RELEASE YOURSELVES FROM SELF-LIMITING THOUGHTS AND ACTIONS.

COME AND WALK WITH ME AND THE THOUSANDS OF OTHERS IN THE NEW ENERGY OF YOUR PLANET. It is time to step into the Universal Energy Transformation that is happening on your planet. WALK OUT OF YOUR COAT OF FEAR AND STEP INTO THE LIGHT OF THE NEW ENERGY. WE ARE HERE REJOICING WITH THE HOPE THAT YOU WILL BE COMING TO JOIN US.

COME AND BE WITH US. CHOOSE TO SHARE YOUR LIGHT WITH THE WORLD. WE ARE HERE SHARING OUR LOVE AND LIGHT WITH YOU.

Know that you only need call my name and I will be there.
In Love, Mother Mary
1/7/11

LETTER 74
WHAT IS GOING ON!!

Dear Ones,

Now that you have stepped into the energy of 2011 many of you are finding chaos, confusion, fear and despair have popped up into your lives. The energy of 2011 is the energy of the Universal Energy Transformation. All that is in your lives that needs to be let go of will come sharply into focus.

You will find that old fears that you have not thought of for a while, but were still lurking in the background, are now out front. Relationships that have not worked for a long time are now ending. Jobs that you have suffered through for the money or fear of not finding another will be ending. All things in your lives that have been helping you to stay stuck in one place will now be falling away.

The energy is urging you to step forward and only allow people, jobs, and places in your lives that feed, nurture, and support your growth. The energy is urging you to become all you are meant to be. This is the time when the energy is all about you taking the best care of you. Working at jobs that honor who you are. Being in relationships that honor both beings that are in the relationship. Having people in your lives that honor and encourage each other to be all that you can be.

Remembering now that the games you played with yourself about all that has not been working in your lives will no longer work. This year, 2011 does not leave room for any of those games that have been played in your minds and hearts. I SAY THIS TO YOU WITH GREAT LOVE AND SUPPORT FOR YOU. YOU NOW HAVE TO STOP THE MIND GAMES AND LOOK AT WHAT IS REALLY GOING ON IN EACH OF YOUR PRIVATE WORLDS.

The energy of this New Year has no room for mind games or non-reality thinking. It is constantly urging you out of those behaviors and asking you to step forward. For a good share of you this must feel like someone is pounding on your bodies and turning your world's upside down. The one word to describe what it must feel like would be devastation. For others, it will feel like someone is gently pushing you to go faster and in a different direction. Yet again for others it will feel good to be right here where they are.

I AM SPEAKING VERY LOUDLY RIGHT NOW, ESPECIALLY TO THOSE OF YOU WHO ARE FEELING DEVASTATION. WE ARE RIGHT HERE WANTING TO HELP YOU. THERE ARE THOUSANDS OF US ON THIS SIDE SENDING YOU LOVE AND SUPPORT. ANY OR ALL OF US CAN STEP FORWARD TO BE RIGHT BESIDE YOU IN A SECOND. PLEASE JUST SAY THE WORDS AND WE WILL BE THERE.

KNOW THAT WE ARE LOVING YOU, EACH AND EVERYONE. WE FIND YOU BEAUTIFUL AND WONDERFUL BEINGS. WE ARE HONORED TO BE HERE WITH YOU AND FOR YOU.

Know that you only need call my name and I will be there.
In Love, Mother Mary
1/9/11

LETTER 75

Dear Ones,

I want to keep repeating this for you time after time. WE ARE RIGHT HERE WAITING TO HELP YOU. WE ARE LOVING YOU AND IN SOME CASES WE ARE WHAT IS HOLDING YOU UP. WE ARE THE INVISIBLE HAND AND ARMS THAT ARE HELPING TO KEEP YOU STANDING.

The changes that are happening in your lives and your world are appearing very large and overwhelming to you right now. SO WE CONTINUE TO STAND RIGHT BESIDE YOU, HOLDING YOUR HAND AND STEADYING YOU. WE ARE KNOWING THAT YOU HAVE ALL THAT YOU NEED INSIDE OF YOU TO MAKE THE CHANGES THAT ARE BEING CALLED FOR. Your courage and strength is beyond measure. You are unaware of all that you are capable of doing. Each of you has immense courage and strength. You have the will and determination to become all that you are meant to be.

The changes that are happening in your world are scary and frightening. IT GOES AGAINST WHAT IS INSIDE OF EACH OF YOU, THAT ONE PERSON CAN HATE ANOTHER FOR THEIR OPINIONS AND BELIEFS. IT IS EXPECTED BY MOST PEOPLE IN THE UNITED STATES THAT ALL OF THAT HAPPENS IN OTHER COUNTRIES. The answer to that is no; it has been happening right here in your country for sometime. Now all of the anger and hate has come to the surface and it is bursting out all over.

Just as with each of you individually, whatever needs to be taken care of and let go of is up in your face and there is no where to hide. It is the same for your countries, whatever has been out of balance and harmful is sharply into focus and is bursting out in the open.

In this year of 2011, it is time for truth, honesty, integrity, and courage. All that has been hidden in the past and needs to be let go of will suddenly appear in your lives. It is the same for your countries. All that has been hidden will suddenly be on the front page of your paper or in your news programs.

This is all as it should be. The Universal Energy Transformation is happening as we speak. All that has been hidden away must be removed to make way for the New Energy. All that has not been let go of will come forward to be looked at and released. The Universal Energy Transformation is about love and caring for others; all others no matter their culture or beliefs. It is about personal honesty, governmental honesty, integrity of the highest order, courage, and bravery to stand for yourselves and others.

There is no more turning your back on the injustices of others. There are no more excuses for harm or neglect of other beings. It will truly be in all ways what is done to another will also be done to each individual. You each are at a crossroad in your lives and your countries are at a crossroad in its life.

I AM SAYING IT AGAIN, WE ARE RIGHT HERE BESIDE YOU. WE CAN HELP YOU MAKE THESE TRANSITIONS. OUR PURPOSE FOR BEING HERE IS TO HELP AND SUPPORT YOU. ONCE AGAIN, I AM SPEAKING VERY LOUDLY, YOUR ASKING FOR HELP IS NOT A BOTHER. NO REQUEST IS TOO SMALL OR TOO BIG.

KNOW THAT WE LOVE YOU AND HONOR YOU. YOU EACH HAVE IMMENSE COURAGE AND STRENGTH, REMEMBERING ALWAYS THAT EVERY BEING NEEDS HELP AND SUPPORT. WE ARE HERE RIGHT BESIDE YOU OFFERING ALL OF THAT TO EACH OF YOU.

Know that you only need call my name and I will be there.
In Love, Mother Mary
1/10/11

LETTER 76
THE DARK ENERGIES AT WORK

Dear Ones,

Today I want to talk to you about the negative or dark energies that are very active on your Mother Earth right now. As your Mother Earth is going into the Universal Energy Transformation, the light is growing and building on your planet. Just as each of you are becoming more light filled and your lights are shining even brighter.

Negativity or dark energies will be trying harder to stop the light from growing. They will not succeed in what they are trying to do. They will attempt to stop the Keepers of the Light from spreading the light or increasing the amount of light on the planet. This will become uncomfortable for the Keepers of the Light. As each of you are unique, so will be the way in which they try to stop you.

ONCE AGAIN, I AM TALKING VERY LOUDLY. WE ARE RIGHT HERE BESIDE YOU. WE ARE STANDING WITH YOU AND WE ARE ASKING EACH OF YOU TO CONTINUE TO STAND WITH US. THIS IS A STRUGGLE THAT HAS GONE ON FROM THE BEGINNING OF TIME. THIS STRUGGLE WILL CONTINUE UNTIL THERE IS ONLY LIGHT SHINING BRIGHTLY FROM ALL AREAS OF YOUR WORLD.

Anna/Barbara experienced struggle with the dark energies this morning. I will step away for now and let Barbara tell you what happened for her. "I woke up this morning feeling depressed and heavy. Not wanting to do anything least of all to scribe a letter for Mother Mary. My mind or what I thought was my mind kept arguing with me, saying you don't have to scribe every day. There were all kinds of reasons not to scribe the letter. The thoughts just kept coming and I was finding things or interruptions to stop me from going to the computer and sitting down at our appointed time. The energy in my apartment became very chaotic matching exactly what was going on in my mind. My animals were up and restless and normally they always sleep during my time with Mother Mary. I believe the dark energies started coming in yesterday as old feelings of not fitting in, not belonging were surfacing. I was just shaking my head wondering where all of this was coming from and how did I get back here.

Finally, this morning through all the fog and chaos in my mind I was able to have my own thought, which was I need to talk to Mother Mary. As I sat at the computer writing my thoughts and feelings out to her, she showed me what was happening and how the dark energies had worked their way in.

I need to let you know that for me, scribing Letters From Mother Mary is an honor and privilege that I regard highly. It is one of the most important things in my life and I feel it is my purpose for being here on Mother Earth during these times. It has been scary and awakening to see how the dark energies could use my own insecurities and old emotions to stop me from going forward."

THANK YOU ANNA/BARBARA FOR SHARING WHAT HAPPENED THIS MORNING. I asked her to share this with you so that you each can see how the dark energy is working right now. They will be confronting each of you in your own unique way. They will work on your insecurities, old emotions, and bringing chaos into your life as their way to stop you.

When the thoughts, emotions, and situations in your lives seem unreal, they probably are. When you find yourself amazed at all the strange goings-on in your lives right now, STOP AND QUESTION YOURSELVES AND QUESTION US. IS THIS REAL OR ARE THESE SITUATIONS, THOUGHTS, AND FEELINGS BEING DISTORTED?

ARE THEY ATTEMPTING TO DIM YOUR LIGHT AND THE LIGHT OF YOUR WORLD? KEEP A CLOSE WATCH ON WHAT IS REAL AND NOT REAL IN YOUR WORLD NOW.

ALWAYS REMEMBERING THAT WE ARE RIGHT HERE STANDING BESIDE YOU AND WE WILL ALWAYS BE RIGHT HERE STANDING BESIDE YOU. THERE ARE TIMES WHEN YOU MAY NOT KNOW WE ARE HERE, BUT WE ARE ALWAYS HERE.

THIS LETTER IS NOT ABOUT PRODUCING FEAR IN YOUR HEARTS AND MINDS. IF THAT IS WHAT COMES UP WHEN YOU READ THIS LETTER THEN I WOULD SAY THAT THE DARK ENERGIES ARE WORKING ON YOU RIGHT NOW. SO I SAY TO

YOU, ASK FOR HELP IN CLEARING THEM AWAY, KNOWING THAT WE WILL BE RIGHT THERE TO HELP YOU. THIS IS A STRUGGLE BETWEEN THE LIGHT AND THE DARK ENERGIES OF THE WORLD. THE LIGHT IS WINNING AND WILL CONTINUE MOVING FORWARD UNTIL THE WORLD IS LIGHT FILLED.

Know that I am here and you only need call my name.
In Love, Mother Mary
1/11/11

LETTER 77

Dear Ones,

Today let us talk about standing up for what you believe and speaking out for what you believe. This is not an easy thing to do, sometimes it means taking risks and being rejected. Sometimes it means walking away from people or a certain way you have lived in the past.

In the weeks and months ahead you each will find it necessary to speak out and stand up for the Universal Energy Transformation. You will find yourselves taking your thoughts, actions, and beliefs into the next level of your being. Many of you are aware of the Universal Energy Transformation. You embrace and honor it inside of yourselves. In the days ahead that will not be enough. You will find yourself being asked by US to speak out and talk about your thoughts and beliefs.

There are many of you saying right now, but I do that. YES, I know that you do, but we will be asking you to speak louder and in different places to different kinds of people. You all have the courage and strength to do this, which is why you are here on planet earth at this time.

ONCE AGAIN, I AM GOING TO BE SPEAKING VERY LOUDLY AND SAYING THE SAME-OLD THING TO YOU. WE ARE STANDING RIGHT HERE BESIDE YOU, BEHIND YOU, AND ENCIRCLING YOU. THINK OF US AS YOUR HONOR GUARD. AT TIMES THERE WILL BE 5 OF US OR TEN OF US AND THE NEXT TIME THERE WILL BE TEN THOUSAND OF US WITH YOU. NEVER WILL YOU BE STANDING ALONE.

During the weeks and months ahead it is vital that you each take care of yourself in a loving, generous, and caring way. We are asking you to think of yourself as the most precious and beautiful creation you have ever known. Stop and think for a moment, how would you treat one of us if we came to stay at your home? What kind of food would you feed us, what about the space where we would sleep and the clothes that you would offer for us to wear? Take the time to contemplate this, what would you do differently in your daily life?

What I am saying to you is that to each of us, you are precious and beautiful beyond words. We here wish for you to be treated that way. So we are asking you to honor yourselves, by feeding yourself good healthy food and making sure you have time to sleep and rest; providing yourselves with a place to live free of clutter and old stagnant energy; remembering to clean and clear your energy field and the energy field of your home and work place. Think of yourselves in terms of a brand new beautiful child. That is what you are coming to in 2011. Treat yourselves accordingly. KNOWING ALWAYS THAT WE ARE RIGHT HERE WITH YOU.

Know you only need call my name and I will be there.
In Love, Mother Mary
1/12/11

LETTER 78

Dear Ones,

Today let us talk about reaching out a helping hand. There are many beings on your planet that have no idea about what is going on energetically with your Mother Earth. They have no knowing of why there are changes happening in their lives and why the changes on Mother Earth are happening.

Let us stop and think of how you are feeling right now. You have the knowledge to explain to yourselves, the why and why not of what is happening. Imagine now if you did not know about the Universal Energy Transformation and all the shifts and changes in the energy.

Would not fear, confusion, anger, and despair be running rampant in your mind and heart at all that is happening? Since you have no knowing of what or why, you would have no way of fixing or lessening what is happening. I have such a clear image of individual after individual standing on a street corner. Their arms are raised, hands with palms open, heads shaking, with a look of utter confusion on their faces. They are saying loudly to the heavens, "what is happening and what is going on?"

Those are the beings I am asking you to reach out to. Share with them what is happening and why everything is in the process of change. They will listen and hear what you are saying. They are desperate to know what is happening?

This is one of the things we will be asking of you as the Wayshowers and the Keepers of light. We are asking those of you who know, to share with those who have no knowing of the energy changes. This sharing will help to decrease the negative flow of energy on your planet. It will help each of you to share your knowledge of love and light. The light will shine so much brighter as you reach out to connect with your brothers and sisters of Mother Earth.

KNOW THAT WE WILL BE STANDING WITH YOU, HELPING YOU WITH THE WORDS AND THOUGHTS TO SHARE. LETTING YOU KNOW WHAT EACH ONE NEEDS TO HEAR. OUR BEING WITH YOU WILL BE VERY EASY. YOU WILL NOT EVEN BE

AWARE THAT WE ARE HELPING YOU TO SAY EXACTLY WHAT THAT BEING NEEDS TO HEAR. WE REJOICE IN YOUR BEING WILLING TO HELP US AND TO SHARE THE NEW ENERGY ON YOUR MOTHER EARTH.

KNOW THAT WE ARE LOVING YOU AND APPLAUDING ALL THAT YOU ARE DOING. WE HONOR YOUR STRENGTH AND COURAGE AS YOU WALK THROUGH YOUR MANY SHIFTS AND CHANGES.

Know that you only need call my name and I will be there.
In Love, Mother Mary
1/13/11

LETTER 79

Dear Ones,

Today I am going to ask you to stop ignoring your inner voice. I am speaking of the voice that talks to you about what your body needs to stay healthy and well. The voice speaks to you about your energy field and the energy fields around you.

It is a voice that you ignore most of the time. It is the voice you need to listen to always. Some of you may not realize that the voice is there. You have become accustomed to it and now it is simply background noise. The voice you pay attention to is the one that argues with you and says unkind, disrespectful things.

The voice I am talking about does not beat you up or cause confusion in your mind or body; your inner voice, or we could call it your higher self-voice!! Your higher self-voice is telling you how to take care of your bodies, meaning all your bodies; spiritual, emotional, mental and physical. The higher-self voice has wisdom beyond your knowing. It comes with the wisdom of all the ages.

That voice, carries the knowledge to care for you, knowing the best foods for your unique physical body. The knowledge it carries covers every aspect of your life and needs. We have already spoken of the need and necessity for learning to care for yourself this year. In this year of 2011, there is no room for the disregard of who you are. There is no room for not loving yourselves to the highest degree.

THE TIME HAS COME FOR YOU TO HOLD YOURSELVES IN THE HIGHEST REGARD. IT IS TIME TO KNOW AND BELIEVE IN YOUR HEARTS THAT YOU EACH ONE ARE PRECIOUS AND IMPORTANT TO THE WORLD. IT IS YOUR RIGHT, AS BEINGS ON YOUR PLANET AT THIS TIME TO BE TREATED WITH THE UTMOST RESPECT AND HONOR.

THIS TREATMENT HAS TO START WITH YOU. YOU ARE THE ONE TO SHOW THE REST OF THE WORLD HOW YOU ARE TO BE TREATED. IF YOU TREAT YOURSELVES SHABBILY AND WITH DISREGARD, THAT IS WHAT YOU CAN EXPECT FROM

OTHERS. IF YOU TREAT YOURSELF WITH LOVE, RESPECT AND CARING, THAT IS HOW OTHERS WILL TREAT YOU.

LOVE, RESPECT AND CARE ALL STARTS WITH YOU. THE TREATMENT THAT YOU DESERVE AND WANT, STARTS WITH HOW YOU TREAT YOURSELF. THE TIME HAS COME TO CHANGE THE WAY YOU TREAT YOURSELF. YOU CAN MAKE THAT CHANGE BY STARTING TO LISTEN TO YOUR INNER VOICE.

RIGHT NOW, BE HERE WITH ME. CLOSE YOUR EYES, CALL MY NAME AND I WILL BE HERE WITH YOU. Breathe easily and stay right here with me. Empty your minds for a moment. Yes, I know that is not an easy thing to do. Place all your thoughts in a different room in your home. Send those thoughts to your bedroom for a time out. As those thoughts pop back into your mind, send them once again back to the bedroom. As you have found your quiet place, ask your inner voice to speak. Let the voice know that you are ready to listen. The voice will not be speaking loudly; it is very quiet, gentle, and loving. Let yourselves understand what the voice is saying. Listen and understand what it is asking you to do.

NOW THE VERY IMPORTANT PART OF ALL OF THIS IS, USING THE INFORMATION THAT YOUR INNER VOICE HAS GIVEN YOU. USING THE KNOWLEDGE AND INFORMATION THAT HAS BEEN GIVEN TO YOU IS THE GIFT. YOU WILL NEED TO TAKE THE TIME DAILY TO PRACTICE LISTENING TO THE INNER VOICE AND USING THE INFORMATION GIVEN.

AS ALWAYS, WE ARE RIGHT HERE WITH YOU. LOVING YOU AND KNOWING HOW WONDERFUL AND BEYOND COMPARE THAT YOU EACH ARE. YOU EACH ARE GIFTS GIVEN TO YOUR MOTHER EARTH. WE CHERISH AND HONOR WHO YOU ARE AND WHAT YOU DO FOR YOURSELVES AND OTHERS.

Know you only need call my name and I will be there.
In Love, Mother Mary
1/14/11

LETTER 80

Dear Ones,

I want to reassure you that all is as it is supposed to be in your world. It is difficult; I am sure, to understand how I could be saying that after last week. There is a much bigger plan in motion than what you are aware of. Much of this plan will never be clear to you until you pass over to my side.

This is a year in which it will be necessary for you to trust as you have never trusted before. There will be much that transpires on your Mother Earth that will be beyond your understanding. There will be many changes in each of your lives and in the life of Mother Earth. You will find yourselves in amazement for all that is shifting and changing.

Remembering always as you go through this year that change is growth, progress and the way of life. Your lives were never meant to stay the same year after year. All life becomes stagnant and stuck when there is no change.

You and everything on your Mother Earth is made up of energy. I am saying EVERYTHING on your Mother Earth is made up of energy! That means you are energy, the rocks, trees, ocean, animals, every insect, and bug is made up of energy. Energy is about movement and connection. You are about movement and connection.

The connection is LOVE. The movement is ENERGY or the LIFE FORCE that flows through all on your planet. Over the last centuries there has been no movement on your planet. Stagnation has occurred and the negative energy that occurs because of the stagnation contaminates all that it touches. That contamination grows and feeds on itself, drawing in all in its path.

SO I SAY TO YOU TODAY GO OUTSIDE SHAKE YOURSELVES AROUND. CAUSE MOVEMENT TO HAPPEN IN YOUR PHYSICAL BODIES. ALLOW THAT MOVEMENT TO SPREAD AND TOUCH ALL IT COMES INTO CONTACT WITH.

OPEN YOUR HEARTS AND WELCOME THE CHANGES, SHAKE OFF THE FEAR. GO OUT AND DO A DANCE IN THE GRASS SHAKING OFF THE FEAR AND ALLOW THE MOVEMENT AND CHANGE TO BEGIN.

TAKE JUST A MOMENT RIGHT NOW TO THINK ABOUT WHAT HAS JUST HAPPENED. ARE YOU SMILING AND MAYBE, JUST MAYBE, GIGGLING OR LAUGHING. IMAGINE HOW SILLY TO BE OUT HERE DANCING IN THE GRASS, SHAKING YOUR BOOTY.

CHANGE HAS STARTED. CHANGE IS HAPPENING. WHEN WAS THE LAST TIME YOU WENT DANCING IN THE GRASS? IT IS OK! YOU CAN BLAME ALL THIS CRAZINESS ON ME.

ALLOW THIS CHANGE, THIS CRAZINESS TO MOVE OUT AND TOUCH YOUR FAMILIES, YOUR FRIENDS, YOUR CO-WORKERS AND THE PEOPLE WALKING DOWN THE STREET. LET'S SPREAD IT AROUND UNTIL IT REACHES EVERY CORNER OF YOUR MOTHER EARTH.

WE ARE HERE LOVING YOU AND JOINING YOU ON THE GRASS, SHAKING OUR BOOTY RIGHT ALONG SIDE OF YOU. WE ARE MOVING AND DANCING WITH YOU. THE JOY AND CRAZINESS OF THIS FILLS YOUR HEART TO OVERFLOWING WITH LAUGHER AND LOVE.

Know you only need call my name and I will be there.
In Love, Mother Mary
1/17/11

LETTER 81

Dear Ones,

In the last letter, I said there had been no MOVEMENT on your Mother Earth for the past centuries. I wish to talk about that today and what that means in my terms. Movement meaning energy, life force and the flow of life.

There have been many changes on your Mother Earth in terms of technology, computers, cell phones, and iPhones. You all stay connected to the world through your technology. There have been great advances in all things associated with WAR. Those advances have given you the power to intimidate and win wars.

In my eyes that is not movement or growth in the area for which your planet was formed and put into existence. THE PURPOSE OF YOUR PLANET AND YOURSELVES WAS TO LEARN TO LOVE YOURSELVES AND ALL OTHER LIVING CREATIONS. REMEMBERING ALWAYS THAT EVERYTHING ON YOUR MOTHER EARTH IS A LIVING CREATION. LIVING CREATIONS ARE ROCKS, TREES, OCEANS, RIVERS, MOUNTAINS, BUGS, HUMANS, AND INSECTS. EVERYTHING ON YOUR PLANET IS LIVING INCLUDING YOUR MOTHER EARTH. ALL OF THIS IS CALLED A LIVING CREATION.

Your wars and all your advances in that area are the direct opposite from your purpose and existence. All your advances in technology have provided useful tools and enabled you to move through your life with ease. They have allowed your lives to move faster and you are able to get more accomplished each day. MY QUESTION IS, "WAS THE INTENTION AND PURPOSE FOR YOUR LIVES TO MOVE FASTER AND FASTER AND ACCOMPLISH MORE AND MORE???" Your advances in technology have also allowed human one on one connection to deteriorate. The human physical touch and eye-to-eye contact is being lost.

WHERE DOES LOVE FIT IN ALL OF THIS??? WHERE HAS LOVE GONE??? LOVE IS WHAT EACH OF YOU AND YOUR MOTHER EARTH ARE IN NEED OF. YOU EACH ARE DESPERATE TO KNOW THAT YOU ARE LOVED. YOU ARE DESPERATE TO

KNOW THAT YOU HAVE A PLACE AND THAT YOU FIT, THAT YOU ARE NOT ALONE.

HUMAN ONE ON ONE CONTACT IS AS IMPORTANT AS FOOD OR WATER TO YOUR MINDS AND BODIES. THERE SHOULD BE A RULE OR LAW ON YOUR MOTHER EARTH THAT EACH BEING IS REQUIRED TO GIVE AND RECEIVE AT LEAST 5 HUGS EACH DAY. I AM NOT TALKING ABOUT THE PRETEND HUGS THAT SOME HUMANS GIVE, BUT I AM TALKING ABOUT THE KIND OF HUGS THAT MAKE YOU SMILE. THOSE HUGS THAT FILL YOUR HEART WITH LOVE, JOY, AND LAUGHTER. THOSE HUGS SAY TO YOU, "YOU ARE LOVED, AND YOU ARE WELCOME HERE."

I am asking you today to go out into your world and practice hugging each other. I am saying practice, because it seems like the art of hugging has been lost or misplaced on your Mother Earth. Hugging can be a genuine and honest expression of love and caring. I AM SPEAKING OF HUGGING EVERYONE, THE PEOPLE ON THE STREET, YOUR FRIENDS, YOUR FAMILIES, YOUR CO-WORKERS, AND YOUR PETS. EACH AND EVERY LIVING CREATION IS IN NEED OF LOVE AND ACCEPTANCE.

OPEN YOUR HEARTS AND STEP OUT INTO THE WORLD AS AN EXPRESSION OF LOVE AND CARING. THERE ARE SOME ON YOUR PLANET WHO HAVE STEPPED OUT INTO THE WORLD IN THAT WAY. THEY HAVE MADE SIGNS AND GONE TO YOUR MALLS. THEIR SIGNS READ, "FREE HUGS." THOSE BEINGS STAND THERE IN YOUR MALLS GIVING HUGS TO ONE AND ALL. I APPLAUD THEM AND ASK YOU TO ALL GO AND JOIN THEM.

WE ARE RIGHT HERE HUGGING EACH OF YOU. WE ARE LOVING YOU AND ACCEPTING YOU. YOU ARE TREASURED AND IMPORTANT TO ALL OF US. PLEASE CALL ON US TO HELP YOU OPEN YOUR HEARTS AND ARMS. WE ARE RIGHT HERE WAITING.

Know you only need call my name and I will be there.
In Love, Mother Mary
1/22/11

LETTER 82

Dear Ones,

Today let us talk of EMOTIONS: JOY, LAUGHTER, LOVE, HOPE, ANGER, HATE, SORROW, SADNESS, DESPAIR, AND GRIEF. Yes, there are many others, but these TEN are the main emotions experienced by all on your planet. They are the common thread that weaves through every being's lifetime.

Of course, they come in different degrees depending on the situation and individual. The first four emotions are the ones everyone wants to have in their lives. The last six are the emotions humans most try to ignore.

It is important for all humans to know and be aware that ignoring these emotions causes harm to your body, mind and soul. The hiding away or ignoring of these emotions causes energy to become stagnant in your bodies, all of your bodies. We spoke of this not too long ago in a different letter. But it seems that you were not listening or you have chosen to ignore the words, just as you have chosen to ignore the emotions.

PLEASE LISTEN. IT IS MOST IMPORTANT THAT YOU LEARN TO LET YOURSELVES EXPERIENCE ALL THE EMOTIONS. ALL TEN OF THESE EMOTIONS ARE NORMAL FOR HUMAN BEINGS TO EXPERIENCE DURING THEIR LIFETIMES. There is not one human who escapes experiencing every single emotion during their lifetime. These emotions are part of your being. You have been programmed to experience all emotions. EMOTIONS ARE NOT THINGS YOU GET TO PICK AND CHOOSE, AS IF YOU WERE BUYING A PARTICULAR BRAND OF FOOD. THEY ARE ALL RIGHT THERE IN YOUR EVERYDAY LIVES, WAITING FOR YOU TO EXPERIENCE THEM.

NOW I AM SPEAKING VERY LOUDLY. PLEASE HEAR ME. THIS IS THE TRICK OF BEING WITH YOUR EMOTIONS, ALL OF THEM. THE TRICK IS TO LET YOURSELF EXPERIENCE THEM AND THEN TO LET THEM GO. IT IS NOT NECESSARY OR MEANT TO BE THAT YOU EXPERIENCE THEM AND THEN HANG ON TO THEM FOR THE REST OF YOUR LIFE. THE HANGING ON IS AS HARMFUL AS NOT EXPERIENCING THEM AT ALL.

SO WHAT I AM TALKING ABOUT RIGHT NOW IS IF YOU ARE SAD, LET YOURSELF BE SAD. THINK ABOUT WHY YOU ARE SAD AND WHAT YOU CAN DO TO CHANGE THE SITUATION. IS THERE ANOTHER WAY TO LOOK AT IT? DO YOU NEED TO CHANGE YOUR PERCEPTION? DO YOU NEED TO ASK FOR HELP IN UNDERSTANDING AND CLARIFYING? MAYBE YOU JUST NEED TO LET YOURSELF BE SAD FOR A LITTLE WHILE.

DO NOT HANG ON TO THE SADNESS, LET IT GO AND LET YOURSELF GO ON TO LIVE YOUR LIFE. Do not stop yourself and live the rest of your life being sad. That is not living life. This is stopping life and being stuck. Being stuck ends life. There is no longer a chance to experience the emotions that all humans enjoy. What happens to love when you are stuck in anger, hate, sadness, or grief? REMEMBERING NOW THAT LOVE IS THE REASON FOR YOUR MOTHER EARTH BEING HERE. LOVE IS THE REASON FOR ALL OF YOU BEING HERE ON YOUR PLANET.

So allow yourselves to experience all of the emotions that come into your lives, but also allow yourselves to let them go. ALL BEINGS NEED HELP IN LEARNING TO LET THE EMOTIONS GO. WE ARE RIGHT HERE READY TO HELP YOU. WE CAN SHOW YOU HOW TO EXPERIENCE AND LET GO OF THE EMOTIONS. THERE WILL BE SUCH FREEDOM IN YOUR LIVES ONCE YOU HAVE THIS KNOWLEDGE, ONCE YOU ARE WILLING TO LEARN AND USE WHAT WE ARE OFFERING.

KNOW WE ARE HERE AND WILL CONTINUE TO BE RIGHT HERE. WE ARE READY TO HELP YOU ONLY NEED ASK.

Know you only need call my name and I will be there.
In Love, Mother Mary
1/23/11

LETTER 83

Dear Ones,

What should we talk about today? I think we should talk about you and the people who support you, nurture you, and love you. I am speaking of those precious ones who are always there for you.

There are those of us here on this side that will always be there for you. We, of course, are always loving you, supporting you and nurturing you. There is great need in each being for what I will call earth angels. Those are the beings that are in physical form doing the supporting, loving, and nurturing.

There are those of you who can feel my arms around you when I am hugging you. There are many who know in their minds that I am hugging them or they are wishing and praying that I am hugging them. IT IS OF THE UTMOST IMPORTANCE THAT THERE ARE EARTH ANGELS WHO ARE RIGHT THERE WITH YOU IN PHYSICAL FORM HUGGING AND LOVING YOU.

EVERY LIVING CREATION ON YOUR PLANET NEEDS AFFECTION AND TOUCHING. IT IS A WELL KNOWN FACT THAT BABIES ON YOUR PLANET DO NOT SURVIVE WITHOUT PHYSICAL AFFECTION AND WARMTH. BEING TOUCHED IS AS VITAL TO YOUR BEING AS FOOD AND WATER.

Take the time to let those who support you know how important and precious they are to you. Let them know that you appreciate their caring, listening, their loving and hugging you. Just as others are providing you with what you are in need of, I am asking you to turn around and provide that for someone else. REMEMBERING THAT LOVE AND CARING GROWS AS IT IS PASSED BACK AND FORTH AMONG YOU.

THE GIVING AND RECEIVING OF LOVE AND CARING IS THE GREATEST GIFT YOU CAN GIVE OR RECEIVE. REMEMBERING THAT THIS IS WHY YOU ARE HERE ON YOUR MOTHER EARTH. IT IS THE REASON FOR YOUR MOTHER EARTH BEING HERE. LEARNING TO LOVE BOTH THE GIVING AND RECEIVING IS WHAT THE WORLD IS ALL ABOUT.

You have come to the time on your planet when LOVE will triumph over all things and all beings. Greed, lust, hate and vengeance can never win over LOVE. LOVE IS BIGGER, BRIGHTER, MORE ENCOMPASSING THAN ANYTHING ELSE ON YOUR PLANET. IT IS TIME FOR ALL OTHER THINGS TO BE RELEASED AND WASHED AWAY.

So during these times ahead when the energy seems intense and the old feelings are coming up to be released, remember there are earth angels right there to help. There are thousands and thousands of angels here on my side to help.

All is as it is meant to be on your planet at this time. The energy is strong and intense. Old ways of being are coming up to be released. It may feel as if you are being tested to see if you have really let go of the old. If the old is still hanging around there will be other opportunities to release and find your truths.

We are here loving you and offering you love and support. We will always be right here with you.

Know you only need call my name and I will be there.
In Love, Mother Mary
1/24/11

LETTER 84

Dear Ones,

Today I want to talk about working together. It has been thought on your Mother Earth that it is a good thing to be strong, independent and able to do everything for yourself, by yourself. That is not a truth. It is truth that you need to be working together.

All beings need to be supporting one another, helping one another. Human beings were never meant to function in the world in separateness. Remembering now that your world was created so love could flourish and grow. You each came to Mother Earth to learn about loving, both the giving and receiving of love. It is impossible for that to take place if you each are concentrating on being in your separateness.

Separateness breeds isolation, depression, and despair. If there were room for love in these very heavy dense emotions, it would be of the mind and not heart-centered. All in your world must be directed from your heart centers.

During this year of 2011, heart-centered will become the key words and chant for all of Humanity. Living a Heart-Centered life leaves no room or want of separateness. Separateness will no longer exist and will be banned from your Heart-Centered world.

It is time for each of you to begin to be conscious of your every thought and action. It is time to begin questioning yourselves before speaking or doing. Is this a heart-centered thought, is this action based in my heart-centeredness? The time has come to let go of the logical and common sense directed life. All life is to be directed from your heart center.

Yes, I know there are those of you who are thinking; this is crazy I am not going to let go of what is logical and makes sense. I say to you to go very, very slow with this and try going with some heart-centered ideas and see how it feels. Once you have let yourself try the heart-centered idea, look back and see what your logical mind would have said for you to do. What would the outcome have been if you had stayed with the logical? Would you have been happy with that, would you feel completed and fulfilled? Where is your heart and passion with your logical thoughts and actions?

There are those of you who will find this an easy transition, for you have been living this way at least part of the time. There are others of you who will need to go a little slower, but by the time that this year draws to a close all beings will be living a heart-centered life. LOVE FLOURISHES AND GROWS LIVING IN THE ENVIRONMENT OF HEART-CEN-TERED-NESS. REMEMBERING ONCE AGAIN THAT LOVE IS THE REASON FOR YOU AND YOUR WORLD BEING HERE.

AS ALWAYS, WE ARE HERE TO HELP YOU WITH THESE TRANSITIONS WHETHER THEY ARE BIG OR SMALL. EVERYTHING ON YOUR PLANET IS MADE EASIER AND GENTLER WITH HELP AND SUPPORT. So remember that we are here waiting to help and support you and of course, we are here loving you.

Know you only need call my name and I will be there.
In Love, Mother Mary
1/25/11

LETTER 85

Dear Ones,

Today let us talk about bringing sweetness and light back into your lives. What do I mean by sweetness and light? I am talking about the things that stop you and instantly make you smile, laugh, or you can just feel your heart growing larger. I am talking about the wonders and miracles that happen every day in your world.

When was the last time you stopped to watch a baby smile? Did you watch a sunset last night? Where are the rainbows? Have you noticed the flowers are starting to come up? I am talking about all the little miracles that happen every single day that fill your heart up with joy.

It seems that for many, their lives are moving way too fast to be able to slow down and taste the miracles of life. There is an old saying in your world and it is fitting for now. "STOP AND TAKE TIME TO SMELL THE ROSES." In this case, the roses are the sweetness and lightness of your life.

Each and every being on your Mother Earth requires sweetness and light in their lives. In the intenseness of your world during this year, it is imperative for each of you to see, hear, and taste the miracles. As you move forward into the 5D world, the journey has been long and challenging. The miracles that are happening every day are there for you. The miracles are meant to lighten the journey and to lift your hearts up to the next level.

Yes, I do know it is winter in much of your world, so there may not be sunsets or rainbows.

Take the time to think of those things that stop you and lift your heart to new levels. I SAY TO YOU RIGHT NOW TO STOP AND TAKE A DEEP BREATH. BE RIGHT HERE WITH ME, CLOSE YOUR EYES AND TAKE SEVERAL DEEP BREATHS. PUT YOUR HAND ON YOUR HEART AND FOCUS YOUR MIND ON YOUR HEART CENTER. LET ALL THE OTHER THINGS RUNNING THROUGH YOUR MIND STOP AND TAKE A BREAK RIGHT NOW. Just be right here with me, with your mind focused on your heart. TELL ME WHAT MAKES YOUR HEART SMILE? YOU DO NOT NEED TO SAY IT OUT LOUD, JUST THINK IT IN YOUR MIND. WHAT MAKES

YOUR HEART SMILE? ALLOW ALL THE DIFFERENT THINGS TO COME UP AND BE PUT INTO YOUR MEMORY BANKS.

JUST STAY RIGHT THERE WITH YOUR HAND ON YOUR HEART AND YOUR MIND FOCUSED ON YOUR HEART. WHAT IS YOUR HEART SAYING TO YOU? WHAT DOES IT NEED? ONCE AGAIN ALLOW ALL THAT INFORMATION TO COME UP AND BE STORED IN YOUR MEMORY BANKS.

Now the challenge of all this is, can you allow yourselves to slow down and do what it is that your heart needs to make it smile? For most of you there are many small things you could do several times a day and you would be using no more than 15 minutes of your time. 15 minutes is a small amount of time to pay for such a huge reward.

THERE IS NO PRICE TOO HIGH TO PAY FOR HAVING THE SWEETNESS AND LIGHTNESS OF LIFE IN YOUR WORLD. ALL THESE WONDERFUL MIRACLES THAT HAPPEN IN YOUR WORLD EVERY DAY, ALMOST EVERY SECOND HAVE BEEN FORGOTTEN. Your lives have been moving too fast for too long and there are many things that have been lost along the way.

So today I am asking you to slow down and give yourself 15 minutes to lift up your heart and add sweetness into your lives. WE ARE RIGHT HERE WITH YOU EVERY STEP OF THE WAY. WE ARE URGING YOU TO SLOW DOWN AND SMELL THE ROSES, TO SLOW DOWN AND SEE, HEAR, AND TASTE THE MIRACLES AROUND YOU. WE ARE LOVING YOU NOW AND ALWAYS.

Know you only need call my name and I will be there.
In Love, Mother Mary
1/27/11

LETTER 86

Dear Ones,

Some of what I say today may be difficult to hear. There are some of you who will say no that is not right. We have always done life, relationships, and raising our children in this way. Yes, what you say is true you have always done it this way and now it is time to do it another way. Your way of the past has not worked. Look at your families, friends, and your world. What you have been doing is not working.

2011 is the year of change, growth, and enlightenment. Your world is working towards becoming heart-centered, where your lives will be lived directly from your heart. Each one of you will be living from your own heart-centered space. Your responsibility first and foremost will be caring for your heart, your life, and how you choose to live that life. What are your passions, dreams, hopes and goals?

This new world we are stepping into will be occupied by beings that live from their heart center. They will be fulfilling their individual purposes here on Mother Earth. They will be living their passion and honoring themselves. You will also be loving and honoring others but never at the expense of your purpose or lives. Honoring someone else, but not yourself has never worked and there is no place in the new world for those kinds of actions.

When each being is caring, loving, and honoring self, you will automatically offer and provide the same for others. In saying you will provide the same for others, it is not saying you will put their passion or dreams ahead of yours. That would be going right back to the old way of being and thinking. I am aware this is a most difficult concept for husbands and wives, parents and children, brothers and sisters. It is important to understand that when you put others before yourself, you are not being as loving and caring as you think. That kind of loving and caring turns into resentment, anger, and in extreme cases hate. Remembering now that the energy from those emotions is what is going out to the ones that you say you are loving and caring for. Do you see why it is time for a change? This old way is not working nor has it ever worked.

For most of you this will be a huge transformation and change. This change also calls for the letting go of all the old feelings caused by the way you have interpreted what loving and caring means. This change will allow you to love and care for yourselves and others in a heart-centered way. The heart-centered way allows you each to love and care for yourself first and then to reach out and care for others. There will be no frustrating and intense emotions caused from this form of loving and caring. No one will become stuck and unable to live his or her lives to the fullest.

CAN YOU SEE THAT THIS NEW WAY OF LIVING WILL PROVIDE YOU AND YOUR WORLD WITH A PEACE AND HARMONY NOT KNOWN ON EARTH BEFORE? These are huge changes I am talking about and it is important for each of you to know that we are truly here waiting to help you. We are aware of the turmoil and confusion that will occur in your lives and your families as you make these changes. REMEMBER THAT WE ARE ALWAYS HERE OFFERING YOU OUR LOVE AND SUPPORT. There are many ways to make these changes and we have many options to share with you. Just as you are each individuals so it follows that how you make your changes will be in your own unique way.

REMEMBER THAT WE ARE HERE AND THERE ARE HUNDREDS OF THOUSANDS OF US WAITING TO HELP YOU.

Know you only need call my name and I will be there.
In Love, Mother Mary
1/28/11

LETTER 87

Dear Ones,

Today let us talk about what makes you smile. It seems as if that has not been happening often enough lately. I know that the energy right now is intense and heavy. The letting go and releasing of old energy can be consuming and overwhelming.

It is essential to your well-being that you also allow yourselves to take a break. What do I mean by a break? When was the last time you smiled because something made you feel happy or joyful? When was the last time you laughed? Laughter is a wonderful way to release stress and tension. Laughter feels good. It allows your whole being to be involved. Laughter involves your heart, body, mind, and soul.

Balance is the key word for this year of 2011. Just as you are working very hard with all the intense energy on the planet, it is also needed that you enjoy laughter and fun. Laughter and fun are reactions and actions of the heart-centered being. Learning and being in a heart-centered world is about experiencing joy, love, and laughter all the time.

Most beings on your planet know more about anger, greed, frustration, and hate then they know about joy, love, and laughter. Your world, for many centuries, has been focused on the negative emotions found in humans. The softer emotions of joy, love, and laughter have been lost and hidden away as weak and un-necessary. That is not a truth.

The truth of your world, your Mother Earth, and your very beings is that you must have joy, love, and laughter. You and your Mother Earth need joy, love, and laughter to grow and survive. When you look around your Mother Earth and see all the things that are not working, know that it is because there is a lack of joy, love, and laughter.

As you work and study at becoming a heart-centered human, you will find that joy, love, and laughter automatically starts coming into your life. As you study and grow, so joy, love and laughter will grow and become so important to your life. You will find that you cannot survive without it. Love, Joy, and Laughter allows your heart to open and grow larger and larger.

THE OPENING OF YOUR HEART AND ITS GROWING LARGER AND LARGER IS WHAT YOU ARE HERE TO LEARN. IT HAS TAKEN MANY CENTURIES FOR YOU TO ARRIVE AS THIS POINT IN TIME. WE HERE ARE SO GRATEFUL THAT YOU HAVE COME TO THIS TIME IN YOUR GROWTH. WE HAVE BEEN WAITING AND WAITING.

AS ALWAYS, WE ARE HERE READY TO HELP YOU AND BE WITH YOU. REMEMBER WE HAVE BEEN WAITING FOR YOU AND WE ARE STANDING HERE WITH OPEN ARMS AND HEARTS. PLEASE BLESS US WITH YOUR REQUESTS FOR HELP AND CARING.

Know that you only need call my name and I will be there.
In Love, Mother Mary
1/31/11

LETTER 88

Dear Ones,

My wish for you today is that you will allow yourselves to have a day filled with peace, light, and love. I AM SPEAKING OF ONE OF THOSE DAYS WHERE ABSOLUTELY EVERYTHING IS RIGHT IN YOUR WORLD. Just for today, let go of the worries and in a small way recognizing that your worrying will never change the outcome of a situation.

Today your eyes will only see a bright blue sky; you will feel warmth from the Sun, and be totally encircled by the love of your friends and families. All resentments and anger have released from your body. Feelings of lack and unworthiness have vanished from your being. Sorrows and regrets have returned to the past where they belong.

TODAY IS ABOUT RIGHT NOW AND THIS ONE MOMENT IN TIME. IN THIS TIME, THE WORLD BELONGS TO YOU. YOU ARE THE BRIGHTEST STAR IN THE SKY. JUST FOR THIS ONE DAY WILL YOU ALLOW YOURSELVES TO BE RIGHT HERE, RIGHT NOW?

Some of you will be able to go instantly to this place I am speaking about. Some of you will need help getting to this place. SO FOR THOSE OF YOU WHO NEED HELP REACHING THIS PLACE OF RIGHT NOW, CLOSE YOUR EYES, TAKE A DEEP BREATH AND COME WITH ME. PLACE YOUR HAND ON YOUR HEART AND CALL MY NAME.

JUST KEEP GENTLY BREATHING, TAKE MY HAND AND WALK WITH ME. TAKE ME TO YOUR FAVORITE PLACE IN THE WHOLE OF THE WORLD. WE CAN GO ANYWHERE YOU WANT. We are in your favorite place and we are staying right here in this moment, not in the past and not in the future. This moment right here and right now is all there is. Allow the energy of this place to absorb into your heart, mind, and body. Feel the glory of it. Your body is totally empty of everything but the joy of being right here, right now, and sharing it with me. Know that I am totally right here with you. My heart is open to just you at this moment in time. You are my total focus. I am surrounding and filling you with love.

We are one. You are me and I am you. We are the brightest stars in the sky.

Allow your heart, mind, and body to absorb all the love and joy that is here right now for you, remembering that any time and any day you can come right back to this time and this space. You can read the letter again or remember in your mind how to return here. Know that it is possible to bring all that you find here in this place back into your world today. STEP ONE IS LEARNING TO BE IN THIS PLACE, RIGHT HERE, AND RIGHT NOW. KEEPING YOUR MIND AND BODY FOCUSED ON NOW AND LETTING GO OF ALL THOUGHTS ABOUT THE PAST AND THE FUTURE. EVERYTHING IN YOUR WORLD IS ABOUT RIGHT NOW. BEING IN THE PRESENT WILL ALLOW YOU TO LIVE IN A HEART-CENTERED WORLD.

REMEMBERING THAT THIS IS YOUR PURPOSE TO BE AND LIVE IN A HEART- CENTERED WORLD, GIVING AND RECEIVING OF LOVE WITHOUT STRINGS OR CONDITIONS.

Know that I am right here with you and there are thousands of others here with me. We are wanting to help you find your way to living in the NOW. Please call on us and allow us to help you find this path.

Know you only need call my name and I will be there.
In Love, Mother Mary
2/1/11

LETTER 89

Dear Ones,

In the last few letters, we have talked about Joy, Love, Laughter, Sweetness, and Light. We have talked of giving yourself a break. Today let us talk about a different kind of break. Some of you are already living in this way and many of you are talking about it. What I am speaking of is learning to follow your heart and letting go of the old way of being.

This is a big shift for most of you, going from what your common sense mind says to what your heart is telling you. This speaks to saying YES to what the universe and the ones here with me are offering you, remembering that what we offer you may not make sense at the moment, but understanding will be sure to follow. That could mean that understanding will follow but not for about 2 or 3 months. So I am saying that common sense understanding is not the most important thing in your world right now.

There are opportunities being presented to each of you at this time. Opportunities that will increase your ability to share your gifts. Opportunities to open your heart wider and wider, allowing the real you to come into the light. Each of you is learning who and what you are. You each are becoming aware of what your gifts are that you have come to share with the world. These opportunities that are being presented to you are portals or windows into your growing and blooming into the light.

What your Mother Earth needs right now to continue to grow and flourish is light. As each of you brings your gifts out into the open, your light increases and shines brighter and brighter. THESE OPPORTUNITIES THAT ARE BEING PRESENTED TO YOU ARE GIFTS TWICE OVER. AS YOU ACCEPT OUR GIFTS AND BEGIN TO OPEN UP YOU WILL BE INCREASING YOUR PERSONAL LIGHT IN THE WORLD. AS YOU INCREASE YOUR LIGHT, YOU WILL ALSO BE FEEDING AND NURTURING YOUR MOTHER EARTH WITH MORE LIGHT.

PERHAPS THESE GIFTS THAT WE ARE SENDING YOU ARE THREE TIMES OVER GIFTS. YOU ARE GIFTED WITH MORE LIGHT. MOTHER EARTH IS GIFTED WITH MORE LIGHT FROM

YOU AND WE HERE ON THIS SIDE ARE BLESSED AND GRATEFUL THAT OUR GIFTS HAVE BEEN ACCEPTED AND APPRECIATED.

WE IN TURN, ALL OF US, ARE PRACTICING WHAT YOUR WORLD WAS MEANT TO BE ABOUT. THESE GIFTS THAT WE ARE SHARING WITH YOU AND THAT YOU ARE APPRECIATING AND ACCEPTING ARE ALL ABOUT LOVE. ALL OF THIS IS PART OF THE GIVING AND RECEIVING OF LOVE.

REMEMBERING NOW THAT THE GIVING AND RECEIVING OF LOVE IS WHAT YOUR MOTHER EARTH IS ABOUT AND HER PURPOSE FOR EXISTING. YOUR PURPOSE FOR BEING HERE ON YOUR MOTHER EARTH IS ABOUT LEARNING TO GIVE AND RECEIVE LOVE. WE HERE ARE APPLAUDING AND LAUGHING IN JOY AND BLESSINGS THAT PURPOSES ARE BEING FULFILLED. LOVE IS RUNNING RAMPANT.

WE HERE ARE FEELING BLESSED AND HAPPY. WE ARE HOPING THAT YOU ALSO ARE FEELING BLESSED AND HAPPY. REMEMBERING THAT WE ARE ALWAYS HERE FOR WHATEVER YOU MAY NEED. KNOW THAT YOU ARE GREATLY LOVED AND APPRECIATED.

Know you only need call my name and I will be there.
In Love, Mother Mary
2/2/11

LETTER 90

Dear Ones,

Each one of you is so precious and unique. Each of your gifts will come in different ways and at different times. You each will present yourself and your gifts to the world differently from anyone else.

What makes your world so wonderful is that you are all so different. It is a crime against each of you that it has been thought that everyone should be like everyone else. Your young people strive to look and be like all their friends, never knowing or learning that it is so wonderful to be different than everyone else.

Some of you are well into your adult lives before you discover that it is not only ok to be different, but that it is absolutely wonderful to be different. Many, many of you never discover that it is ok to be just who you are and that it is ok to be different. There is huge pain, stress, frustration, and desperation caused from trying and working to be the same as everyone else. It is not something that you can ever accomplish, because the truth is there is no one like you or no one like the person you are trying to be.

This battle or war that goes on inside of you trying to make yourselves into being normal or like everyone else, is never ending. There will be no winners in this battle or war, only losers. In working to be as everyone else it causes you to think less and less of your worth and value to the world and yourself. It is a constant re-enforcing voice in your head saying you are not ok as you are.

I AM SPEAKING VERY LOUDLY RIGHT NOW. MAYBE I AM EVEN SCREAMING BECAUSE THIS IS SO IMPORTANT. YOU ARE WONDERFUL JUST AS YOU ARE. YOU WERE NEVER MEANT TO BE LIKE ANYONE ELSE. YOU WERE MEANT TO BE DIFFERENT THAN ANYONE ELSE ON YOUR EARTH. YOU ARE PRECIOUS AND ONE OF A KIND. YOU ARE TO BE CHERISHED, ADORED AND HONORED BECAUSE YOU ARE WHO YOU ARE.

BECAUSE YOU ARE DIFFERENT AND ONE OF A KIND, YOU BRING YOUR OWN SPECIAL GIFTS TO THE WORLD. YOU EACH ARE A SEPARATE AND UNIQUE FORM OF ENERGY THAT IS

NEEDED TO MAKE UP THE WHOLE OF YOUR PLANET. Your world is made of hundreds of thousands of separate and unique energy forms, each form having its own place and space to fill. If you are trying to change yourself and your energy form, how will you fit into your own special place and space? If you change your energy form and make it different, you will never find your place or how you fit into the world.

SO I AM SAYING TO YOU AND EVEN BEGGING YOU TO PLEASE PAY ATTENTION AND HEAR MY WORDS. YOU EACH ARE WONDERFUL AND UNIQUE AND WERE NEVER MEANT TO BE LIKE ANYONE ELSE. WE HERE ARE HONORING YOU FOR YOUR DIFFERENCES AND THE COURAGE, IT TAKES TO BE WHO YOU ARE. IT TAKES GREAT COURAGE AND STRENGTH TO STEP OUT OF OLD THOUGHT PATTERNS AND HONOR YOURSELVES AND US BY BEING WHO YOU ARE MEANT TO BE. DIFFERENT, UNIQUE AND MAYBE EVEN STRANGE SOMETIMES, BUT THAT IS WONDERFUL BEYOND WORDS.

KNOW THAT I AM LOVING YOU AND EVERYONE HERE IS LOVING YOU FOR YOUR DIFFERENCES. WE ARE STANDING RIGHT HERE TO HELP YOU TAKE THOSE STEPS TO ALLOW YOURSELVES TO BE DIFFERENT AND UNIQUE. WHAT COULD BE MORE WONDERFUL THAN BEING WHO YOU ARE?

Know that you only need call my name and I will be there.
In Love, Mother Mary
2/3/11

LETTER 91
HONESTY & RELATIONSHIPS

Dear Ones,

Is it feeling like your relationships are a little stretched thin these days? With each of you having a constant barrage of old emotions and situations coming up, relationships are suffering. For most of you relationships have never been easy. They take work, honesty, love, and forgiveness to flourish and grow.

The honesty I am speaking of concerns honesty with yourself first and then honesty with the person you are in relationship with. We are not just speaking of husbands and wives, but every possible relationship you can think of. There are hundreds of different kinds of relationships in your world.

HONESTY SEEMS TO BE THE MOST DIFFICULT THING FOR EACH OF YOU TO SHARE WITH ONE ANOTHER. HONESTY TAKES TRUST. TRUST THAT THE PERSON YOU ARE BEING HONEST WITH WILL NOT REJECT YOU, ABANDON YOU OR RIDICULE YOU. ALL OF THOSE THINGS ARE GOING ON INSIDE EACH OF YOU AS YOU TRY TO HAVE HONESTY IN YOUR LIVES AND RELATIONSHIPS.

Indeed all of those things are on the line when you take the risk to be honest. You could be rejected, abandoned and ridiculed. Let us look at the price you pay for not being honest with yourself and others. When I am talking about being honest, I am not talking about the lie that says you are going to the store when you are going to have a beer with friends. The honesty I am talking about is not sharing the truth of who you really are. Not sharing the truth of how you feel and think about life, yourself, the world, God, ME (Mother Mary), and hundreds of other important things in your world.

WHAT IS YOUR TRUTH? WHO ARE YOU? WHEN WILL YOU COME OUT OF THE CLOSET? IT IS TIME TO LET THE WORLD KNOW WHO YOU REALLY ARE. How does one do that? You do that by starting very slowly to tell those that you are in relationships with the truth. It is the time for honesty and courage.

In the world of 2011 there is no more time or room for hiding all that you are away behind physical doors or energetic doors. In the year of 2011 it is time for all the doors to come down. IT IS TIME TO BE HONEST WITH YOURSELVES AND HONEST WITH THE BEINGS THAT YOU ARE IN RELATIONSHIP WITH. IF YOU ARE SAYING TO YOURSELF RIGHT NOW THAT THIS LETTER HAS NOTHING TO DO WITH YOUR LIFE. I WOULD ASK YOU TO READ IT AGAIN.

THERE IS NO BEING ON YOUR MOTHER EARTH WHO HAS BEEN TOTALLY HONEST WITH THEMSELVES LET ALONE ALL THE OTHERS IN THEIR LIVES.

BEING HONEST WILL BE A NEW WAY OF BEING FOR ALL OF YOU. EACH OF YOU HAS BEEN TAUGHT FROM YOUR FIRST BREATH TO HIDE WHO YOU ARE. EACH OF YOU HAS BEEN TAUGHT THAT IT IS MOST IMPORTANT TO HIDE FROM THE ONES YOU SAY YOU LOVE. THEY HAVE THE MOST POWER TO HARM YOU.

LOOK AROUND YOU. WHO ARE YOU THE MOST OPEN WITH? WHO ARE YOU THE MOST HONEST WITH? ARE YOU THE MOST OPEN AND HONEST WITH YOUR FAMILIES, YOUR HUSBAND OR WIFE, OR THE PEOPLE WHO HAVE LESS IMPORTANCE IN YOUR LIVES?

This lack of honesty about who you are and what you feel and think has not worked well. Families end up being torn apart and marriages end up in divorce. In most cases, all parties are standing and looking as if they have been hit by a car. They have no understanding of what has happened and who this other person is. The truth is they don't know who the other person is, because there has been no honesty, no being real, only this façade or pretend person.

TIME AFTER TIME, YOU HAVE BROKEN YOUR OWN HEART AND THE HEART OF OTHERS TRYING TO PROTECT YOURSELVES FROM BEING REJECTED, ABANDONED OR RIDICULED.

IN THE PROTECTING OF YOURSELF FROM OTHERS, YOU HAVE ENDED UP REJECTING YOURSELF, ABANDONING YOURSELF AND RIDICULING WHO YOU REALLY ARE. It is time to stop all this pain. It is time to take the risks to be who you are and to share with the rest of the world who you are.

KNOWING AS I SAY THESE WORDS TO YOU, THAT I AM RIGHT HERE WAITING TO HELP YOU MAKE THESE CHANGES. WE WILL MAKE THESE CHANGES AS GENTLY AS POSSIBLE, VERY SLOWLY, AND WITH LOVE AND CARING FOR WHO YOU TRULY ARE. THERE ARE HUNDREDS OF THOUSANDS OF US WAITING HERE TO HELP YOU.

Know you only need call my name and I will be there.
In Love, Mother Mary
2/7/11

LETTER 92

Dear Ones,

Again today I wish to write more about Honesty & Relationships. Remembering now that when I speak of relationships, I am including the relationship you have with yourself! After all, the relationship that you have with yourself is the most important one that you will ever have.

You may not think that this is so, that your relationship to yourself is more important than any other. You may think you don't have to work at this relationship, make compromises, keep promises, be honest, nurturing, and supportive. If that is what you are thinking, that is so untrue. All of those statements are untrue.

This is the one relationship where you must do all of those things or "YOUR LIFE WILL NEVER WORK FOR YOU, AND IT WILL NEVER BE WHAT YOU WANT."

Those are harsh words but they are truth. You are the one and only person who can take care of yourself in the way in which you need to be cared for. There is no other being on your planet who can do this as well as you can. OFTEN IT IS THOUGHT, IF I JUST FIND MYSELF THE RIGHT PARTNER OR SPOUSE, THEY WILL TAKE CARE OF ALL MY NEEDS. EVERYTHING WILL BE ALL RIGHT IN MY WORLD. THEY WILL FIX IT FOR ME.

NOW LET'S TRAVEL BACK TO YESTERDAY AND THE LETTER "HONESTY & RELATIONSHIPS." Remember now what I spoke of yesterday. That most people find it almost impossible to be honest and who they truly are with the people they love. SO LET US STOP FOR A MOMENT AND THINK ABOUT THIS. IF YOU ARE SOMEONE WHO IS THINKING THEY JUST NEED TO FIND THE RIGHT PARTNER OR SPOUSE AND THEY WILL TAKE CARE OF ALL MY NEEDS. HOW IS THIS GOING TO WORK? YOU ARE BUSY BEING THE PRETEND FAÇADE PERSON BECAUSE YOU LOVE THIS PERSON AND ARE AFRAID OF ABANDONMENT, REJECTION AND RIDICULE. AT THE SAME TIME, YOU ARE THINKING THEY WILL TAKE CARE OF ALL YOUR NEEDS.

I AM TALKING VERY LOUDLY RIGHT NOW. YOU ARE BEING

A PRETEND OR FAÇADE PERSON, AND YOUR PARTNER HAS NO IDEA WHAT YOUR NEEDS ARE. HE OR SHE DOESN'T EVEN KNOW THE REAL YOU, LET ALONE TRYING TO FIGURE OUT WHAT YOU MIGHT NEED.

Is this craziness? This is setting yourself up for more hurt and pain. This is a continuing, on-going cycle that is running rampant on your Mother Earth. This cycle is like living your life on a roller coaster. IT IS TIME TO TURN OFF THE ROLLER COASTER AND JUST STOP.

IT IS TIME TO STOP AND FIND OUT WHO YOU TRULY ARE. IT IS TIME TO STOP BEING THE PRETEND OR FAÇADE PERSON. If you are in the cycle long enough, pretty soon you start to believe that the pretend or façade person is who you really are. CAN YOU SEE THIS IS NOT THE TRUTH?

THIS IS AN ONGOING CYCLE OF HURT, PAIN, AND DISAPPOINTMENT. THIS IS NOT SOMETHING THAT THE OTHER PERSON IS DOING TO YOU, BUT SOMETHING THAT YOU ARE DOING TO YOURSELVES.

IT TAKES GREAT COURAGE TO TURN OFF THE ROLLER COASTER AND CHOOSE TO BECOME HONEST IN THE RELATIONSHIP WITH YOURSELF. IT TAKES GREAT COURAGE TO BECOME HONEST WITH THE ONES YOU LOVE. YOU MAY FIND THAT SOME OF THE THINGS YOU ARE AFRAID OF WILL HAPPEN. BUT AT THE SAME TIME YOU WILL FIND HUGE REWARDS, ENORMOUS PERSONAL REWARDS FOR BEING HONEST AND GETTING TO LIVE A LIFE BEING WHO YOU TRULY ARE.

YOU WILL FIND SUCH JOY AND WONDER IN THE DISCOVERY OF WHO YOU ARE AND BEING ABLE TO LIVE THE LIFE YOU NEED AND WANT.

OF COURSE, REMEMBERING ALWAYS THAT WE ARE RIGHT HERE WAITING WITH OPEN ARMS AND HEARTS TO CARE, NURTURE AND LOVE YOU. WE ARE WAITING TO HELP YOU WITH IT ALL.

Know that you only need call my name and I will be there.
In love, Mother Mary
2/8/11

LETTER 93

Dear Ones,

Let us today talk about choices. The choice that I am interested in today is the one you make in the morning after you get out of bed. Will it be a good day? Will it be a bad day? Will it be an OK day?

Did you know that you have a choice about what your day will be? You can get out of bed feeling a little tired, crabby and saying, "Yuck, it is raining." Guess where the day will go from there. What kind of day do you think you will have if you CHOOSE to stay in that mindset? First off, is the energy that you wake up with all yours or is it part of the collective consciousness? Have you cleared and cleaned your energy field lately? Have you cleared and cleaned the energy field of your home and car?

The condition of your energy field has a direct connection to the kinds of days you choose for your life. Isn't it incredible that these are your choices about what kind of days you can have? Have you been thinking it was a random thing that just happened to you? I WANT YOU TO KNOW THAT YOU HAVE CHOICES ABOUT HOW YOUR DAY WILL BE.

The energy of your world right now is very intense and heavy. There is great turmoil going on in many countries and cities all over the world. You have a choice, whether or not to bring that energy into your car, your home, and your life. People walking through your grocery stores and malls have great turmoil going on inside of them. What about the people who are struggling to find a job or they are worrying about losing their homes?

You can change nothing for these people who are in turmoil by bringing it into your lives and homes. That will not change anything for them. In fact it is more harmful for them when that happens. The harm comes from you increasing that turmoil by bringing it home and allowing it to grow and expand. It is so much better for you, your world, and those in turmoil if you CHOOSE to stay in your own energy field, simply sending love and caring to them.

There is another kind of turmoil going on in your world right now. We have talked before about old emotions and situations coming up to be released and let go. If you CHOOSE to hang on to these old emotions and situations, how do you think you will feel in the morning when you get out of bed? REMEMBERING NOW THAT YOU TOOK THEM TO BED WITH YOU OR IN SOME CASES THEY CAME TO YOU DURING THE NIGHT IN YOUR DREAMS.

WHETHER TO LET GO OF THESE OLD EMOTIONS AND SITUATIONS IS A CHOICE THAT IS FOR YOU TO MAKE. PLEASE CONSIDER WHEN YOU ARE MAKING YOUR CHOICE THAT IT AFFECTS THE KIND OF DAY YOU WILL HAVE. IT WILL AFFECT THE KIND OF MOTHER/FATHER YOU WILL BE, THE KIND OF WIFE/HUSBAND YOU WILL BE AND THE KIND OF WORLD CITIZEN YOU WILL BE.

What is your energy field bringing into the world today? Are you bringing turmoil and unrest or WILL YOU BRING YOURSELF INTO THE DAY AS A HEART-CENTERED, LOVING, CARING BEING?

AGAIN, IS IT NOT INCREDIBLE THAT YOU GET TO CHOOSE WHAT KIND OF DAY YOU CAN HAVE? YOU GET TO CHOOSE WHAT KIND OF ENERGY FIELD YOU BRING INTO THE UNIVERSAL ENERGY FIELD.

KNOW THAT WE ARE HERE LOVING YOU AND WE ARE WAITING AND WILLING TO HELP YOU WITH WHATEVER YOU WOULD LIKE HELP WITH TODAY. WE ARE ALWAYS HERE AND THERE ARE HUNDREDS OF THOUSANDS OF US SUPPORTING AND LOVING YOU.

Know you only need call my name and I will be there.
In Love, Mother Mary
2/4/11

LETTER 94

Dear Ones,

Today for the first time my letters will be able to come to you in audio form. So not only can you read my letters but you will also be able to hear my letters. You will find as you listen to my letters that the energy waves will go directly to your ears and then directly to your heart.

Your mind will no longer be able to filter out the bits and pieces that it might find uncomfortable. Our connection will be heart to heart, bringing us to a whole new level of communication.

I am excited today that you will be able to hear me say I LOVE YOU, I LOVE YOU BEYOND YOUR WILDEST IMAGINATION. You are unaware of the depth of love and caring that everyone here feels for you. You are unaware of the respect and praise we have for the work that you each are doing in your world.

YOU ARE THE ONES WHO HAVE MADE IT POSSIBLE FOR YOUR WORLD TO STEP INTO THE NEXT PHASE OF ITS GROWTH. WITHOUT EACH AND EVERY ONE OF YOU, THERE WOULD BE NO NEXT PHASE. WE KNOW IT HAS TAKEN GREAT STRENGTH, DETERMINATION AND COURAGE TO ACCOMPLISH ALL THAT YOU HAVE ACCOMPLISHED.

WE KNOW THAT EACH OF YOU CAME BACK TO YOUR EARTH AT THIS TIME TO BE PART OF THIS GREAT TRANSFORMATION. YOU EACH HAVE CHOSEN TO BE WAYSHOWERS AND KEEPERS OF THE LIGHT DURING THIS TIME ON YOUR MOTHER EARTH. WE HONOR YOU FOR THE PATH YOU HAVE CHOSEN AND THE WAY YOU ARE WALKING YOUR PATH.

I HAVE SAID MANY TIMES IN MY LETTERS THAT WE ARE RIGHT HERE WAITING TO HELP YOU. NOW YOU CAN HEAR ME SAY, "WE ARE RIGHT HERE WAITING TO HELP YOU." KNOW THAT NO REQUEST FOR HELP IS TOO BIG OR TOO SMALL. WE ARE HONORED AND PRIVILEGED TO BE ABLE TO HELP YOU IN ANY WAY.

Thank you for reading my letters and today, thank you for listening to my letters and connecting with me in a new way.

Know you only need call my name and I will be there.
In Love, Mother Mary
2/9/11

LETTER 95

Dear Ones,

Today let us talk about Change, Renewal, and Growth. Each of you thinks and daydreams about having more exciting lives. Those daydreams could be about traveling to a strange and new place, having a new job, or maybe it is thoughts of a new person in your life. All of those thoughts and daydreams are about changing things in your lives.

These daydreams are exciting to think about, but when it comes to the reality of your everyday life, they mean change. Something will need to change if those thoughts and dreams are to come true.

Immediately, the whole process of you manifesting your dream's stops. THE DREAMS STOP BECAUSE TO HAVE THESE THINGS YOU ARE THINKING ABOUT, YOU WILL HAVE TO CHANGE. Adding change into the process of what you are thinking and dreaming about stops you in your tracks.

Most beings on your Mother Earth perceive CHANGE as a scary and bad thing. Change is something to be avoided as long as possible. IT IS TIME TO CHANGE YOUR PERCEPTION OF WHAT CHANGE MEANS IN YOUR LIFE. CHANGE CAN BRING JOY, LAUGHTER, LOVE, AND HAPPINESS INTO YOUR LIVES. WOULD ALL OF YOU NOT WANT TO HAVE THOSE THINGS IN YOUR LIVES?

Change often happens with the letting go of the known in your lives to accept and try out new people, places, and things. Change can be exciting and fulfilling. Growth and renewal are the rewards of change. Every being on your planet needs to experience growth and renewal. It is vital to your beings that you continue on a path of growth and renewal of self.

Sickness of the mind and body comes to beings that find they are unable to go forward in their lives. Becoming stuck in the same-old thing year after year causes tremendous wear and tear on the mind and body. Staying in the same place year after year comes from the fear of CHANGE. The fear tells you that change is bad, that it will cause you pain and suffering. THAT IS NOT A TRUTH.

CHANGE CAN BRING JOY, LAUGHTER AND LOVE INTO

YOUR LIVES. ACCEPTING CHANGE CAN ALLOW THOSE THINGS THAT YOU DREAM AND THINK ABOUT TO COME INTO YOUR LIVES. There are times when change can bring pain and suffering into your lives, but that is usually the effect of your not being able to let go and move forward.

REMEMBERING NOW THAT WE ARE HERE TO HELP. WE CAN HELP YOU TO RELEASE THE FEAR THAT IS STOPPING YOU FROM HAVING WHAT YOU WANT IN YOUR LIVES. HELP WITH MAKING THOSE CHANGES IS RIGHT HERE AS CLOSE AS A WHISPER. ALL YOU NEED DO IS TO THINK I NEED HELP AND HELP WILL APPEAR.

I AM REMEMBERING THAT YOU CAN HEAR ME NOW, SO AGAIN, I WILL SAY VERY LOUDLY, I LOVE YOU, I LOVE YOU, I LOVE YOU, AND I LOVE YOU. WHAT JOY IT BRINGS TO MY HEART TO KNOW THAT YOU CAN HEAR THOSE WORDS SAID OUT LOUD IN YOUR WORLD.

Know you only need call my name and I will be there.
In love, Mother Mary
2/11/11

LETTER 96

Dear Ones,

Are some of you wondering why I keep writing about the same things over and over? I do that because not everyone understands or can take in what I am saying. Many times the ones reading The Letters tell themselves that The Letter is for someone else. Their lives are totally fine; they are not afraid of change or they have no fear in their lives. Whatever I have written about has nothing to do with them.

So I keep writing letters about fear, change and all the other things that cause challenges in your lives. Each of you will become awakened to the stumbling blocks in your lives in your own time and own way. You may read ten of my letters all about change and it will not click in for you until you read the eleventh letter.

For some of you, it may never click in. You may choose to stay right where you are at in your lives. That is your choice or your free will and it is to be honored and respected. For those in your lives who are moving into different directions it can be difficult to let you stay right where you are at. They want to bring you along on their journey forgetting that you have your own journey. Your journey may be to stand right where you are.

Those that are taking steps in different directions and those that are standing still it is vital that you each honor the other. It may be difficult for each of you to understand as you stand on opposite sides of the road, but it is not necessary to understand. It is only necessary to love one another and to allow each other the peace and dignity to do what each one needs.

WATCHING AND LOOKING INTO SOMEONE'S LIFE WITH EYES OF JUDGMENT IS NOT ABOUT LOVE AND CARING. THE EYES OF JUDGMENT COME FROM FEELINGS OF BEING BETTER THAN THE OTHER PERSON. THE EYES OF JUDGMENT SAY YOU KNOW BETTER THAN THEY DO, BETTER THAN SPIRIT DOES, AND BETTER THAN ANYONE ELSE DOES.

So I will ask you now, is that what you are meaning, that you know better than anyone else how someone other than yourself should live? I can almost see you shaking your head, wondering how all this got to this point.

With your eyes of judgment, you have never taken the next step to see what you are doing or why you might be doing it. So I will say to you now to stop and look at your life to see if there are changes you need to make. Now I will ask you, "What are you going to do about your changes?"

The eye of judgment is one way that beings can stop themselves from taking the next steps in their own lives. Most often the eye of judgment comes up when there are challenges in your own lives that you are unable to look at.

NOW I WILL ASK YOU TO LISTEN TO ME VERY CAREFULLY WHETHER YOU ARE THE ONE BEING JUDGED OR THE ONE DOING THE JUDGING. EACH OF YOU ARE IN CHALLENGING AND DIFFICULT PLACES IN YOUR GROWTH. CAN YOU STEP OUT OF YOUR OLD PATTERNS AND PUT THE EYES OF JUDGMENT AWAY? CAN YOU GO TO YOUR HEARTS AND FEEL THE LOVE AND CARING YOU HAVE TO GIVE? I ASK YOU TO SHARE THAT LOVE AND CARING WITH YOURSELF AND OTHERS. ACKNOWLEDGE WHERE YOU ARE AT AND SEEING WHERE OTHERS ARE AT WITH EYES OF LOVE AND CARING.

Each and every one of you is different and unique. You each grow and change at different levels and different times. You will go forward or you will stand still at different times in your lives. REMEMBERING NOW WHAT MAKES YOUR WORLD SO WONDERFUL IS THAT YOU ARE EACH DIFFERENT AND SEPARATE BEINGS. LEARNING TO LOVE YOUR SEPARATENESS AND DIFFERENCES IS PART OF YOUR PURPOSE HERE ON EARTH.

EACH ONE OF YOU IS PERFECT IN WHATEVER PLACE YOU MIGHT BE IN YOUR LIVES. YOU ARE EACH DOING THE VERY BEST THAT YOU CAN DO. WE ARE RIGHT HERE READY TO HELP YOU WITH EYES OF LOVE AND CARING. WE ARE HONORING WHERE YOU HAVE CHOSEN TO BE IN YOUR LIVES.

WE ARE ASKING ONLY TO BE ABLE TO LOVE YOU AND HELP YOU. PLEASE CALL ON US. WE ARE HERE WAITING TO HELP YOU.

Know you only need call my name and I will be there.
In Love, Mother Mary
2/12/11

LETTER 97

Dear Ones,

Today let us talk about Stress and the role it is playing in your life. Stress is the biggest obstacle in your everyday life. There are a hundred thousand different things that can cause you to feel stressed. Everyone picks and chooses what they want to be stressed about and it changes from day to day.

In your world, stress is so common it is thought to be part of your life. "It is just the way it is" are the thoughts that many of you have. Stress is not to be part of your life. It is something you have learned and passed down through the generations.

I do not understand why a parent would want to pass STRESS on to their child and tell them it is just the way it is. No, you do not say that verbally but your actions say it very loudly. How you each act around them, how you treat yourself, how you treat your friends, and families. Every action and many times your words express that STRESS is just a part of life. Without saying a word your actions are saying to them "GET USED TO IT, THIS IS HOW LIFE IS."

TODAY, I WANT TO SAY VERY LOUDLY IN YOUR WORLD, "DO NOT GET USED TO IT, AND THIS IS NOT HOW LIFE IS MEANT TO BE."

STRESS IS AN ADDICTION, JUST LIKE YOUR CIGARETTES, FOOD, ALCOHOL, AND DRUGS. All of these things are harmful to your physical, mental, spiritual, and emotional bodies. There are no redeeming qualities in any of these addictions. Anything in your world can be turned into an addiction. Overuse turns anything into an addiction.

Today, we are going to talk just about the addiction of STRESS. ASK YOURSELF NOW, WHAT DOES STRESS DO FOR ME? TELL ME WHAT GOOD IT BRINGS TO YOUR LIFE? TELL ME HOW IT ENRICHES YOUR LIFE? TELL ME WHY YOU LIKE IT IN YOUR LIFE? TELL ME WHY IT IS IN YOUR LIFE? I AM NOT SPEAKING ABOUT WHAT IS HAPPENING WITH PEOPLE, PLACES AND THINGS OUTSIDE OF YOU. I AM ASKING WHY YOU ARE CHOOSING TO HAVE IT IN YOUR LIFE?

There are times in everyone's life that situations come up and stress occurs. That is a normal reaction to trauma, death, divorce, and illness. I am speaking of keeping it after these situations have passed and allowing it to grow and become part of you.

I am speaking of making stress your way of life, an everyday part of who you are. STRESS is not who you are. It is an addiction you have allowed in your life. NOW IS THE TIME TO LAY IT DOWN AND WALK AWAY. YES, I DO KNOW THAT IT IS NOT QUITE THAT EASY. BUT TODAY LET US START TO CHANGE THIS ADDICTION. IT IS TIME TO LEARN HOW TO RELAX AND STAY THAT WAY.

SO RIGHT NOW CLOSE YOUR EYES, BREATHE DEEPLY, PUT YOUR HAND ON YOUR HEART AND CALL MY NAME. I AM RIGHT HERE WITH YOU, TAKE MY HAND AND LET US TAKE A JOURNEY TO THE LAND OF RELAXATION.

JUST CONTINUE TO BREATHE DEEPLY. WE ARE BREATHING IN A SOFT GOLDEN LIGHT AND IT WILL GENTLY TRAVEL THROUGH YOUR BODY. ALLOW THE LIGHT TO DO ITS JOB. IT IS COLLECTING ALL THE PARTICLES OF STRESS THAT LIVE IN EVERY CELL OF YOUR BODY. AS YOU BREATHE OUT, ALLOW THE GOLDEN LIGHT TO LEAVE. NOTICE THAT ALL PARTS OF YOUR BODY ARE STARTING TO SLOW DOWN. YOUR MIND IS NOT RACING SO FAST, YOUR BREATH IS COMING SLOWER AND YOUR HEART BEAT IS BECOMING MORE EVEN AND BALANCED.

STAY HERE WITH ME AS LONG AS YOU CAN, JUST BREATHING IN THE GOLDEN LIGHT. BREATHING OUT NOW AND ALLOWING THE LIGHT TO LEAVE, CARRYING THE STRESS OUT AND AWAY FROM YOU AND YOUR BODY. THE GOLDEN LIGHT WILL TRANSFORM THE STRESS BACK INTO CLEAR AND HEALTHY ENERGY.

IT IS IMPORTANT FOR YOU TO KNOW AND LOOK AT WHAT STRESS IS TO YOUR LIFE. TAKE AN HONEST LOOK AT THE WAYS THAT STRESS IS STOPPING YOU FROM HAVING WHAT YOU WANT IN YOUR LIFE.

We, of course are here waiting to help. We are here to help you do some soul-searching about the addiction of stress and how it is affecting your life. Call on us, we are right here, ready and willing to help you. KNOW THAT YOU ARE LOVED AND CARED FOR BY HUNDREDS OF THOUSANDS OF US HERE ON THIS SIDE. REMEMBERING THERE IS NO GREATER GIFT TO GIVE OR RECEIVE THAN LOVE.

Know you only need call my name and I will be there.
In Love, Mother Mary
2/14/11

LETTER 98

Dear Ones,

I wish to continue talking about STRESS as an addiction today. Have you given any thought to STRESS in your life after reading or listening to my letter yesterday? Is STRESS an addiction in your life? Do you find yourself missing out on much of the life that is going on around you? Are you so stressed that you are unable to focus and be present with your life?

If you are finding that the answers to all of these questions IS YES, then it is time to do something about your addiction. It is time for you to be in charge of how you live your life. It was never meant for STRESS to be the one in charge of your life and how you live it. STRESS is a chemical reaction that occurs in all your bodies after you experience trauma, death, divorce, or illness.

STRESS is a reaction to certain life-altering situations that happen in your life. It comes with life-altering situations and is then meant to disperse after a short amount of time. Living in a continual state of STRESS causes your physical, mental, and emotional bodies to become ill and out of balance. Ongoing stress over an extended period of time causes you to live in the mode of hyper alert. You are always watching and waiting for the next thing to happen and there is no relaxation or enjoyment of your life. WATCHING AND WAITING BECOME THE KEY WORDS AND THE STANCE OF HOW YOU LIVE YOUR LIFE.

SO NOW LET US GO TO THE ADDICTION PART OF STRESS AND WHAT YOU CAN DO ABOUT IT. One part of addiction is habit; it is the way you have learned to operate in the world. Today we are only going to be addressing addiction as it relates to your STRESS.

WHEN was the last time you attempted to find some form of relaxation for yourself? First, do you know what you can do to help yourself relax? What works for you? Is it music, massage, talking, writing, listening to the ocean or doing visualization? What is it that works to relax you? Maybe it is as simple as walking out the door and taking a deep breath. We are looking for one small thing that will get you started.

Each one of you will find their relaxation and change of lifestyle in their own way. We are willing to work one on one with each of you to help you find your path to be STRESS-FREE.

I AM SAYING THIS VERY LOUDLY, THERE IS NO ROOM OR SPACE IN THE 5D WORLD FOR STRESS ADDICTIONS. THE 5D WORLD IS ABOUT THE CONSTANT AND STEADY FLOW OF LOVE ENERGY. THE ENERGY OF STRESS ADDICTION IS CHAOTIC AND ALWAYS IN THE MODE OF WATCHING AND WAITING FOR THE WORST TO HAPPEN.

SO I AM ASKING YOU RIGHT NOW TO START WORKING ON THE RELEASING AND LETTING GO OF ANY PARTS OF YOUR LIFESTYLE ASSOCIATED WITH STRESS ADDICTION. REMEMBERING THAT WE ARE RIGHT HERE WAITING AND WILLING TO HELP YOU FIND YOUR OWN PERSONAL PATH FOR RELEASING THE STRESS IN YOUR LIFE. LOVE, JOY, LAUGHTER, AND HAPPINESS COMES WITH A CONSTANT, STEADY, AND GENTLE FLOW OF ENERGY. We are here offering you the path of love, joy, laughter, and happiness. Come and take my hand and we will find that path together.

Know you only need call my name and I will be there.
In Love, Mother Mary
2/16/11

LETTER 99

Dear Ones,

Today I want to talk about something new I would like to start. It will be an addition to Letters from Mother Mary. I am going to call it "Footnotes to Mother Mary's Letters."

Barbara or "Anna" as I call her will be posting the first Footnotes in a few days; she hasn't written it yet. Footnotes will be letters or comments from all of you about how you have used The Letters to help yourselves.

I know that you read The Letters and sometimes it feels like, oh no, that letter was written just for me. Darn, what do I do now? Maybe the words are a little stronger than that. There are two choices at this point. Either you ignore the letter or decide you want to do something about what you read in the letter.

The letter has reminded you that you have some unfinished business to take care of. Perhaps it reminds you that there are things you need or want to change in how you are living your life. Maybe The Letters remind you that you are not telling the people in your life how much they mean to you and how much you love them. None of these things are easy to consider or think about. They all mean change, personal risk, and letting yourself be vulnerable to others.

So now I am going to ask you to go one step further and share with the other readers of The Letters how you were able to move forward, how you were able to change the things in your life that you needed and wanted to change.

I realize that for some of you this is one step beyond impossible. For others, you may consider doing this, after you think about it for a while. There are others of you who are saying, "Why would I want to do this or why would anyone want to do this?" THAT IS A WONDERFUL QUESTION.

MY ANSWER IS TO HELP YOURSELF AND TO HELP OTHER PEOPLE. YOU MAY FIND A WAY TO CHANGE SOMETHING IN YOUR LIFE THAT SOMEONE ELSE WOULD NEVER EVEN THINK OF. WHAT A GIFT TO REACH OUT AND SHARE SO THAT MAYBE SOMEONE ELSE COULD USE YOUR WONDERFUL IDEAS.

THIS IS ALL GOING BACK TO YOUR PURPOSE FOR BEING HERE ON YOUR MOTHER EARTH. REMEMBER THE PURPOSE IS TO LEARN TO GIVE AND RECEIVE LOVE. PART OF LOVING IS SHARING YOURSELF, YOUR THOUGHTS, YOUR IDEAS AND YOUR TIME WITH OTHERS. THIS IS WHAT FOOTNOTES IS ALL ABOUT.

This may be a huge risk for some of you to take and I honor and respect that. I also know and trust that you each will do exactly what you want and need to do to take the very best care of yourselves. As Barbara or Anna is thinking about writing her Footnote, she also is not totally comfortable with putting herself out there either. It is a risk to make yourself vulnerable to others. It is also a wonderful growing experience to step out and say to the world, "Here I am and this is how I feel."

We are right here loving you. You each are cherished and loved beyond what you can even imagine. We are here offering our help.

Know you only need call my name and I will be there.
In Love, Mother Mary
2/19/11

PS: IT IS IMPORTANT TO KNOW THAT YOU DO NOT NEED TO HAVE YOUR NAME ATTACHED TO YOUR FOOTNOTE. IT IS OK TO HELP WITHOUT DISCLOSING WHO YOU ARE. There will be more information about Footnotes and how it will work in my next letter. Please email to Barbara anything you would like to have included in Footnotes. Each correspondence received will be treated with the utmost respect and love.

LETTER 100

Dear Ones,

I would like to talk a little more about Footnotes and how all of it might work. You will send your Footnote items directly to Barbara. Each entry received will be treated in a respectful and loving manner. All emails will be confidential. It is entirely up to you whether your name is posted with your footnote or not. It can simply say, "A Reader from Portland, Oregon" or wherever you may live.

There are no rules or regulations that go along with this. The size of the entry is up to you. Big or small, it doesn't matter. What matters is that you each are reaching out to help someone else and in turn you will end up helping yourselves. Footnotes will not be recorded at this time. There is always room for change, so by the time next week gets here, it may all need to be changed and done differently.

Barbara's Footnote will be included with this letter. REMEMBER, WE ARE RIGHT HERE WAITING TO HELP YOU IN ANY WAY. FROM OUR HEARTS TO YOUR HEARTS, WE ARE LOVING AND CARING FOR YOU.

Know you only need call my name and I will be there.
In Love, Mother Mary
2/23/11

FOOTNOTES TO MOTHER MARY'S LETTERS

Footnote from Barb Beach, Seaside, OR
Hi everyone,

Well, I have to say I am a little nervous about writing this. I need to say right up front that I love all The Letters From Mother Mary, but I am not crazy about Letter 83 & 84. Who in the world would ever think that Stress is an addiction? Certainly not me. I think Mother Mary should have started those two letters addressed to "Dear Barbara' not 'Dear Ones".

I am making a guess that stress started in my life while I was still in my mother's tummy. Since that time, the amount has increased by 200%. Some of that was due to my childhood and the rest from how I have chosen to live my adult life.

I live in the mode of hyper alert, always watching and waiting, working very hard to always be prepared for what might happen in the future. The future could be hours away or months and years ahead. Of course, we know there isn't any way I can control all of that but I keep looking and trying to cover all my bases.

I was not pleased when Mother Mary said there was not room or space for Stress Addiction in the 5D world. About a week before her letters 83 & 84, Mother Mary gave me a taste of what it is like to be in the 5D world. The 5D world is wonderful. It seemed to me like I was seeing everything in a new light. I was amazed by the beauty of everything. I felt almost giddy and so light-hearted with a child-like amazement of the world. My trip into the 5D started while I was performing a wedding and it was wonderful. I felt so solid and right there and the words flowed as if someone else was speaking. I want to live in the 5D world.

So needless to say, her words about no space or room for stress addiction motivated me to action. I called on a friend who is very connected to spirit and has lots of wisdom and knowledge about life in general and the 5D world, in particular. I was not prepared for her to say step one was letting go of the caffeine. There had never been a thought in my mind that caffeine helped me to sustain my 200% stress level. No denial going on in my life.

Breaking away from this way of operating in the world is going to take some changes in my life, one being letting go of caffeine. I am a constant coffee drinker, strong coffee. Boy, I did not want to hear that. I felt kind of sick at heart. I don't want to give up my coffee. I also don't want to give up going to the 5D world. So yesterday I bought my first can of decaffeinated coffee. I will start mixing the two coffees together, letting myself down slowly.

I have started taking very hot baths. That is so relaxing to me and I had just stopped doing that a long time ago. Listening to relaxation tapes is something that works well for me, but I don't let myself do that very often. Well, I will be listening at least every other day. The other big change I need and want to make is to start living in the present moment. It is very difficult to live in the present moment if you are always watching and waiting.

Stress addiction for me is all about control, living in the future and trying really, really hard to always be prepared for whatever might come my way. So for now, I am starting to let go of the caffeine, taking hot baths, and listening to relaxation tapes. I'm working at catching myself when I start going into the future and then bringing myself back to right now. Hope these words are helpful to someone else. For my part, it feels good to put all these thoughts and feelings down on paper and get them out of my head.

Love & Light, Barb

LETTER 101

Dear Ones,

As you watch your TV's and talk to your friends and neighbors, you, are seeing the great transformations that are taking place here on your Mother Earth. People everywhere are saying very loudly that it is not all right for anyone to abuse them or mistreat them in any way.

This has all been simmering for many years, many decades and many centuries. As the whole of your world, all of your Mother Earth is preparing itself to go into the 5D world, all must be transformed. REMEMBERING NOW THE ENERGY AND THE WHOLE OF THE FORM OF THE 5D WORLD IS LOVE. IN 5D, THERE IS NOTHING BUT LOVE. NOTHING WILL PASS THROUGH THE WALLS OR VEILS TO GO INTO THE 5D UNLESS IT IS GENERATED AND PROPELLED BY LOVE.

LOVE is the only energy of 5D, so that anything that is not of the Love energy will not be part of the 5D world. Meaning that foods, cigarettes, alcohol, cars, drugs, and materials that are not for the highest good of the people of earth will not be allowed. They simply will not be able to be in the 5D world. The energy of 5D will not sustain anything that will not be for the good of human kind.

Are you thinking now how is that possible? Everything you can imagine in your minds is possible. Is there panic in your hearts and minds at some of the things you might need to let go of? Know that there is plenty of time for you to release these things that are harmful to your body, mind, and spirit. As you each become more prepared to pass into the 5D world, all things that do not sustain the energy of Love will pass away. You personally will no longer want them in your life. So it will not be that someone or something has taken these things away from you. You will simply be walking away from them. You will no longer want them or crave them in your life.

Just as you are seeing countries making huge changes you will also see individual people making huge changes and transformations. I AM SAYING THIS VERY LOUDLY NOW, EVERYTHING ON YOUR PLANET IS GETTING READY TO MAKE THE CHANGES AND TRANSFOR-

MATION NECESSARY TO PASS INTO 5D. You each are being carried along by the energy waves that are coming into your plant. These energy waves have been arriving for several years now and the power of the waves has increased by 200% percent since the beginning of 2011.

This is a time of joy and celebration that each and every one of you will be making their way into a new world. A world where Love is the power that sustains it and each of you. Where what is offered to you each day will be loving, supportive and caring. This is not something that any of you has ever experienced. It is only something many of you have been dreaming about for years. REMEMBERING NOW THAT DREAMS DO COME TRUE AND MIRACLES DO HAPPEN.

We are right here taking this journey with you. We are offering that love, support and caring to you today and every day. REMEMBERING NOW THAT I LOVE YOU, I LOVE YOU, AND I LOVE YOU. I AM STILL LOVING THAT YOU CAN HEAR THOSE WORDS SAID OUT LOUD.

Know you only need call my name and I will be there.
In Love, Mother Mary
2/24/11

FOOTNOTES TO MOTHER MARY'S LETTERS

From Barbara Rogers, Happy Valley, OR

A few weeks ago, I was working on my motor home putting a new tarp on before the rain hit. It took me most of the day and into the night but I finally got the tarp on. My day had not gone all that great and I was tired, sore, my knees hurt from crawling around on the roof but as I said I got it done. I laid on my back for a minute to look up at the sky. The clouds were black and rolling in fast. I knew that rain was not far behind. Still feeling out of sorts, for some reason, I felt like crying but I closed my eyes and asked Mother Mary to come to me and bring me some love. I had never asked her for anything before but I really needed to know that if I did she would be there for me.

I then said, "Mother Mary, I ask that you give me a sign that you have heard my prayers. Touch me, pull my hair, just to let me know you are with me." Well, I lay there a bit longer; eyes closed, and under my breath, I said to myself, " I know, just show me the moon."

I opened my eyes and there right in front of me the dark clouds parted, and there was the moon, full and so beautiful I couldn't believe my eyes. The feeling that came over me at that moment was full of joy and I started to smile, even laughed out loud, and in a second the clouds covered it and it was gone. I know that was meant for me to see and that Mother Mary was with me and she did hear me loud and clear. I felt very blessed and wanted to share this story with anyone out there that might have doubts about whether Mother Mary is out there, or whether she hears us. I am here to tell you that she is out there and she does listen. Barbara Rogers, Happy Valley, OR

LETTER 102

Dear Ones,

Today let us talk about forgiveness. There are many parts to forgiveness. Forgiving yourself, forgiving others, asking for forgiveness and accepting apologizes. All four of these are complicated and life altering.

So today let us look inside and see if there is forgiveness that has never been resolved or released. We can think of this as spring-cleaning your file of forgiveness. Are there things in your forgiveness file that need to be released and disposed of? Are there issues of forgiveness in the files that you have forgotten about or buried so deep they have been hidden away? These unfinished pieces of forgiveness cause all your bodies to be out of balance and in distress. You may be totally unaware of the distress that is going on in your body, because you are accustomed to it and think it is normal for you.

SO RIGHT NOW LET US TAKE THE TIME TO LOOK INTO THE FILE OF FORGIVENESS. CLOSE YOUR EYES, TAKING SEVERAL DEEP BREATHS. SAY MY NAME AND I WILL BE THERE. ALLOW YOUR MIND TO WONDER. ALLOW IT TO FIND THE PLACE WHERE YOU NEED TO BE, TRUSTING YOURSELF NOW TO KNOW WHAT YOU NEED TO SEE. JUST CONTINUE TO ALLOW YOUR MIND TO DO WHAT IT NEEDS TO DO. WHEN YOU COME TO YOUR RIGHT PLACE IT WILL BE AS IF A MOVIE IS PLAYING FOR YOU. YOU WILL BE ABLE TO SEE ALL PARTS OF THIS PLAY. YOU ARE NOT IN THE PLAY, YOU ARE OBSERVING THE PLAY. YOU ARE WATCHING YOURSELF AND OTHERS. YOU ARE SEEING THE TRUTH FROM EVERY ONE'S POINT OF VIEW. Take a moment now and just be with yourself.

WHAT IS IT THAT YOU NEED TO DO? DO YOU NEED TO FORGIVE YOURSELF OR DO OTHERS NEED TO FORGIVE YOU? DO YOU NEED TO FORGIVE OTHERS AND ACCEPT THEIR APOLOGIZES? Take the time right now to do whatever it is that you need to do to release yourself from these old stagnant energies.

You may need to return to this exercise many times to thoroughly clean out your forgiveness file. Be aware of how your body feels after releasing these old energies. You will find that your body feels lighter. Your moods will shift and your energy level will increase. Think about how good you feel after doing the spring-cleaning in your homes. It is as if the sun is shining brighter and so are you.

REMEMBERING NOW THAT YOU WILL HAVE THE RECORDING AND CAN RETURN TO IT AND USE IT AS MANY TIMES AS YOU NEED. KNOW THAT WE WILL BE RIGHT THERE WITH YOU EACH TIME YOU COME TO DO MORE SPRING CLEANING. WE ARE LOVING YOU AND HOLDING YOU IN OUR HEARTS.

Know you only need call my name and I will be there.
In Love, Mother Mary
2/26/11

FOOTNOTES TO MOTHER MARY'S LETTERS

From Victoria M. in Arizona

Mother Mary and The Letters have changed my life. Mother Mary has brought me and continues to bring me the peace of mind and joy. Thank you, Victoria M. in Arizona

LETTER 103

Dear Ones,

Today lets us talk about the energy of the collective consciousness. Yes, I know that we have talked about it many times. As I look in on each of you in the past days, I can see that your lives are being greatly affected by what you are picking up from the collective consciousness as you go about your daily lives.

It is so important that you start to have a daily routine of clearing and cleaning your personal energy field. Making a habit of cleaning and clearing your energy everyday when you return home is imperative. Even if it is no more than a few words as you are turning the key in the lock at your front door. My question to you is, why would you want to take other people's energy into your sacred space? Your sacred space is what your home is. Home is where you blossom and grow. It is your safe place here on your Mother Earth.

If there are those of you out there right now who know this is not what your home is all about, then I say to you. "CALL ON ME TO COME AND WORK WITH YOU ONE ON ONE, NOT THROUGH THE LETTERS. WE, HERE ON THIS SIDE, CAN HELP YOU TO FIND YOUR SACRED SPACE AND SAFE HOME. JUST ASK ME TO COME AND HELP AND I WILL BE THERE."

I cannot put into words how important it is for each of you to keep your energy field clear and clean. The allowing of other people's energy or energy from the collective consciousness to come into your energy field is stopping your growth. It slows you down and causes confusion in all your bodies. Your emotions become chaotic and fearful.

So I will say to you again to start yourselves a daily routine of clearing and cleaning your energy fields. Pay attention to how you are feeling. If old emotions and patterns come into play and you are not feeling like who you are today, then clear and clean your energy. Ask yourself, is this my energy or does it belong to someone else?

So the words for today are CLEAR AND CLEAN. PLEASE CALL ON US TO HELP WITH YOUR CLEARING AND CLEANING. WE WOULD BE HONORED TO ASSIST YOU. REMEMBERING THAT I LOVE YOU AND THERE ARE MANY THOUSANDS OF OTHERS HERE WHO ARE LOVING YOU ALSO.

Know you only need call my name and I will be there.
In Love, Mother Mary
2/28/11

LETTER 104

Dear Ones,

Today let us talk about your Inner Knowing. I am speaking of that small voice inside your head, or maybe it comes in the form of energy in your stomach or some other place in your body, the voice that tells you when things are OK or when things aren't OK.

As you travel further into 2011 and more of the energy waves continue to enter your Mother Earth, that voice is going to become much louder. The voice will be helping and directing you on your individual path to the 5D world. The inner voice can also be called intuition. It is the connection you each have with energy of the universe, both the seen and unseen worlds.

This is the voice or the knowing that most of you have been taught to ignore. So now it is a matter of re-training yourself to listen. You each will be able to do that easily. First, do you know the voice I am talking about? Most of you are going to be shaking your heads yes, you do know, but you most often don't pay attention to it.

If you are one of the people who doesn't understand what I am speaking about please just stop for a minute. Let yourself relax and allow me to come to you and show you what I am speaking about.

Now is the time to start paying attention to what the voice is saying to you. Start following up on what the voice is saying or pushing you towards. Once you recognize that the voice is leading you in the direction that you want to travel, it will be easier to pay attention.

This all leads back to trusting yourself and once again most of you were trained or taught not to trust yourselves. In your growing up you were taught to listen to others, which in turn told you that someone else knew more or better than you. Of course now you are starting to learn this is not the truth. Each and every being knows exactly what is best for them. There is not one thing on your Mother Earth that someone else would know better than you what is best for you.

SO NOW IS THE TIME FOR YOU AND YOUR INNER VOICE TO BE RECONNECTED. WHETHER THAT MEANS FORMING A NEW CONNECTION OR JUST INCREASING THE CONNEC-

TION THAT YOU HAVE. NOW IS THE TIME TO LISTEN AND TRUST THE INFORMATION THAT YOU ARE BEING GIVEN. BY LISTENING YOU WILL FIND THE INNER RESOURCES TO ACCOMPLISH YOUR GOALS AND LIVE THE LIFE THAT YOU HAVE BEEN ASKING FOR.

Know that we are here waiting to help you increase your connection or to help you find it if that is what you need. I AM LOVING YOU. WE ARE LOVING YOU AND WE ARE HOLDING YOU IN OUR HEARTS.

Know you only need call my name and I will be there.
In Love, Mother Mary
3/2/11

LETTER 105

Dear Ones,

Today I am writing you a letter of gratitude and thanks for all that you have been doing to help your world transform. We, here on this side, are so aware of everything that is happening to each of you. We know of your tiredness, your feelings of being overwhelmed, and your physical struggles with the energy waves that are coming to your planet.

We are aware that there are times when you feel completely alone and without support. KNOW MOST ASSUREDLY THAT WE ARE HERE, WE ARE ALWAYS HERE, AND WE ARE DOING ALL THAT WE ARE ABLE TO ASSIST YOU. This transformation that is happening on your planet is something that must be accomplished and completed by the beings (you) that occupy Mother Earth.

Part of your purpose for being here on Mother Earth at this time is to accomplish this transformation. You are the ones who are solely responsible for the completion of this transformation. The work that each of you has accomplished towards your goal is remarkable and awe inspiring. Your courage, determination, and willingness to prepare yourself for your personal entry into the 5D world has been wondrous to see.

As each new energy wave comes to your planet, you each are standing and walking through whatever is necessary to reach the other side. You have opened your hearts and minds to the many different kinds of help that we have been sending you. The welcoming and rejoicing that we see you offering to each of the new and different kinds of guidance you are receiving is rewarding to us. For we see you living your purpose for being here on your planet, the purpose being the giving and receiving of love without judgments and restrictions. Your hearts and minds have opened and are welcoming whatever is coming to support you on your journeys.

We thank you and send you our gratitude for all that you have accomplished. We are loving and supporting you in every moment of everyday. We are here and we are ready to help you in whatever way you may need. I know that I have said this many times in the past, but I will continue to say it over and over. I LOVE YOU, I LOVE YOU, AND I LOVE YOU.

DO YOU HEAR ME? REMEMBERING NOW THAT THERE ARE THOUSANDS OF OTHERS HERE WITH ME SAYING THAT THEY ARE LOVING YOU ALSO.

    STAND FIRM IN YOUR BELIEFS IN YOURSELF, YOUR DREAMS, YOUR MOTHER EARTH, AND THE POWER OF LOVE. REMEMBERING THAT WE ARE STANDING RIGHT HERE BESIDE YOU.

Know that you only need call my name and I will be there.
In Love, Mother Mary
3/4/11

LETTER 106

Dear Ones,

Today let us talk about Gathering Your Forces around you. Let me explain to you what I am talking about. You each have people and places that give you support, strength, courage, love, and hope. So by Gathering Your Forces I am speaking of those things.

It is time to pay more attention to those things that help you to walk your path. Sometimes it is easy to get so busy walking your path and trying to survive the energy waves that you forget the ones who are helping you. Remembering now that each of those people who are helping you are also walking their path and trying to survive the energy waves just as you are.

So for today let us call this a day of appreciation, gratitude and joy for each person and place in your life that is supporting and assisting you. Remembering now that you also are assisting and supporting others, so there will be appreciation, gratitude and joy coming back at you for what you have offered to others.

Can you see it now? We are making an unending circle of gratitude, appreciation and joy. As you give out to others, others are giving back to you. Each of you is being showered with love, and strength. This energy of gratitude, appreciation and joy provides you with strength and hope to move forward and continue on your journey.

When and if those days come when you no longer think you can brave one more energy wave then I say to you gather your forces about you. Allow the energy of your forces to rejuvenate and support you. With help and support you will find the energy waves are not nearly so intense.

You each are doing a wondrous job dealing with the increase in the energy waves that are coming to your planet. I know there are times when you say to yourselves when is this going to stop? Enough is enough. There will come a day when the energy waves will stop and the 5D world will arrive. Then you will rejoice and celebrate that the energy waves did not stop.

KNOW THAT WE ARE HERE AND WE ARE PART OF YOUR FORCES. SO GATHER US CLOSE AND KNOW THAT WE HAVE GATHERED YOU CLOSE. WE ARE HOLDING YOU IN OUR

HEARTS. YOU ARE BEING SHOWERED FROM ABOVE WITH GRATITUDE, APPRECIATION AND JOY FOR ALL YOU ARE DOING AND ALL YOU HAVE DONE. I LOVE YOU, I LOVE YOU AND I LOVE YOU. CAN YOU HEAR ME, I AM SAYING THIS VERY LOUDLY.

Know you only need call me name and I will be there.
In Love, Mother Mary
3/6/11

LETTER 107

Dear Ones,

Oh my children, I want to reach out and hold each one of you in my arms, giving you the freedom to do whatever it is that you each need. Is it tears you need to shed, or burdens that need to be gone, warmth and comfort to energize you, or maybe just to be held?

Today I ask you each to tell me what it is that you believe you need to be able to continue walking your path. Let us see if together we can provide you what you believe you need. Remembering now that what you believe you need does not always turn out to be what you think and plan.

I am asking you today to open your minds, your hearts, and the whole of your body to all the options available to you. Tunnel Vision is a disease that is wide spread on your planet. This disease only allows you one outcome, one path, one journey, and only one road you get to travel during your lifetime. The disease of Tunnel Vision lies to you and there is no truth in its words.

So I am asking you each today do you have this disease, are you encased in Tunnel Vision? Have you taken away all your options and opportunities? The disease of Tunnel Vision places you in a cage with no way to turn or move and no way to see other options. You are trapped in limits and restrictions.

Is that what is happening in the whole of your life or in certain parts of your life? Have you become trapped and encased in narrow thoughts and visions? TODAY I INVITE YOU TO COME ON A JOURNEY WITH ME TO CURE YOURSELF OF THE DISEASE OF TUNNEL VISION.

STOP WHAT YOU ARE DOING RIGHT NOW. CLOSE YOUR EYES, TAKE SEVERAL DEEP BREATHS, PLACE YOUR HAND ON YOUR HEART AND CALL MY NAME. TOGETHER YOU AND I WILL TAKE THIS JOURNEY OF FREEDOM AND OPPORTUNITY. CONTINUE YOUR BREATHING AND TAKE MY HAND. JUST ALLOW YOURSELF TO BE HERE IN THE STILLNESS ACCEPTING THE ENERGY I AM SENDING YOU. KNOW THAT YOU ARE NOT ALONE, FEEL MY PRESENCE, MY ENERGY AND MY HAND.

VERY SLOWLY NOW, SEE WHERE WE ARE. CAN YOU SEE THE BARS ON YOUR CAGE, AND CAN YOU SEE THE DOOR? ARE YOU READY TO REACH FOR THE DOOR HANDLE? ALLOW YOURSELF A MOMENT TO GATHER YOUR STRENGTH. NOW I ASK YOU TO OPEN THE DOOR AND WALK THROUGH THE DOOR WITH ME. IT IS LIKE WAKING UP FROM A VERY LONG SLEEP, OR COMING OUT OF THE DARKEST CAVE. THE LIGHT MAKES IT ALMOST IMPOSSIBLE TO SEE FOR A MOMENT. GIVE YOURSELF TIME NOW TO BECOME ACCUSTOMED TO THE LIGHT, JUST STAYING STILL AND QUIET FOR A MOMENT.

OPEN YOUR EYES FULLY NOW AND KNOW THAT I AM STILL RIGHT HERE WITH YOU. CAN YOU SEE ALL THE PATHS, ALL THE OPTIONS AND ALL THE OPPORTUNITIES BEFORE YOU? IT IS NOT NECESSARY FOR YOU TO CHOOSE A CERTAIN PATH TODAY.

Today is about recognizing that there are other paths, other options, and other opportunities that are available for you. Over the next few days and weeks take the time to look closely at all these things that are available. NOW WHAT DO YOU WANT? WHAT IS YOUR PASSION? WHAT DO YOU WANT TO TRY? AND MOST IMPORTANTLY WHERE DOES YOUR HEART WANT TO BE? ALLOW YOURSELF PLENTY OF TIME TO ANSWER THESE QUESTIONS.

Remembering now to come back to today and to this letter, bringing back with you all that you have learned. KNOW THAT WE ARE HERE TO HELP YOU IN MAKING YOUR DECISIONS AND CHANGES. WE ARE HERE HONORING YOUR COURAGE AND STRENGTH. WE ARE LOVING YOU AND HOLDING YOU IN OUR HEARTS.

Know that you only need call my name and I will be there.
In Love, Mother Mary
3/8/11

LETTER 108

Dear Ones,

Today let us talk about Worry and Frustration. If these two feelings or emotions are your best friends, then it is time to look around and make some changes. Worry and Frustration are not your friends. They do not feed your soul or uplift you in any way.

What they do is to rob you of your energy, and drain your body of laughter and joy. Worry and frustration are very powerful and all encompassing. They have the ability to absorb all energy from happiness, laughter, love, and joy. It is as if they are two little PAC MAN figures running through your body with their big mouths open and they are eating up every good warm loving piece of energy in you.

I am hoping in your mind that you can vividly see what I am talking about. Because those two little PAC MAN figures have the ability to stop you in your tracks. When they are doing their best work, your body becomes very heavy with your mind going over and over the same problem. Your mind is unable to find any solutions. It just goes right back to worry and frustration. You no longer have the ability to co-create your life. You have given that power over to these two little PAC MAN figures.

Are you in shock now that those two little figures are the ones who are deciding how you live your life? They have complete power over what you do; how you think and act. This is an eye-opening experience to realize what havoc and destruction that Worry and Frustration can bring into your life. Are you going to tell me now that this is how you have always lived your life? That you learned to live this way when you were very young? If that is what you are thinking or wanting to tell me, then this is what I want to say back to you.

IT IS TIME TO STOP LIVING YOUR LIFE IN THIS MANNER. IT IS TIME FOR EACH OF YOU TO BE CO-CREATING YOUR OWN LIVES. THERE IS NEVER ANY TIME IN YOUR LIVES WHEN IT IS APPROPRIATE TO GIVE YOUR POWER OF CO-CREATION TO ANYONE OR ANYTHING ELSE. CO-CREATION IS YOUR LIFE SOURCE. It is a gift to be honored and cherished; it was never meant to be given over to two little PAC MAN figures.

Worry and Frustration are habits and another addiction. So as in all addictions, it is necessary to first realize that you have the addiction and then to proceed to do something about the addiction. SO MY QUESTION TO YOU IS, DO YOU HAVE THIS ADDICTION OR HABIT? If the answer is yes, then it is time to do something about this. Start out small, start to recognize when you go into Worry and Frustration, now learning to put it aside and choosing to walk in a different direction.

When you first recognize that you are going into Worry and Frustration that is the time to call on us. We will be right here to show you a different way to handle your life and what is going on in your life. Letting go of this habit is not something that you need to do by yourself. Changing old habits is much easier to accomplish when you allow yourself to use the help and support that is offered. WE ARE RIGHT HERE WAITING TO HELP AND SUPPORT YOU IN EVERY WAY. KNOW THAT WE ARE LOVING YOU AND HOLD YOU IN OUR HEARTS. I LOVE AND CHERISH EACH OF YOU.

Know you only need call my name and I will be there.
In Love, Mother Mary
3/10/11

LETTER 109

Dear Ones,

Let us talk today about Moving Forward in your lives. In most of your lives Moving Forward causes a huge conflict. It is as if you are divided into two parts: the part that desperately wants to Move Forward, Change, and Grow and then there is the other part of you that has its feet planted firmly in one spot and hanging on for dear life to that one spot.

This is a constant battle that goes on inside each of you. One side wanting to Move Forward and one side wanting to stay in the same-old place. This battle has been going on since the first being was placed on your Mother Earth.

Today I want you to know that it does not have to be this way. It is possible to learn to accept change and growth in your lives without the constant companion of fear. There are beings on your planet that are learning to process and accept change in a different and new way.

That new way is about trusting with your whole being that you are being guided and taken care of. It is about knowing that we are right here with you always. You are not alone nor have you ever been alone. Yes, I do know that often during your lifetime you have felt alone and abandoned. In truth, we have always been here, you just were not seeing us or sensing our presence, but we were here.

Many beings on your planet are learning or have learned to reach out and ask for help with their Moving Forward. The acceptance of help during these times has changed their whole out look on what Moving Forward means. No longer is there conflict and fear running rampant in their bodies and minds. They have replaced those feelings with excitement and anticipation of the new and wondrous things they have allowed to come into their lives.

Moving forward or staying in the same-old place is your personal choice. How you choose to co-create those times in your lives is also a personal choice. Allowing yourself to ask for help and believing that we will be there is also a personal choice. I will tell you that there has never been a time when you have asked for help that we have not been right beside you. It is our honor and purpose to be of help to each of you.

Know that we are here and we are ready to help you in anyway. It is our wish for you that you will be asking for help with your Moving Forward. There is a whole world of wondrous things for you to try and experience. REMEMBERING NOW THAT DREAMS DO COME TRUE AND MIRACLES DO HAPPEN. SOMETIMES IT IS NECESSARY TO MOVE FORWARD TO ALLOW ALL OF THAT TO HAPPEN IN YOUR LIVES.

Know that we are loving and caring about you. We are holding you in our hearts. I am once again going to say those words. I love you, I love you, and I love you.

Know you only need call my name and I will be there.
In Love, Mother Mary
3/14/11

LETTER 110

Dear Ones,

Let us talk of the shifts and awakenings that are happening on your planet. This weekend you will be experiencing a full moon and then going into the Spring Equinox. This is a time of awakening and new beginnings. Life is awakening and coming awake after the winter isolations. CHANGE and NEW BEGINNINGS are in the air of your planet.

Mother Earth's energy is shaking off the old and preparing herself for what is to come. Just as it is time for you to shake yourselves off and let go of the dark and isolation of the winter. Open your eyes and allow yourselves to see the world with new perspectives and attitudes, letting go of the old fears and doubts.

Just as the bear comes awake after his winter hibernation, it is time for you also to come out of yourself-induced hibernation; your hibernation being the closed eyes and ears that you have chosen to see and hear the world through.

You each are on the brink of a new world, a new way of being. To step into this world it is necessary to let go of your coat of hibernation and to open your eyes and ears. Your new world is about your heart and the heart of Mother Earth. We, here, are calling this new world "HEART SPACE." In this new world called HEART SPACE you will learn to live inside of your heart. Your actions and reactions to people, places, and all things around will be heart directed. There will no longer be a place for judgments, restrictions, and limitations that hold and keep you in old, stuck, mind imposed patterns.

In this new place called HEART SPACE you will find yourself stepping into doing what you each have dreamed of doing. In some cases, there will be those who go on to do much more than what they could have ever dreamed of. REMEMBERING NOW IN THIS NEW PLACE THERE ARE NO LIMITS IMPOSED ON YOU OR PLACED ON YOU BY YOURSELVES. LIMITS AND RESTRICTIONS WILL NO LONGER EXIST. THERE WILL NO LONGER BE ANY NEED OR WANT FOR SUCH THINGS.

FEARS, DOUBTS, AND FEELINGS OF UNWORTHINESS WILL SLIP AWAY AND STAY IN THE OLD WORLD. YOU WILL FIND IT DIFFICULT TO UNDERSTAND WHY YOU PAID SO MUCH ATTENTION TO THOSE KINDS OF THOUGHTS AND FEELINGS. THERE WILL BE NO DOUBT IN YOUR MIND ABOUT YOUR WORTH OR WHAT YOU ARE CAPABLE OF DOING. ALL WILL BECOME POSSIBLE.

YOU WILL BE SEEING YOURSELF AND THE WORLD WITH NEW EYES. YOU WILL BE SEEING FOR THE FIRST TIME WHAT A UNIQUE AND MARVELOUS BEING THAT YOU ARE. YOU WILL FIND THAT YOU ARE WITHOUT LIMITS AND ALL IS POSSIBLE IN YOUR NEW WORLD CALLED "HEART SPACE."

IT WILL NO LONGER BE NECESSARY TO HIDE YOURSELF AND BE WHAT THE WORLD SAYS YOU SHOULD BE. THIS IS ABOUT FREEDOM. THIS IS ABOUT LOVE. THIS IS ABOUT TRUTH. WELCOME TO WHAT YOUR MOTHER EARTH WAS ALWAYS MEANT TO BE ABOUT.

We are here loving you and looking forward to seeing you in your new world. You will finally be able to see what we, here, see as we look at each of you. WE ARE SEEING LOVE, LIGHT, AND BEAUTY BEYOND COMPARE. REMEMBERING NOW THAT WE ARE WALKING RIGHT HERE BESIDE YOU.

Know you only need call my name and I will be there.
In Love, Mother Mary
3/17/11

LETTER 111

Dear Ones,

We are in the times when it is necessary for each of you to stand up and allow the world to see who you really are. Yes, I do know that there are many of you out there who are still not quite sure of who they are. So it is in this time that you each will be discovering the truth of who you are. Each of you will then have the opportunity to stand and claim your space in the world.

Over the next few months, you will become more aware of the truth of who you really are. You will find it is like putting together a puzzle. Little pieces of awareness will be flowing into your minds. One more piece to place in the grand picture of you.

During this time, you will also be letting go of the parts of you that are not truth. By that I mean the pictures of you that someone else has painted and said to you this is who you are. In your doubts about who and what you are, you believed what they said without looking for the truth yourself. Some of you have found the pictures of the false you are almost too heavy to carry at times. Others of you have struggled so hard trying to be all that you were supposed to be.

You each will find that it is a relief and great freedom to let go of other people's ideas and pictures of who you should be. COME WITH ME RIGHT NOW AND LET US REMOVE SOME OF THESE ROBES YOU HAVE BEEN GIVEN TO WEAR. TAKE A FEW DEEP BREATHS, PLACE YOUR HAND ON YOUR HEART, AND CALL MY NAME. JUST CONTINUE TO TAKE A FEW MORE DEEP SLOW BREATHS. LET US NOW WALK INTO A LARGE ROOM FILLED WITH YOUR FAVORITE FLOWERS, BEAUTIFUL CANDLES, AND THE WALLS ARE PAINTED YOUR FAVORITE COLOR.

YOU ARE LOVING THIS ROOM. IT IS SO SAFE, WARM, AND COMFORTABLE. JUST SLOWLY ALLOW YOURSELF TO LOOK IN THE MIRRORS. INSTANTLY, YOU CAN TELL WHICH ROBES DO NOT BELONG TO YOU. SIMPLY ALLOW THEM TO FALL AWAY. THOSE ROBES DO NOT TELL THE TRUTH OF WHO YOU ARE. ALLOW YOURSELF TIME NOW TO JUST STAND IN FRONT OF

THE MIRRORS. CAN YOU SEE ALL THE DIFFERENT ROBES YOU HAVE BEEN GIVEN THROUGHOUT YOUR LIFETIME? LETTING GO OF THE ONES YOU ARE SURE DO NOT FIT YOU, KEEPING THE ONES THAT YOU WANT TO EXAMINE A LITTLE MORE CLOSELY.

OVER THE NEXT DAYS AND WEEKS, YOU WILL FIND THE TIME TO EXAMINE THE ROBES THAT YOU KEPT. CHECK EACH ROBE CAREFULLY TO SEE IF THEY ARE PART OF THE TRUTH OF WHO YOU REALLY ARE. ALSO NOTICE THAT IN THE FAR CORNER OF THE ROOM ARE MANY BOXES HOLDING MORE ROBES. YOU MIGHT WANT TO TRY ON SOME OF THESE ROBES AND SEE IF THEY FIT AND TELL THE TRUTH OF WHO YOU REALLY ARE.

Time now to return to this letter and this day, knowing that over the next days and weeks you will have time to examine all the robes, both trying on and taking off. This is a time of discovering who and what you are. Many of you are in for some big surprises. Some of you have already had wonderful surprises and discoveries.

For us here on this side it is like watching someone turn on the light inside each of you and it is shining out from every part of your body. We are honored to watch those lights being turned on. WE ARE LOVING YOU AND WANTING YOU TO REMEMBER THAT WE ARE RIGHT HERE WAITING TO HELP IN ANY WAY.

Know you only need call my name and I will be there.
In Love, Mother Mary
3/20/11

LETTER 112

Dear Ones,

Is this a Good Morning? Are you feeling refreshed and rested? What were you dreaming about last night? Was your mind quiet while you slept or was it going 200 hundred miles per hour? I have asked you all these questions and now I want you to stop. JUST COMPLETELY STOP. LET YOUR MIND BE QUIET. CAN YOU JUST FOR ONE MINUTE LET YOUR MIND BE EMPTY?

I know that in these times of the intense energy waves that it is difficult to allow your minds to stop and be still. The minds of most beings on your planet are going so fast right now that they can hardly hold one thought for more than two seconds. Your physical body's reaction to this is to go into overload and be unable to process what it is it needs to do next. It is like walking around in a fog. Are you running around and around trying to focus and get one thing completed?

SO AGAIN I WILL SAY STOP. JUST STOP RIGHT NOW. REACH OUT AND HOLD ON TO MY HAND AND I WILL HOLD YOU STEADY. TAKE A BREATH AND LET YOURSELVES BE FOR JUST ONE MOMENT.

Now is that better? Can you take a deep breath and shake yourself off? Ask for help in clearing your energy fields. For the next several days and weeks, it will be necessary to allow yourselves these few seconds of down time. If you are out in the world or at work, just stop and then go to one of your restrooms and give yourself a moment. If you are in your home, it will be easier to provide yourself with a precious moment to catch your breath.

The energy that is coming into your planet right now has speeded up and increased beyond 500 hundred times what you are accustomed to. It has turned your mind's and body's upside down and sideways. Know that these increased intense energies are necessary for the transformation of you and your Mother Earth. If there was another way to accomplish this transformation, it would surely be done in a different way.

SO AT THIS TIME, I AM SAYING MOST LOUDLY TO YOU "HANG ON AND KEEP ON HANGING ON." You are doing well beyond what anyone from our side or yours could expect. Each of you is doing a wonderful job working your way through the energy waves and keeping yourselves walking and talking. I am thinking that there are times when you are not sure where you are walking or what you are saying. Did that make you giggle just a little? I hope so.

Know that we are right here holding our hands out so you can grab a hold to slow yourselves down or to help you stop for just a moment. We are loving you and honoring all that you are walking and talking your way through. I LOVE YOU, I LOVE YOU AND I LOVE YOU.

Know you only need call my name and I will be there.
In Love, Mother Mary
3/24/11

LETTER 113

Dear Ones,

Good Morning beloved beings of earth. I often think in my mind that you are small children and I can just gather you up in my arms and hold you safe and loved. But the truth is you are grown men and women. You each have chosen to be here on earth at this time and you each have a grand purpose to fulfill.

You each made the personal choice to be Wayshowers or Keepers of the Light during this lifetime. There is excitement and adventure in the path you have chosen. There is also extreme turmoil and confusion during this time of grand energy waves. In previous letters, I have said that the grand energy waves will continue throughout the next weeks and months and so they will.

It is important for you to know that the gentlest way to ride these waves is in flexibility. Know that nothing in your life will be as it once was. Allow yourselves to ride the waves without expectation, letting go of your old way of thinking and your knowing of how things should be in the world. REMEMBERING NOW THAT ALL IS NEW AND DIFFERENT IN THE 5D WORLD. The grand energy waves that are coming into your planet is all about the 5D world. So allowing yourselves to just be open and freethinking without expectations or assumptions during this time is imperative.

Each of you are learning or will be learning new ways of thinking and being. Your minds are being expanded and reaching out into the far ends of the universe for information and knowledge unknown to you before this time. It is important to let go of old limiting thought patterns and rigid ideas of how the world should be.

You each are pioneers going into this new world, no different than your ancestors who traveled into the unknown of your planet back in the beginning. Your role as a pioneer is easier than your ancestors. You have been told what your new 5D world will be about. You know that it is a heart-centered world where all connections, all life forms will come from the HEART SPACE. You have also been told that your new 5D world is called HEART

SPACE here on this side. Your mind and the rest of your body will coordinate and process all information through the heart. Your lives will begin and end within your own personal heart space.

Spend time over the next few days allowing yourselves to daydream about what that might be like. REMEMBERING NOW THAT EVERYTHING THAT COMES INTO YOUR WORLD WILL BE PROCESSED INTO AND OUT OF THE HEART. HOW YOU DEAL WITH PEOPLE, PLACES AND ALL THINGS WILL COME ONLY FROM THE HEART. YOUR MIND WITH ITS LIMITS, JUDGMENTS, RESTRICTIONS AND PREJUDICES WILL NO LONGER PLAY A PART OR HAVE THE FINAL WORD.

Can you even imagine or comprehend what this will mean to you and all the other beings of earth? IS IT ALMOST BEYOND UNDERSTANDING HOW ALL THAT WILL HAPPEN AND BE POSSIBLE?

KNOW THAT IT IS SO AND ALL OF THIS WILL BE TAKING PLACE TOWARDS THE END OF 2011. Daydreaming about this is a way of preparing yourselves for the coming of the 5D world. You may even find yourselves slipping into the 5D world for brief periods of time as you contemplate all the possibilities of that world.

Know that we are here offering our help. Know that we are loving each of you. Know also that we have answers to many of your questions and we are ready to share with you. YOU ONLY NEED ASK.

Know that you only need call my name and I will be there.
In Love, Mother Mary
3/26/11

LETTER 114

Dear Ones,

Are you becoming accustomed to the craziness that is happening on your planet? Each and every being on your planet is being effected in someway by the grand energy waves that are coming your way.

IT IS MOST IMPORTANT THAT YOU JUST ALLOW THE ENERGY WAVES TO WASH OVER YOU AND GO ON BY. THE EFFECTS OF THE GRAND ENERGY WAVES ARE CAUSING MANY OF YOU TO BECOME UNFOCUSED AND CONFUSED. You are finding it difficult to complete any task that you set out to accomplish. It may seem at times that what you call time is slipping away without you even being aware. Hours and minutes are disappearing and you are wondering where they have gone.

In truth, it is not your hours and minutes that are disappearing, it is you!!!! Many of you are floating out of your bodies to go and be somewhere else. Some of you are going into the 5D world. Others are just floating around in space daydreaming about who knows what. Normally, I would say these are lovely things for you to be doing, as long as you are aware that you are doing them. Floating off into space and daydreaming is most relaxing and helpful in your stressful world. It is not helpful if you are unaware that you are doing that until you come back and wonder why it is 3:00 instead of 2:00.

It is even less helpful if you are floating away while you are driving and then we have to snap you back into your car and you are wondering where you are and where you were going. WE ARE WATCHING OVER EACH OF YOU VERY CAREFULLY RIGHT NOW, MAKING SURE YOU DO NOT HURT YOURSELVES IN YOUR FLOATING AND DRIFTING AWAY.

IT IS MOST IMPORTANT THAT YOU TRY VERY HARD TO PAY ATTENTION TO YOUR BODY RIGHT NOW. YOUR BODY CAN GIVE YOU THE SIGNALS WHEN THE ENERGY WAVES ARE COMING IN THE STRONGEST. THE ENERGY WAVES ARE NOT ALWAYS ON CONSTANT HIGH VOLTAGE, THEY DO COME IN LIKE THE WAVES OF YOUR OCEAN. SO THE TRICK NOW IS FOR YOU TO FIGURE OUT WHEN THE WAVES ARE COMING. Your lives will become less stressful and chaotic once you get a sense of how the waves work.

SO CLOSE YOUR EYES, TAKE SEVERAL DEEP BREATHS, PUT YOUR HAND ON YOUR HEART AND CALL MY NAME. JUST CONTINUE YOUR STEADY DEEP BREATHING. TAKE MY HAND AND I WILL TAKE YOU INTO A VERY DARK ROOM. THIS ROOM IS IN TOTAL DARKNESS. KEEP HOLDING MY HAND AND WE WILL FIND CHAIRS TO SIT IN. I WANT YOU TO JUST KEEP LOOKING AROUND AND BECOME ACCUSTOMED TO THE DARK. IN A MOMENT, YOU WILL START TO SEE THE WAVES OF ENERGY THAT ARE COMING TO YOUR PLANET. THE ENERGY WAVES ARE VERY BRIGHTLY COLORED. CAN YOU SEE THEM NOW? ALLOW THE WAVES TO WASH RIGHT ON THROUGH YOUR BODY. DO NOT HOLD ON TO ANY OF THE ENERGY.

STOP FOR A MOMENT NOW AND JUST WATCH THE WAVES. ACKNOWLEDGE THE FEELING OF THEM MOVING RIGHT ON THROUGH YOUR BODY. CAN YOU SEE AND FEEL THE DIFFERENCE OF WHAT HAPPENS WHEN YOU KEEP SOME OF THAT ENERGY IN YOUR BODY AND WHEN YOU LET GO OF IT? TAKE TIME RIGHT NOW TO SEE HOW YOUR BODY FEELS WHEN YOU HOLD ON TO THE ENERGY. NOW SEE HOW IT FEELS WHEN YOU LET IT ALL WASH ON THROUGH YOUR BODY.

NOW I WANT YOU TO VISUALIZE YOURSELF TAKING A SHOWER, WASHING YOUR BODY OFF INSIDE AND OUT. WASHING AWAY ANY RESIDUE FROM THE ENERGY WAVES.

When you are finished in the shower come back to the letter and this day. Your life will become more focused and less stressful if you will allow yourself to do this exercise several times a day. Become more aware of how your body feels when the energy waves come and then follow it up with a very short shower. All of this is happening very quickly in your mind. It is not necessary to think it will take great amounts of your time to do this. I am speaking of no more than 15 seconds once you allow yourself to become accustomed to doing this.

We are right here willing to help you learn to do this for yourself. We are loving you and holding you in our hearts. I LOVE YOU, I LOVE YOU AND I LOVE YOU.

Know you only need call my name and I will be there.
In Love, Mother Mary
3/29/11

LETTER 115

Dear Ones,

Some of you are experiencing great amounts of sadness and regret. There is an awakening to the fact that you will be letting go of many things in your lives to move forward into the 5D world. This is as it should be. Grief is a releasing and acknowledging of what is occurring in your life at this moment.

Many of you are becoming aware of the people you know who may choose not to be joining you in the 5D world. You also are aware of old dreams that are washing through, never to come into being. The letting go of the known and walking into the unknown is a two-sided coin. There is great joy and excitement about the new world, the new way of being, and most of all about living in a heart-centered world based in love. It is also imperative to recognize that you are walking away from the way you have lived for years.

It becomes easy during these times to think in terms of the old way being all about struggle, unhappiness, feelings of being unloved, and loneliness. REMEMBERING NOW THAT THERE IS SO MUCH MORE TO THE WAY YOU HAVE LIVED YOUR LIVES HERE ON MOTHER EARTH THAN STRUGGLE AND UNHAPPINESS. It is time to take off your one-sided glasses and see all that your life here on Mother Earth has been. There have been great challenges and great joys. There have been times of love and times of feeling unloved. In other words, I want you to see the whole of the picture, both the challenges and the joys.

True and complete letting go does not happen until you can see the whole of the picture. The letting go will take place slowly over the next few months. It is important for each of you to be aware that this is a process that you each will need to go through. You each will decide your own time and speed in which to do this. Some of you have already started and others will be waiting until the time is closer to move into the 5D.

Being aware that this is a process that you each will need to go through will make it less chaotic and confusing when it pops into your life. We already have chaos and confusion happening with the coming of the grand energy waves. REMEMBERING NOW THAT BOTH OF THESE EVENTS CAN BE HANDLED IN THE SAME MANNER. Acknowledging the grief as it comes and allowing it to release and wash through your body. It works the same with the grand energy waves; acknowledge, release and allowing the waves to wash right on through your body.

This is a process that you will work with throughout the next weeks and months. It is part of your preparation for moving forward into the 5D world. We will be walking with you as you journey through these processes. We will be right beside you to help in anyway. We are holding you in our hearts. Know that you are greatly loved and honored.

Know you only need call my name and I will be there.
In Love, Mother Mary
3/31/11

LETTER 116

Dear Ones,

Today I am asking you to come and spend some time with me. Amid all the confusion and chaos of your world right now it is most necessary for you to take time for self-care. Now I will treat you as a small child and tell you that it is time for a time out. Not as a punishment for wrongdoing, but as a reward for all your work and effort.

You each have put so much energy into this journey to the 5D world, that it is time for a time out. It is time to allow yourself to be loved and cared for even if it is for only a few of your moments.

SO I ASK YOU NOW TO COME AND BE WITH ME. CLOSE YOUR EYES, TAKE SEVERAL DEEP BREATHS, PUT YOUR HAND ON YOUR HEART AND CALL MY NAME. KNOW THAT I AM RIGHT HERE BESIDE YOU, TAKING YOUR HAND. LET US TAKE A WALK IN MY GARDEN. CAN YOU SEE MY GARDEN NOW? I HAVE FLOWERS OF EVERY COLOR. THE SMELL OF THE GARDEN IS MAGNIFICENT. IT ALMOST MAKES YOU DIZZY AND LIGHT HEADED. LOOK AT THE TREES. HAVE YOU EVER SEEN ANYTHING SO BEAUTIFUL? THEY ARE ALL IN FULL BLOOM WITH BEAUTIFUL FLOWERS OR LEAVES OF ALL DIFFERENT COLORS AND VARIETIES. Take a moment now to just look around.

JUST KEEP WALKING WITH ME NOW. NOTICE HOW YOUR BODY IS FEELING. THERE IS NO MORE HEAVINESS OR TIREDNESS. YOU ARE BEGINNING TO FEEL LIGHTER AND LIGHTER. BEING IN THE BEAUTY OF NATURE AND ALLOWING YOURSELF TO REALLY SEE THE BEAUTY CAN REFRESH AND LIFT YOUR SPIRITS.

LET US SIT ON THE BENCH AND ENJOY EACH OTHER'S COMPANY. WE CAN SIT HERE IN SILENCE OR WE CAN VISIT, IT IS YOUR CHOICE. YOU CAN REST YOUR HEAD ON MY LAP OR JUST CONTINUE HOLDING MY HAND AND BEING HERE WITH ME.

IT IS OK TO JUST BE HERE WITH ME AND NOT TO WORRY ABOUT TIME AND ALL THE THINGS YOU BELIEVE YOU HAVE TO DO. ALLOW YOUR BODY TO ABSORB ALL THE LOVE, JOY, BEAUTY, AND KINDNESS THAT FLOURISHES AND GROWS HERE IN THE GARDEN. KNOW THAT THIS GARDEN WAS GROWN FOR JUST SUCH A DAY AS THIS. THE GARDENS PURPOSE IS TO REJUVENATE AND SHOWER YOU WITH ALL THAT YOU ARE IN NEED OF. Take the time now to absorb all that is here for you.

WHEN YOU ARE RESTED AND REVITALIZED COME BACK TO THIS LETTER AND THIS DAY. ALLOW YOURSELF TO LOOK AROUND SLOWLY. ARE YOU SEEING THE WORLD WITH DIFFERENT EYES? ARE YOU SEEING YOURSELF WITH DIFFERENT EYES? WHAT ABOUT ALL THE THINGS THAT ARE ON YOUR TO DO LIST, ARE YOU SEEING THEM WITH DIFFERENT EYES ALSO?

Life becomes easier and gentler when you allow yourself to take a time out. Your time out has given you the time to allow your body, mind, and spirit to rejuvenate and revitalize itself. Thank you for spending time with me. I am loving you and holding you so dearly in my heart. Please come and walk with me in the garden often.

Know you only need call my name and I will be there.
In Love, Mother Mary
4/2/11

LETTER 117

Dear Loved Ones,

Today I am over come with my feelings for all of you. There are hundreds of millions of people who live on your Mother Earth. I love and hold each and everyone as most precious in my heart. It is thrilling to see the steps you are each taking and the changes you are making. Your minds and hearts are opening up so wide, taking in all the new that is happening in your world as it prepares for transformation.

It is a wonder to watch each of you as you journey on your own individual paths. Enjoyment and delight runs through my heart as I watch your amazement when life falls into place. You each have been struggling and drudging along for several years and it is a joy to know that all of that is in the past. You and your world have come to a time of awakening and new ways of doing and being.

If you are reading this letter and thinking that you are still in the struggling and drudging along phase, then I say to you it is time to wake up. It is time to look at your life and decide how you would like it to be. Are you ready for new ways of thinking and being? Are you ready to let go of the past and the old tired roles of victim and martyr?

If those words seem harsh, they were meant to be harsh. Even if my words are harsh I am still loving you and holding you most dear to my heart. My words are harsh because it is time to wake up and take responsibility for who you are and what you bring to the world. Do you know that each and every being's energy affects the whole of the universe? You, each and everyone make a huge difference in your world and the whole of the universe.

The heaviness and denseness of your world and the universe comes from the energy of the beings who inhabit these worlds. So each being makes a huge difference. If your personal world is not good, then it is up to you to change it. REMEMBERING NOW THAT THERE ARE THOUSANDS OF US HERE ON THIS SIDE WAITING TO HELP YOU. YOU ONLY NEED ASK. You are not alone nor have you ever been alone. Yes, I know that there have been many times that you have felt alone. Those feelings come when you shut us out and block all feelings of our love and energy.

KNOW THAT WE ARE STILL STANDING RIGHT HERE BESIDE YOU AND WE WILL NOT BE LEAVING YOU.

DO NOT BE AFRAID TO OPEN YOUR EYES. YOUR WORLD IS CHANGING AND SO CAN YOU. YOU EACH HAVE SO MUCH COURAGE AND STRENGTH, YOU CAN DO SO MUCH MORE THAN YOU KNOW.

NOW IS THE TIME OF AWAKENING. SO COME AND TAKE MY HAND AND I WILL WALK WITH YOU THROUGH THESE DAYS OF CHANGE AND NEWNESS. SOON YOU WILL NO LONGER NEED MY HAND AND WILL BE ABLE TO FINISH THIS JOURNEY ON YOUR OWN. YOU WILL FIND THAT ONCE YOU ALLOW YOURSELF TO AWAKEN; THERE IS JOY, EXCITEMENT, AND HAPPINESS WALKING THIS JOURNEY WITH YOU. COME AND ALLOW YOURSELF TO BE ALL YOU WERE MEANT TO BE. FOR YOU ARE WONDROUS INCREDIBLE BEINGS WHO SHINE SO BRIGHTLY.

I AM LOVING YOU SO DEARLY AND HOLDING EACH AND EVERY ONE OF YOU IN MY HEART.

Know you only need call my name and I will be there.
In love, Mother Mary
4/5/11

LETTER 118

Dear Ones,

Today let us talk about relationships. First, the very most important relationship you have is with yourself. It is a fact that if you are not taking care of that relationships, then all your other relationships are not being taken care of either.

I am thinking that you are saying NO; I take care of my relationships with partners, children, family, friends, work and the people at the grocery store. I can almost hear you saying relationships are so important to me and I take care of them. I am always there for the people I love and care about, honoring my commitments, listening and being present for the important people in my life.

All of those things are important and so necessary if you are wanting to have healthy loving relationships. THE RELATIONSHIP I AM WONDERING ABOUT IS THE ONE WITH YOURSELF. Do you pay 90% of your attention and time to the other relationships in your lives and 10% of your attention and time to yourself? How often do you walk around feeling empty and wrung out? No energy, no time, feeling like you have not one more thing to give.

Those are the feelings and the way you live when you are taking care of all your other relationships except the most important one. If your body, mind, and spirit is not fed and cared for how can it continue to give and give. It can't and that is why I am saying to you that your most important relationship is the one with yourself.

SELF-CARE AND LOVE IS OF THE UTMOST IMPORTANCE. I KNOW THAT YOU HAVE HEARD THIS OVER AND OVER. YET IT IS ONE OF THE MOST IGNORED STATEMENTS IN YOUR WORLD. YOU HAVE BEEN TAUGHT TO BELIEVE THAT OTHERS AND EVERYONE ELSE MUST BE CARED FOR FIRST. YOU MUST BE LOVING, KIND, AND PRESENT FOR EVERYONE AND EVERYTHING ELSE IN YOUR LIVES.

I AM SAYING TO YOU MOST LOUDLY TODAY THAT THIS IS NOT A TRUTH. YOU MOST URGENTLY HAVE TO START CAR-

ING FOR YOURSELVES FIRST. DO YOU NOT SEE THAT YOU HAVE REALLY NOTHING LEFT TO GIVE UNTIL YOU FILL YOURSELVES UP FIRST? EVERYONE ON YOUR PLANET IS WASTING AWAY FROM THEIR LACK OF CARING ABOUT SELF.

WOULD YOU CARE AND TREAT ME IN THIS MANNER THAT YOU ARE TREATING YOURSELF? I KNOW THE ANSWER TO THAT QUESTION, NO YOU WOULD NOT YOU WOULD NEVER DREAM OF DOING THAT.

I AM GOING TO SAY AGAIN MOST LOUDLY. WE ARE ALL ONE. YOU ARE ME AND I AM YOU. SO INDEED WHEN YOU ARE UNCARING AND LEAVE YOURSELF TILL THE LAST, SO YOU ARE DOING THE SAME TO ME. WHEN YOU HAVE NOTHING LEFT TO GIVE AND FEEL WASHED OUT, THEN I AM LEFT WITH THE SAME FEELING. THAT IS NOT WHAT LOVE IS ABOUT.

LOVE IS NOT ABOUT FEELING EMPTY AND WASHED OUT BECAUSE YOU GAVE IT ALL AWAY. LOVE IS ABOUT LOVING AND CARING FOR YOURSELF FIRST. THIS ALLOWS YOU TO HAVE LIMITLESS AMOUNTS OF LOVE AND CARING TO GIVE TO OTHERS.

ONLY WHEN YOU ARE FULL AND BALANCED WILL THERE BE ENOUGH TO GO AROUND FOR EVERYONE ELSE. THEN YOU WILL COME TO THE END OF YOUR DAY STILL FEELING FULL AND BALANCED.

I AM LOVING YOU AND HOLDING YOU MOST DEARLY IN MY HEART. I AM HOPING THAT YOU WILL START LOVING YOURSELVES AND HOLDING YOURSELVES IN YOUR OWN HEARTS MOST DEARLY. KNOW THAT WE ARE HERE WAITING TO HELP.

Know you only need call my name and I will be there.
In Love, Mother Mary
4/7/11

LETTER 119

Dear Ones,

We here on this side are knowing where you are going and what this new world will be about. You are still wondering and thinking about how all this can happen. So today let us talk a little about how all that can happen.

As most of you are aware there are those of you who are choosing not to go into the 5D world. Those beings are leaving Mother Earth now and they may or may not choose to return to earth and participate in all of this. On the other end of the scale, there are many of you who have chosen to be Wayshowers and Keepers of Light. You are the ones who will be showing the way to the hundreds of thousands or millions of other beings who will be following into the 5D world.

The Wayshowers and Keepers of the Light will pass permanently into the 5D world in the fall and winter of this year. When this happens your realties and existence will be only in the 5D world, the 3D world will still exist for thousands and millions of other beings. The difference will be that they will be able to see all of you Wayshowers living in the 5D. The need and want to join you and live as you do will become so great they will find the courage and strength to change and let go of the old.

In truth what all the beings of the earth need is to live in the land of HEART SPACE. WHERE LOVE IS THE RULING LAW OF THE LAND, WHERE YOUR WORLD AND LIFE IS DIRECTED BY YOUR HEART, WHERE YOUR MIND BECOMES USEFUL ONLY TO OBEY THE VOICE OF THE HEART. Once the beings of earth can see with their eyes and hear with their ears, then they will know which path to follow. Right now, the beings of earth have no role models, no path to follow. They have nothing concrete in their world to show them the way.

That is where you come in, you Wayshowers and Keepers of the Light. You are leading the way. You are the Role Models your people need. You will be the concrete proof your people need. Your Courage and Strength will allow them to step forward and find their Courage and Strength. Once they can see how you are living, loving, and being, they will not be able stop themselves from coming and joining you. For this 5D world that is heart directed is what each and every being on your mother earth has searched for and dreamed of generation after generation.

If you have not had a glimpse of the 5D world yet, know that it will be happening in the next few days and weeks. Each of you Wayshowers and Keepers of the Light will start crossing the footbridge into the 5D world on a regular basis. It is necessary for you to visit many times before you come to the place where you can be there all the time. Imagine yourself walking across a small footbridge into the 5D world. What will it be like, what will you feel like, what will your eyes see, how will it all be different, and how will you be different? Whenever you have a moment in the next days and weeks close your eyes and allow yourself to walk across the footbridge and take a look.

We will be right here waiting to walk across the footbridge with you. We are excited to share this new world with you. WE are excited to watch your reaction to this new world that is governed by LOVE. COME AND JOIN US. WE ARE WAITING!

Know you only need call my name and I will be there.
In Love, Mother Mary
4/10/11

LETTER 120

Dear Ones,

Today let us talk about all that is going on energetically in your world. Most of you are aware that there are solar flares, sunspots and it goes on and on. The planets are aligning and the stars are moving and shifting. Are you getting the idea, your world is being bombarded by all kinds of energy confusion? We have talked before about the intense energy waves that are coming to your Mother Earth.

All of these happenings are about the changes that are coming to your world. This is all in preparation for the coming of the 5D world. Your world is preparing itself for a great transformation. This transformation has long been awaited and prophesied by almost all of the indigenous peoples of the Universe. Even in the book you call, The Bible, it speaks of what is called the end days.

The term "the end days" has been twisted and misrepresented to mean disaster and punishment. All of that is exactly the opposite of what the term means and is calling for. For many years, 2012 has been spoken of in terms of death, disaster, and great huge amounts of fear. It is my wondering if the idea of being fearful of these times has been a plan to stop the wondrous changes that are starting to take place on your planet.

The changes that are coming are not about fear, death, and disaster. These changes are about love and what your world was always meant to be about. These changes are about all beings learning to live from their hearts and not their minds. These changes are about loving and honoring every living life form and I do mean every living life form. You may not realize it but everything that is on your Mother Earth is a living breathing life form. There are hundreds of thousands of different life forms on your planet. Your Mother Earth is a life form herself, one that has never been honored or cared for. Most of the life forms on your planet have been harmed and abused as if they have no value or worth.

For centuries, human beings have been abusing and harming one another at will, without conscious thought of the consequences of their actions. These same humans have been abusing and harming every other life form on your planet without conscious thought of their actions. Each and every human being on your planet has come to the time of knowing the consequences of their actions. In these times before the new 5D world comes into being each of you are being asked to look at your past and what you believe might be your future. In the looking you are also being asked to let go of all the actions and reactions of the past. IT IS A TIME OF FORGIVENESS AND LETTING GO. The past will have no effect on who you are in the 5D world, for you cannot take it with you. Just as the future you have believed might be yours will have no effect on the 5D world, for you cannot take it with you.

THE 5D WORLD IS ABOUT THE PRESENT MOMENT. THE NOW. THERE IS NO YESTERDAY OR TOMORROW. THERE IS ONLY THE PRESENT MOMENT KNOWN AS NOW.

THERE WILL BE NO MORE WARS, NO ABUSE, NO MORE HARMING OTHERS. THOSE THOUGHTS AND ACTIONS CAN NOT LIVE IN THE 5D WORLD. THERE IS NO SPACE OR ROOM FOR SUCH THOUGHTS OR ACTIONS. THERE WILL BE NO ROOM OR SPACE FOR BITTERNESS, OLD GUILT, AND THOUGHTS OF REVENGE OR PAYING SOMEONE BACK FOR INSULT OR INJURY. All of that is gone, never to be again.

REMEMBERING NOW THAT THE NEW 5D WORLD IS ABOUT RIGHT NOW. IT IS ABOUT LIVING AND BREATHING FROM YOUR HEART. REMEMBERING NOW THAT THE HEART IS ABOUT LOVE, LOVE OF ALL LIFE FORMS.

This transformation is in process right now as you are reading this letter. It has been in the process for some time. Open your eyes and be aware of what is going on in the world. It is changing and becoming more than it has ever dreamed of being.

Come and walk with us and we will speak to you of more of what is happening and will be happening. We are loving you and holding you most dearly in our hearts.

Know you only need call my name and I will be there.
In Love, Mother Mary
4/12/11

LETTER 121

Dear Ones,

Again today we are going to talk about the energy coming into your planet. We know that this new kind of energy that is coming is in preparation for the 5D world. What we have not talked about is how each and every one of you is dealing with this new energy.

All of you are trying desperately to speed up your minds and bodies to keep up with the energy waves. For most of you this is not working well. You are walking around confused, unfocused, with memory problems, and exhaustion. So today what we will try to do, if I can get you to slow down for a moment, is to find another way to deal with this new energy.

Because the energy has speeded up does mean that you have to speed up. The truth is you cannot go fast enough to keep up with this new energy. What is needed at this time is for you to join with the energy. Become one with it.

Imagine if you will the speed walkers at your airports, where you can step on and it moves you along very quickly. What if the new energy is like the speed walkers at the airport and all you have to do is to step on?

SO RIGHT NOW CLOSE YOUR EYES, TAKE A DEEP BREATH, PUT YOUR HAND ON YOUR HEART AND CALL MY NAME. JUST CONTINUE TO TAKE SEVERAL DEEP BREATHS. COME WITH ME NOW TO THE AIRPORT. IT SEEMS STRANGE THERE IS NO ONE HERE, BUT YOU AND I. EVERYTHING IS VERY QUIET AND EMPTY. UP AHEAD WE CAN SEE THE SPEED WALKERS. AS WE APPROACH THEM, I WANT YOU TO STOP AND IN YOUR MIND ALLOW THE WALKER TO BECOME A STREAM OF ENERGY.

CAN YOU SEE THE ENERGY? IT IS MOVING SO VERY FAST YOU ALMOST CAN'T SEE ITS MOVEMENT. IT IS SWIRLING AND SWISHING RIGHT ON BY YOU. CAN YOU SEE THE COLORS? WHEN YOU ARE READY, I WANT YOU TO SIMPLY STEP OUT AND STEP INTO THE ENERGY WAVE. DO NOT BE AFRAID, I WILL NOT LET YOU FALL.

THERE IS NO STRUGGLE, NO HURRY. YOU ARE SIMPLY RID-

ING A WAVE OF ENERGY. JUST CONTINUE TO STAY WITH THE ENERGY, NOW JUST MOVING ALONG WITH IT. WHEN YOU'RE READY COME BACK TO THIS LETTER AND THIS DAY.

EACH MORNING BEFORE YOU GET OUT OF BED IT WILL BE NECESSARY FOR YOU SIMPLY STEP INTO THE ENERGY WAVE.

Allow yourself to go through your day riding the energy wave instead of fighting and trying to keep up with it. Riding the wave is not accomplished through struggle and exhaustion. Riding the wave is allowing yourself to be in the flow of the universe. It is about being in the now. REMEMBERING THAT WHAT YOUR NEW 5D WORLD IS ABOUT IS BEING IN THE NOW. Learning to ride the energy waves is good practice and preparation for learning to be in the 5D world. Once you start riding the energy waves your world will actually slow down, become smoother and less chaotic. Your everyday life will be less of a struggle. Your own personal energy level will increase. Your mind will be more focused and your memory will improve. Life will become easier and more joyful.

REMEMBERING NOW THAT WE ARE RIGHT HERE WAITING TO HELP YOU IN ANYWAY. BRING US ALONG AS YOU PRACTICE RIDING THE WAVES. WE ARE HERE TO MAKE THIS TRANSFORMATION AS EASY AND GENTLE AS POSSIBLE. LEARNING TO RIDE THE WAVES OF ENERGY WILL CHANGE THE WAY IN WHICH YOU ARE ADAPTING TO THE WORLD THAT IS COMING. WE ARE LOVING YOU AND HOLDING YOU MOST DEARLY IN OUR HEARTS.

Know you only need call my name and I will be there.
In Love, Mother Mary
4/14/11

LETTER 122

Dear Ones,

Today let us once again talk about the new energy coming to your world and the 5D world that is coming. Many of the beings of your Mother Earth are totally unaware of what is happening. When I speak of unaware, it is consciously unaware. All other parts of their being are totally aware of the shifts, alignments, and adjustments that are happening here on Mother Earth. Remembering now that all beings have free will and there are many beings here on Mother Earth who are choosing to ignore what is happening.

It is appropriate to leave all these beings who wish to ignore what is happening to their chosen path. Each being will find their own time and path into the 5D world. In the past, many of you would have tried pushing and prodding others to join you on your path. You are finding now that you do not have the energy or desire to continue doing that. The letting go of other beings and paying attention to yourself is an important process in each of your journeys to the 5D world.

Now is the time when each of you must provide yourselves with the greatest of care and nurturing. You each are using great amounts of energy, time, and determination on your walk into the 5D world. As you have found there is not energy left over to push or prod others along. The little energy and time that you have left after walking your journey is best used in being with others who are making the same journey as yourselves. It is vital in these times of transition that you join with others who are walking a similar path.

Each of you are in need of support, love, and caring during this journey. Many of you have not had that in your past, but it is imperative that you allow yourselves to join together with others at this time. Many of you have spent time in semi-isolation during the last years to protect yourselves from the energies of the world in general. It is important for you to know that time has passed. Now the time of joining together and becoming part of a community of people who are walking similar paths is imperative.

Allow your inner lights to come together and shine as one immense, brilliant light, allowing all other beings on your planet to see the light and follow you. As the Wayshowers and Keepers of the Light, it is part of your purpose to shine the light as brightly as possible so others can follow in your footsteps. It is important for you to know that indeed your lights are shining very brightly and are being seen by many of the other planets and stars in the universe. All other worlds, planets, and star nations are aware of what is happening here on your Mother Earth. Many are assisting you in their own ways. REMEMBERING NOW THAT IN THE 5D WORLD ALL IS ONE. ALL LIFE FORMS ARE JOINED TOGETHER IN HARMONY, LOVE, MUTUAL RESPECT, AND APPRECIATION. Know that we are one with you. We have the utmost respect and appreciation for all that you are.

Know you only need call my name and I will be there.
In Love, Mother Mary,
4/17/11

LETTER 123

Dear Ones,

Today we will talk of all the different life forms that live throughout the universe. There are hundreds of thousands of different live forms in the universe, all looking different from each other, with different cultures, and different belief systems.

Most of the life forms that inhabit the universe are aware of each other and have learned to honor and respect each other's differences. Each and every one of these life forms has learned that they are all equal. Through the centuries, they have found that each group of life forms has equal intelligence and knowledge. Some groups have special knowledge of certain areas of life, but they are always willing to share and exchange information.

The beings of Mother Earth have been very slow in learning to respect and honor the differences in people and cultures. Beings of Mother Earth from the beginning of time have been most interested in power, power over other beings and other life forms. Wars have been fought many times. People have been enslaved and animals have been dominated for the sake of power. Power and greed have ruled Mother Earth from the moment of her inception. The beings of Mother Earth have never learned to live in love and harmony with other life forms. They have not learned to respect and honor one another for their differences and what they might learn from each other.

It fills my heart and the hearts of all others here with great sadness that such cruelty and harm has existed for centuries there on Mother Earth. WITH THE COMING OF THE 5D WORLD, ALL BEINGS OF MOTHER EARTH WILL BE CHANGING THEIR ATTITUDES AND PERCEPTIONS. REMEMBERING NOW THAT THE 5D WORLD IS A HEART-CENTERED WORLD WHERE EVERY LIVING LIFE FORM IS HONORED AND CHERISHED. NO ONE LIFE FORM IS BETTER OR MORE THAN ANOTHER. Each and every being is honored and cherished for who they are. No one is greater or more important than another. No nation or country is more important than another. ALL ARE EQUAL AND HONORED FOR WHO AND WHAT THEY ARE.

REMEMBERING NOW THAT ALL LIFE FORMS ARE CON-

NECTED AND MAKE UP THE PICTURE OF THE WHOLE. WE ARE ALL ONE WHETHER YOU COME FROM MOTHER EARTH, ONE OF THE STAR NATIONS OR A PLANET FROM THE FAR GALAXIES. WE ARE ALL ONE. EVERYTHING THAT YOU CAN SEE AND HEAR IS A LIVING BREATHING LIFE FORM, be it rocks, water, plants, trees, mountains, Mother Earth, planets, or stars.

SO I SAY TO YOU TODAY OPEN YOUR MINDS AND HEARTS. ALLOW YOURSELF TO LET GO OF THE FEAR OF NEW AND DIFFERENT LIFE FORMS AND NEW AND DIFFERENT WORLDS. FOR YOU ARE ALL ONE. YOU ARE ALL BROTHERS AND SISTERS MEANT TO BE TOUCHING AND CONNECTING WITH ONE ANOTHER.

YOUR WORLD AND ALL WORLDS ARE PREPARING TO COME TOGETHER AS ONE. THIS IS THE WAY IT WAS ALWAYS MEANT TO BE, ALL LIFE FORMS JOINING AND CONNECTING TO COMPLETE THE PICTURE OF THE WHOLE AND THE ONE.

We are loving you and walking with you as you make this journey to connection and wholeness. The 5D world awaits you with open arms. It is time for you to open your hearts and minds as you prepare yourself to become part of the 5D world.

Know you only need call my name and I will be there.
In Love, Mother Mary
4/19/11

LETTER 124

Dear Ones,

Today let us talk about good and bad, light and dark, and all the judgments that go along with those two sets of assumptions. The people of Mother Earth from the beginning of time have been judging each other as good or bad, light or dark. These judgments that have been passed down through the years, have served no purpose.

If you are judging someone else to be good or bad, it is done only to increase your own importance in your own mind. It is also used as a tool to convince others that you are right and that they should follow you and your thinking. Thus in your mind you have elevated yourself into believing that you are right. Your reasoning is that if someone else believes as you do you must be right. Are you thinking that this increases your importance in the world? Are you thinking this has anything to do with your purpose here on earth? Are you thinking you will be more loved and cared about?

PLEASE LISTEN TO ME VERY CAREFULLY AND I AM GOING TO BE SPEAKING VERY LOUDLY RIGHT NOW. YOUR JUDGMENTS OF OTHERS AND OF YOURSELF SERVE NO PURPOSE IN THE WORLD. THERE ARE NO TRUTHS IN YOUR JUDGMENTS. YOU DO NOT KNOW THE WHOLE STORY. YES, YOU MAY BE THINKING RIGHT NOW I DO KNOW THE WHOLE STORY. I AM TELLING YOU THAT NO ONE KNOWS THE WHOLE STORY OF ANOTHER. ONLY WE, HERE ON THIS SIDE, KNOW THE WHOLE STORY OF EACH BEING ON MOTHER EARTH.

THE TIME HAS COME TO LET GO OF JUDGMENTS AND TOOLS OF SELF-IMPORTANCE. THESE WAYS ARE NOT SERVING YOU OR SERVING THE WORLD. In these times of transformation, it is time to let go of the past and the old ways of being. There is no longer room for games of self-elevation or importance. These actions do not come from your heart nor do they belong in a heart-centered world. Your judgments do great harm to the one being judged and also great harm to the one doing the judging.

Once again, I will say please listen very carefully to what I am saying, the judgment of others comes from your own lack of self-worth. It is a tool used to try and elevate yourself so that you will believe you are worthy and important in your world.

AGAIN, I AM GOING TO SPEAK VERY LOUDLY, EACH AND EVERY ONE OF YOU IS WORTHY, PRECIOUS, AND CHERISHED IN OUR HEARTS. YOU DO NOT NEED TO USE HARMFUL UGLY JUDGMENTS TO ELEVATE YOURSELF IN OUR EYES. YOU ARE ALREADY OF THE UTMOST IMPORTANCE. FOR YOU ARE LOVED AND HELD MOST DEARLY IN ALL OUR HEARTS AND MINDS.

I say to you now to let go of your judgments of others. Open your hearts to each other and share your love and compassion. Learning to love and care for each other is one of your many purposes for being here on Mother Earth.

THE MAIN PURPOSE FOR BEING HERE ON MOTHER EARTH IS TO LEARN TO LOVE YOURSELF AND TO BELIEVE WHAT WE ARE SAYING TO YOU. THERE IS NOTHING THAT YOU COULD HAVE DONE THAT HAS NOT BEEN FORGIVEN AND FORGOTTEN. ALL THE REASONS YOU THINK YOU ARE UNWORTHY OR LESS THAN HAVE BEEN WASHED AWAY. THE ONLY THING LEFT TO DO IS FOR YOU TO LET GO OF THESE UNTRUTHS. IT IS TIME FOR YOU TO WRAP YOUR ARMS AROUND YOURSELF AND TO LOVE YOURSELF AS WE LOVE YOU. KNOW THAT WE ARE STANDING RIGHT HERE WRAPPING OUR ARMS AROUND YOU AS YOU HUG YOURSELF. FOR WE ARE LOVING YOU GREATLY AND HOLDING YOU MOST DEARLY IN OUR HEARTS.

Know you only need call my name and I will be there.
In Love, Mother Mary
4/21/11

LETTER 125
HAPPY EASTER BLESSINGS TO EACH OF YOU

Dear Ones,

During this time of the Resurrection of Jesus let us acknowledge that this is indeed a time of awakening and renewal. It is a time of New Beginnings and making ready to enter a New World, which is exactly what Jesus' Resurrection was about. It was a time of awakening and coming back to life and preparing himself and the world for his passing into a different world. Are you not doing the same right now here on Mother Earth? Each being here on Mother Earth is awakening or coming back to life and preparing themselves to go into the 5D world. So indeed it is time for a huge celebration, both of the past Resurrection and the current Resurrections.

Many of you have been awake for sometime but there are others who are literally just awakening from years of being asleep. For those of you who have been awake during these past years of preparation, we are honoring you and appreciating all that you have done. For the many thousands of you who are just now awakening, know that there is more than enough time for you to catch up and prepare yourselves. Everyone who chooses to do so will be traveling into the 5D world. The Wayshowers and Keepers of the Light will be the first to walk across the footbridge into the 5D world. As I have said previously, this will happen in the fall/winter of this year. The rest of you will follow once you have completely prepared yourselves to do so.

For those of you who are just awakening this will be a time of relearning and letting go of the old ways. These old ways are what put you into your trance-like sleeping state, where you were unaware of what was going on in your body, mind and spirit. All the beings that are just now awakening will go through a time of great cleansing and releasing. For many it will seem as though they have awakened into a brand-new world. You will be amazed at all you see and hear as you prepare yourselves to travel into one more new world, the 5D world.

Your new 5D world will be a heart-centered world. All thoughts, actions, and deeds will come directly from the heart. Your mind will be taking second seat to your heart in this new world. All worlds, all nations, all people, and all living life forms will be connected as one. In your preparation for going into the new 5D world you will find your hearts opening and growing larger and larger. Never again will anyone look on another as less than or better than. All life will be equal and connected to one another to make up the whole of the one.

As you each awaken and become aware of what is going on in your own personal worlds you will notice that there is a certain light surrounding you. Know that this light is your guidance from us to help you in your preparation for going into the new world. For you Wayshowers and Keepers of the Light if you have not noticed this light around you before, please do so now. Once you have reached a certain point in your journey to the new 5D world others will be able to see your light and notice the changes in you.

This is a time of following your hearts and letting go of the should and should not's of your mind and all your old ways of being. It is a time of letting your light shine brightly so all can see. We are loving you and holding you most dearly in our hearts.

OUR WISH FOR YOU IS A JOYOUS AND HAPPY EASTER, CELEBRATING THE RESURRECTION OF JESUS AND THE RESURRECTION OF YOURSELVES.

Know you only need call my name and I will be there.
In Love, Mother Mary
4/23/11

LETTER 126

Dear Ones,

Today let us talk of what you might have done in the last few days to feed your Soul. I know that you feed your stomach with food, you feed your brain with new information from books, Internet and TV, but what about your soul. When was the last time you fed your Soul?

Your hearts are opening and beginning to play a more dominant role in your lives. The energy that is coming into your planet is allowing your hearts to grow larger and become more open and less guarded. As you work your way through the forgiveness phase of your preparations, you will find yourselves ready to be more heart-centered in your world. REMEMBERING NOW THAT THE HEART IS THE DOORWAY TO YOUR SOUL. THE MORE OPEN THE DOORWAY, THE MORE COMFORT AND NOURISHMENT IS ABLE TO REACH INSIDE TO YOUR SOUL.

The feeding of your soul can happen in a close spiritual connection with other beings of your planet or it could happen through music, the sight of a rainbow or a beautiful flower or tree. Nourishment of your soul will happen as you have your quick glimpses into the 5D world. You will notice when you have those glimpses that the whole of your body will hum as if it were trying to sing a song. Those glimpses will be as if you have turned a light switch on inside yourself.

We are talking today about the feeding of your soul because on your planet, most beings have paid little attention to their souls. It is as if you are pretending that it doesn't even exist. Your soul is not just the place where information is stored from all your life times. Your soul holds the essence of who you are today and who you have been forever. The soul is your center of divinity, your God source. It is your divine connecting rod to all of us.

Yes, your soul is nourished each time we connect, each time you read my letters, and the writings of other beings from my side. If you are doing a meditation or yoga practice, you are indeed connecting to your center or I call it your soul. In these two practices, you are opening your center point and allowing an energy flow between yourself and the divine. There are many ways to nourish your soul and it is important for each of you to find the way that works best for you. I am asking you to start a daily practice of nurturing and nourishing your soul. I AM ASKING YOU TO FIND SOMETHING BESIDES WHAT YOU MIGHT BE DOING AT THIS TIME. I AM ASKING YOU TO ADD SOMETHING ELSE TO WHAT YOU ARE DOING NOW. YOUR SOUL IS IN NEED OF MORE THAN WHAT IT IS RECEIVING AT THIS TIME.

We will be most honored to help and connect with you in your journey to find the right nourishment for your soul. We are waiting to hear your body hum and purr with divine satisfaction. I am loving you and loving you.

Know you only need call my name and I will be there.
In Love, Mother Mary,
4/26/11

LETTER 127

Dear Ones,

Today let us talk about you, and the world in general. I am sure you are all noticing that the whole of the world is changing and adjusting. Are you also aware of how you are changing and adjusting? I am thinking perhaps you are really wondering if you are adjusting or just getting ready to go over the edge. All the confusion and intense energy waves are disruptive and enough to drive everyone a little crazy.

It is so important for each of you to know that you are not alone. Know that everyone on your planet is being affected by all that is occurring on your planet. Each of you are handling it in different ways with different actions and reactions. You each are so unique and have your own processes for dealing with disruptions and distractions.

I wish that I could tell you this is almost over and the world will calm down and become gentler and easier to be in. The truth of your world right now is that it will not be calming down for the next several months. In fact, I think you will notice that there are times when it will become most intense.

Right now, I want to stress to you the importance of letting go of any control you may think you have. The truth is there is no control of what is happening right now, except for the fact that you can lessen the stress and tension in your lives by riding the waves. REMEMBERING THAT WE TALKED LAST WEEK ABOUT THE SPEED WALKER. ARE YOU REMEMBERING EACH MORNING TO VISUALIZE YOUR ENERGY SPEED WALKER AND THEN SIMPLY STEPPING ONTO THE WAVE? For those of you who have great need to be in control, this is the only way you can be in control right now. Just step on the energy speed walker and go with the flow.

Much of what is happening right now is about letting go of the supposed control that you believe you have. For the truth is you have no control over the past and no control over the future. REMEMBERING NOW THAT YOU ARE ALL LEARNING TO LIVE IN THE NOW. Your new 5D world is only about living in the now. When living in the now there is no need for control for there is nothing to control. When you live in the now there is only the flow of your life with what is happening in the moment.

Can you see yourself with no reason for the dearly beloved control? Can you feel the freedom? Your bodies can relax and let go of their rigid stance. You can be yourself, just allowing yourself the freedom to be. For some of you, I am sure you are not even sure what I am speaking of. For many of you this will be a whole new way of being, or maybe I should say it will be a way of being for the very first time.

Allowing yourself to stand in one spot and not to worry about which way you will step or what will happen if you choose this way or that. Imagine for a moment that you are standing still and then you walk away without thinking about where you are going or what direction you are heading. You are just walking to be walking. Over the next week think about the possibilities of living in this way. IT IS A WONDER, IS IT NOT?

KNOW THAT WE WILL BE WALKING WITH YOU NO MATTER WHICH WAY YOU GO. FOR WE ARE LOVING YOU AND WANTING SO VERY MUCH TO BE WITH YOU.

Know you only need call my name and I will be there.
In Love, Mother Mary
4/28/11

LETTER 128

Dear Ones,

Today let us stop and take a breath. There is always much to say and much to do. So just for today, I wish to stop and take a breath. It is the First day of May, a day of lightness and new energy. It feels as if the weight of your world has lifted and dispersed some of its heaviness. The air of Mother Earth is not so thick with regrets, sorrows, and I wish I had done this or that.

During these times when old unfinished business of the past is coming forward it is only necessary to acknowledge and release. It is not necessary to hang on to them and tell yourself I should have done this or that. The only reason for them coming forward at this time is so you can release them and allow them to leave your body space.

Remembering now that this is indeed a time of clearing and cleaning out of your body space. Each of you holds much energy and memories in your body space. The holding on of the old energies causes you to have a heavy and dense energy field. The heaviness and denseness cause you to stay securely connected to the 3D world of fear, regrets, and great sorrows.

So today in the lightness of this First day of May, it would be a good time to start your energy spring-cleaning. Spending your time holding onto sorrows and regrets serves no purpose but to hold you back and hold you down. So I say to you today to let go of these burdens of the past. Allow yourself to take a moment and tie balloons to each of these burdens and release them. Let the balloons carry your burdens up and out into the ethers never to be seen again.

Become aware of how your body space lightens as you let each balloon float away. Your mind becomes less confused and the chaos floats away with the balloons. Your mind, body, and spirit was never meant to carry these extreme weights of sorrow, old regrets, and should haves. Holding on to these things has only served to hold you back from all that you are meant to be. So today let your balloons float away allowing your light to shine brighter and brighter.

Also, today I want to take time to talk about you, my readers, and to say THANK YOU for reading my letters and sharing them with others you know. I am honored and most humbled by your requests for help. I rejoice each time I hear my name called. All of us here on this side, are most honored to be able to help in anyway. Be are aware of how difficult and intense it can become on your planet during these times. We honor your courage and strength during these times. We are most aware that each of you has chosen to be here during this time. You Wayshowers and Keepers of the Light are providing a great service to your planet and your people. So we say to you, we are honored to be of service to each of you. WE ARE LOVING YOU AND I AM LOVING YOU.

Know you only need call my name and I will be there.
In Love, Mother Mary,
5/1/11

LETTER 129

Dear Ones,

Today let us talk of LOVE and what you are thinking a heart-centered world will be like. In a heart-centered world there will be no space or room for anger, hated, judgments, or distrust of other humans. Each of you will find it necessary to release any of these 3D feelings that you might carry in your energy field before traveling into the 5D world. It will not be just the beings of the Mother Earth, who will need to release all 3D feelings. It will also be each country and nation.

Each country and nation holds the collective consciousness of its citizens. So I am saying that all citizens of each country will need to release old ways of being before traveling into the 5D world. Is there a collective sigh from you when you think of that and how that could ever happen? It will happen. It will not be tomorrow or the next day or next month, but I assure you it will happen. If there are those citizens who find it impossible to let go of the old ways, then they will choose to leave your earth and pass over to our side. REMEMBERING NOW THAT EACH AND EVERY BEING OF MOTHER EARTH AND THE WHOLE OF THE UNIVERSE HAS FREE WILL. There will be and there are beings right now who are making the choice to keep their old ways and are choosing to pass over to our side. Know that each of those beings is being welcomed with open arms and hearts. They are receiving the love and care, they need to heal and transform.

Now let us speak of you who are choosing to stay and change your old ways of being. This journey that you are choosing is not for the weak of heart. As you are already aware, it is trying and challenging at the best of times. I am aware you are wondering when the best of times will arrive. It has now been many months of on-going confusion, memory problems, lack of concentration, and being unable to focus on completing projects. As time passes these things will also move out of your systems and become less important. You will find yourselves being much more flexible and able to joke and laugh about the craziness these things have been causing in your lives. If you have been using the energy speed walker, you will by now have an idea of what being in the flow might mean. All of this craziness is teaching each of you to be in the flow of the energy waves that are coming to your planet. If you are one of the beings who are choosing not to use the speed walker and are resisting going with the flow, then your life must be most difficult at this time.

SO I WILL SAY TO ALL OF YOU LET GO OF RESISTANCE AND GO WITH THE FLOW. YOU HAVE MADE THE PERSONAL CHOICE TO BE HERE AT THIS TIME, SO ALLOW YOURSELVES TO SEE THE HUMOR AND THE PLAY IN ALL THAT IS OCCURRING. Learning to laugh at oneself can bring great joy into your hearts and minds. REMEMBERING NOW THAT WE ARE LOVING YOU NO MATTER WHAT. FOR ALWAYS AND ALWAYS I WILL BE LOVING YOU. IF YOU FIND YOURSELF CHUCKLING AND LAUGHING AT THE THINGS THAT ARE HAPPENING, KNOW THAT I AM RIGHT BESIDE YOU SHARING IN YOUR LAUGHTER. For I love to laugh and play.

Know you only need call my name and I will be there.
In Love, Mother Mary
5/3/11

LETTER 130

Dear Ones,

The energy on your planet for the last couple of weeks and continuing for a few more weeks is most intense and difficult. It may feel as if your world has turned upside down and sideways. All feelings have been intensified and increased two fold and in the case of anger three fold. Have you found yourselves becoming angry at things that make no sense? Are you flaring out at people, places, and things that you have no control over? REMEMBERING NOW THAT THIS IS A TIME OF LETTING GO OF CONTROL.

Going with the flow and letting go of control is a great challenge for many of you. You have held this belief that you have control over everything in your lives. Your belief is that you have control over people, places, and things and this is an untruth. The truth is you have never had nor will you ever have control over people, places, and things. THE ONLY CONTROL THAT YOU CAN HAVE IS THE CONTROL OF BEING AND STAYING IN THE FLOW OF LIFE, WHICH IS TO SAY IF YOU ARE IN THE FLOW THEN YOU ARE LETTING GO OF CONTROL. BEING IN THE FLOW IS LIVING IN THE NOW AND BEING PRESENT FOR WHATEVER MIGHT OCCUR AT ANY GIVEN MOMENT IN TIME.

So the craziness of your world right now is about each of you learning to let go of control and allowing yourselves to be in the flow of life. The energy waves to your planet have increased greatly over the last few weeks and this will continue through the month of May. So it is a time of hanging on to your hat and allowing yourself to be. Resistance of any kind at this point in time will only increase the challenge of these times.

Take the time now and over the next few weeks to spend time with yourselves daily. Take a few moments each day to be silent and be with yourselves and if it is possible then do this several times a day. REMEMBERING TO CLEAN AND CLEAR YOUR ENERGY DAILY OR SEVERAL TIMES A DAY IF YOU ARE OUT IN THE WORLD. Calling on us to come and be with you during your quiet times or at your worst of times will be most helpful. IT IS IMPORTANT TO REMEMBER THAT YOU DO NOT HAVE TO DO THIS ALONE. EVERYONE ON YOUR PLANET IS GOING THROUGH SIMILAR SITUATIONS AS YOURSELF.

REMEMBERING NOW THAT WE ARE HERE AND WANTING TO HELP YOU. WE ARE WORKING HARD TO DEFLECT AND DEFUSE MUCH OF THE ENERGY THAT IS COMING YOUR WAY. THERE ARE LIMITS TO HOW MUCH WE CAN HELP. REMEMBERING THAT THIS IS INDEED A JOURNEY THAT MOTHER EARTH MUST TAKE AND A JOURNEY THAT EACH OF YOU MUST TAKE.

WE ARE HONORING YOU FOR THE WORK YOU ARE DOING AND WE ARE LOVING YOU GREATLY.

Know you only need call my name and I will be there.
In Love, Mother Mary,
5/6/11

LETTER 131

Dear Ones,

Over this past weekend as you celebrated Mother's Day your hearts opened up one more notch. I am asking you today to leave your heart open that one more notch and to start living in your world with a slightly more open heart. There is so much in your world for you to experience from a heart-centered place. You will be amazed at how your attitudes and perceptions will start to change as you learn to live with a more open heart.

Most beings of your planet walk around with their hearts on pause. You may smile and speak to your neighbors, but do you let yourselves care. When was the last time you offered to help one of your neighbors or even your friends? There may be nothing that they need help with right now, but just in your asking you have showered them with love and caring. What a gift you have given just by speaking a few words.

Let us take a step back right now and ask how do you feel after reaching out and asking if someone needs help? What is your heart doing? Can you feel new warmth within yourself? What is happening is you are receiving back from those ones you offered to help. They are sending you back love and gratitude for your asking them. Is this what you call full circle? You have offered love and caring to your neighbors and friends and they have returned it back to you with love and gratitude for your asking.

This is what your world was meant to be about. The accepting of love and caring from others and the returning of that love and caring back to the ones who are giving. A constant interactive thread of love and caring creating full and intertwined circles of love. Can you picture in your mind, the thousands and thousands of inter-connected circles of love? WHO WOULD NOT WANT TO BE PART OF THOSE CIRCLES? WHO WOULD NOT WANT TO BE PART OF LOTS AND LOTS OF THOSE CIRCLES?

THOSE THOUSANDS AND THOUSANDS OF INTER-CONNECTED CIRCLES ARE EXACTLY WHAT THE 5D WORLD IS ABOUT. It is about each of you opening your hearts and minds to welcome and join together with every other life force on your planet. Life as you know will be about loving each other, no matter who or what you are. You each will be giving and receiving love constantly. It will become part of your everyday life. Just as you breathe fresh air to give yourself life, you will be giving and receiving love to also give yourself life.

Life, as you know it today, will cease to exist. It will be replaced with warmth, nurturing, love, and caring. I THINK THAT THIS IS A TRADE WORTH MAKING. WHAT ABOUT YOU? ARE YOU READY TO TRADE IN THIS LIFE AND START LIVING IN A NEW WAY WITH AN OPEN CARING HEART? IF SO, START TODAY TO REACH OUT TO YOUR NEIGHBORS AND FRIENDS AND THEN PREPARE TO RECEIVE IT BACK. START CREATING YOUR CIRCLES OF INTER-CONNECTING LOVE. Know that we here have encircled each of you with love and caring. I AM LOVING YOU GREATLY AND HOLDING YOU IN MY HEART.

Know you only need call my name and I will be there.
In Love, Mother Mary
5/9/11

LETTER 132

Dear Ones,

Good Morning Special Ones, I hold each of you so dear in my heart. You are truly loved beyond your wildest imaginations. Each of you is held in such honor and respect, far more than you love, honor, or respect yourself. I am wondering why that is so, that we here on my side think so much more of you than you think of yourselves. IS THAT NOT STRANGE?

EACH AND EVERY ONE OF YOU HAVE BEEN TAUGHT AND SHOWN FROM THE TIME OF YOUR BIRTH THAT YOU ARE LESS THAN YOU REALLY ARE. WAS THIS DONE ON PURPOSE? THE ANSWER IS NO; IT WAS NOT DONE ON PURPOSE. THIS IS SOMETHING THAT HAS BEEN-HANDED DOWN GENERATION AFTER GENERATION.

It is a crime that has been perpetuated on your Mother Earth from the beginning of time. I am unaware of what started this or why it has continued on and on. I AM SPEAKING VERY LOUDLY NOW. THIS MUST STOP AND IT MUST STOP NOW. I AM PUTTING EACH AND EVERY ONE OF YOU ON NOTICE. From this time forward all beings of your planet will start seeing the truth of who they are. If any parent, teacher, or guardian of one of the children of Mother Earth says or does anything to indicate to a child that they are less than they are, they will find themselves unable to continue. They will find themselves stumbling over their words and wondering why they were going to say that. Just as each of you will no longer to be able speak to yourselves in any way that is not truth.

The voice in your head that shames you, degrades you, or devalues you in any way will find it difficult to speak. The voice will either go away or be quiet, no longer able to exist in your world. AS YOU ALL KNOW WE ARE GETTING READY TO MOVE INTO A HEART-CENTERED WORLD WHERE LOVE IS THE MAINSTAY OF EXISTENCE. There is no space or room in a Heart-Centered world for untruths about who and what you each are. There is room only for love and honoring of each being. REMEMBERING NOW THAT ALL BEINGS ARE NOT THE SAME. EACH BEING IS INDIVIDUAL AND UNIQUE IN WHO

AND WHAT THEY ARE.

THEIR TALENTS AND GIFTS ARE EACH SEPARATE AND INDIVIDUAL. SOME MORE GIFTED IN ONE AREA AND SOME IN ANOTHER. Each being will use their gifts and talents to the best of their ability to aid and help the whole.

ALL BEINGS AND ALL LIFE FORCES WILL COME TOGETHER TO MAKE UP THE WHOLE. EACH OFFERING THEIR PART TO SUSTAIN THE WHOLE AND EACH NEEDED TO SUSTAIN AND MAKE UP THE WHOLE. Each being and life form will play their own separate and individual important role in your new 5D world. It is important to think about and know that all beings of the 5D world will not be looking alike or even speaking alike. All life forms will be accepted and honored as one of the whole. There will be many outside differences between the life forms. THERE WILL BE NO INSIDE DIFFERENCES IN THE MANY LIFE FORMS IN THE 5D WORLD. ALL LIFE FORMS IN THE 5D WORLD WILL BE HEART-CENTERED, REACHING OUT TO ONE ANOTHER WITH OPEN HEARTS AND MINDS.

This is the way your world was meant to be. With all life forms being honored and accepted in love for who and what they are. Know that we here are accepting each of you and loving each of you greatly. I am wanting to say to you once again, I LOVE YOU, I LOVE YOU, AND I LOVE YOU.

Know you only need call my name and I will be there.
In Love, Mother Mary
5/11/11

LETTER 133

Dear Ones,

Today let us talk of your hopes and dreams. Let us talk of the tomorrows to come. All the things that you hope and dream of are possible in the new 5D world that is coming. It is most necessary for you to let go of your old ways of thinking and being. Preparing yourself for the journey into the 5D world is all about learning new ways of thinking and being.

Yesterday we talked about the voices that are constantly talking to you inside your mind. The voice could be your Mother, Father, Teacher, Friend, or even your own voice. This voice you hear is a harmful, cruel, and a vicious voice that abuses you over and over. This has been going on for years. Some of you have been able to quiet your voices during your lifetime, although sometimes it will still raise its ugly head and catch you unaware. Always pushing you down and taking yourself-esteem and self-confidence away.

Now is the time when the voices must stop and each of you will need to participate in stopping the voices. Learning to live without the voices will require work and constant vigilance on each of your parts. REMEMBERING NOW THAT ONLY YOU HEAR THESE VOICES. EVEN IF YOUR FRIENDS OR NEIGHBORS WERE TO HEAR YOUR VOICES THEY WOULD KNOW WITHOUT A DOUBT THAT THEY SPEAK ONLY UNTRUTHS. NOW IS THE TIME FOR YOU TO LEARN THEY SPEAK ONLY UNTRUTHS.

The next time you hear that voice in your head telling you that you can't do something or you're not smart enough, are you going to believe it? NOW IS THE TIME TO EXAMINE WHAT IS BEING SAID TO YOU AND TO CHECK IT OUT. MOST OF THE VOICES ARE WORDS FROM LONG AGO AND YOU ARE STILL CHOOSING TO LIVE BY THOSE OLD THOUGHTS AND WORDS.

REMEMBERING NOW THAT YOU ARE GOING INTO A NEW WORLD WHERE ALL IS POSSIBLE. A WORLD WHERE LOVE IS THE PURPOSE FOR THE WORLD AND THE PURPOSE OF THE PEOPLE LIVING THERE. THERE IS NO ROOM OR SPACE FOR UNTRUTHS AND VOICES THAT SHAME, DEVALUE AND DE-

GRADE THE BEINGS WHO LIVE THERE.

So I say to you are you ready to take the time to quiet and stop the voices. We are right here waiting to help you stop and quiet the voices. THE NEXT TIME YOU HEAR ONE OF THE VOICES IN YOUR HEAD, IT WILL BE UP TO YOU TO STOP AND REALLY HEAR WHAT IS BEING SAID. KNOW THAT WE WILL BE RIGHT BESIDE YOU WHEN YOU DO THAT. WILL YOU CHOOSE TO BELIEVE THE VOICE OR WILL YOU RECOGNIZE THAT IT COMES FROM THE PAST AND HAS NO REASON FOR BEING HERE IN YOUR LIFE NOW OR IN THE FUTURE? The voice will stop and release once you no longer choose to believe what it is saying to you.

IT IS IMPERATIVE THAT YOU ALLOW YOURSELVES THE TIME TO RELEASE AND LET GO OF THESE OLD VOICES OF UNTRUTH. AS ALWAYS, WE WILL BE RIGHT HERE WITH YOU HELPING IN WHATEVER WAY YOU WILL ALLOW. WE ARE LOVING YOU AND STANDING WITH YOU.

Know you only need call my name and I will be there.
In Love, Mother Mary
5/13/11

LETTER 134

Dear Ones,

You each are so special to me and there are not enough words to express my feelings for each of you. Often I say to you, "I LOVE YOU, I LOVE YOU, AND I LOVE YOU." Yet there are many of you who are unable to hear my words. In your hearts and minds, there is no belief that anyone could possibly love you. Others of you hear my voice as a breath of a whisper. In your hearts and minds, there is the small chance you are hoping that what I say is true. Yet there are others who have opened their hearts and minds fully and they are rejoicing and allowing my love to fill them.

My hope, my prayer, and my wish is that the day will come soon that all of you will be able to accept and believe my words. I am aware that your belief is that you are unworthy of love from anyone, let alone me. In your minds, you are thinking how could she possibly love me. My answer back to you is, how could I not love you? You each are wondrous incredible human beings. You each are separate and unique, there is no one else in the whole world like you. It fills my heart with joy just to see each one of you.

Today I ask each one of you to come on a journey with me, a journey where I can share my love with you. SO CLOSE YOUR EYES, TAKE SEVERAL DEEP BREATHS, PUT YOUR HAND ON YOUR HEART AND CALL MY NAME. I AM RIGHT HERE WITH YOU. NOW I WILL ASK YOU IN YOUR MIND TO GO TO YOUR FAVORITE, SAFEST PLACE IN THE WHOLE WORLD. I ALSO ASK YOU TO TAKE ME WITH YOU TO YOUR SPECIAL PLACE. YOU AND I WILL SPEND TIME HERE TODAY JUST BEING WITH EACH OTHER. I ASK YOU NOW TO TAKE MY HAND. CAN YOU FEEL THE WARMTH, COMFORT AND, MOST IMPORTANTLY LOVE FLOWING FROM MY HAND TO YOURS?

CAN YOU FEEL YOUR HEART OPENING NOW? ARE YOUR HANDS, YOUR ARMS, YOUR HEART, AND THE WHOLE OF YOUR BODY BEGINNING TO FEEL WARM? SOME OF YOU WILL START TO TINGLE AND YET OTHERS WILL FEEL LIKE THEY HAVE BEEN FILLED UP WITH JOY. OTHERS OF YOU MIGHT

WANT TO CRY OR LAUGH OUT LOUD. ALLOW YOURSELF TO EXPRESS WHATEVER IT IS YOU ARE FEELING.

I AM GOING TO SPEAK VERY QUIETLY RIGHT NOW, BUT YOU WILL HEAR MY VOICE VERY LOUDLY. YOUR BODY, MIND, AND HEART WILL VIBRATE WITH THE SOUND OF MY VOICE. I LOVE YOU, I LOVE YOU AND I LOVE YOU.

ALLOW MY WORDS TO WRAP AROUND AND FILL YOU UP. STAY HERE WITH ME AS LONG AS YOU WISH. WHEN YOU ARE READY, COME BACK TO THIS LETTER AND THIS DAY. I AM HOPING THAT YOU WILL COME BACK TO THIS JOURNEY MANY TIMES, UNTIL YOU KNOW WITHOUT A DOUBT THAT WHAT I SAY IS SO. I AM LOVING YOU MOST DEARLY AND HOLDING YOU IN MY HEART EVERY SECOND, EVERY MINUTE OF EVERY DAY.

Know you only need call my name and I will be there.
In Love, Mother Mary
5/16/11

LETTER 135

Dear Ones,

Let us talk today about the things you are wanting to change in your lives. When you talk to me or when you pray it is almost always about wanting something in your life to change or even your whole life to change. I am wondering what you are willing to do to make that change happen.

Many times the things you are asking for are things that you yourself can make happen, only you are just not sure of how to go about it. Sometimes you are afraid to take the steps needed to get where you want to be. As we talked about the other day in another letter, all the things you are asking for and dreaming of are possible in the 5D world.

Each and every one of you will be making the journey into the 5D world. Before going into the 5D world you will need to let go of the fears, doubts, limitations, and the old victim thinking. These are the things that are stopping you from having what you want in the 3D world. You each will need to release and let go of these old ways of thinking during your journey into the 5D world. As I have said before there is no room or space in the 5D world for fears, doubts, limitations, and victim behavior or thinking.

If it were possible for me to remove these old ways of thinking by a wave of my hand, I would do so. For I know how tired you are of carrying around your fears, doubts, and victim-hood. ARE YOU REMEMBERING NOW THAT EACH AND EVERY ONE OF YOU HAS FREE WILL? Are you thinking right now, I don't want these things? My free will is to let go of these things that are holding me back. I say to you that is what your mind is saying. What about your emotions, what are they saying? It is not an easy action to simply let go of all the fears, doubts, and victim-hood. Those things have been with you for many, many years, sometimes your whole life. This is how you have learned to live and be. It is what you know.

So now it is time to learn to live without these things in your life. It is about recognizing the fears, doubts, and victim-hood that happens every day in your life. So now we are back to how to do that. HOW DO I LET GO OF THESE BELIEFS? Well, this goes back to listening to the voices in your head. I AM GOING TO SUGGEST THAT YOU GO BACK AND

READ LETTER 119. This letter explains how to listen and release the old beliefs and untruths that govern your lives.

If you are thinking right now, I don't have time to do that, I have this and this and this I need to do. I WILL SAY VERY LOUDLY RIGHT NOW IT IS TIME TO STOP AND PAY ATTENTION. I AM WANTING YOU TO HAVE ALL THOSE WONDERFUL THINGS THAT YOU DREAM AND THINK ABOUT. HOW BADLY DO YOU WANT TO HAVE THEM? WHAT ARE YOU WILLING TO DO TO HAVE THEM AND HOW MUCH TIME WILL YOU PUT INTO HELPING YOURSELVES?

As always, I am right here willing and ready to help you. There are thousands of others here with me ready and willing to help you. We are all hoping you are ready and willing to help yourselves. I AM LOVING EACH AND EVERY ONE OF YOU AND HOLDING YOU IN MY HEART.

Know you only need call my name and I will be there.
In Love, Mother Mary
5/17/11

LETTER 136

Dear Ones,

Let us talk today about something that has been happening to many of you. Are old uncomfortable feelings coming up and swamping you? Are you finding yourself engulfed in those feeling before you even know what has happened? Some of these episodes of old feelings can go all the way back to childhood.

When these episodes come it can feel as if you have been hit by a tidal wave. You are in it and you are back where it first started. It may take some time for you to recognize what has happened and that you are not really back in that old place. Listen to what you are saying to yourself. Once again, it is the voices of untruth.

Stop and take the time to listen to what you are saying about yourself to yourself. These are the same old, degrading, shaming, and devaluing words that are not true. Listen to the voices and then speak the truth out loud. Clearly stating who and what you are today. Give yourself a moment to just stop and allow all of those old untruths to release and be gone as you speak about who you are today. You may even be able to feel the energy of all the words releasing and leaving your body.

This is not something that will just happen all at once and everything will be peachy after you do this one time. Stop and think about all the things that you have said to yourself over the years. Some are much louder and clearer than others, but be aware that there are more than one set of words or sayings to release.

Over the next weeks and months be aware of what is happening in your mind and body.

Each time your hear the voices of untruth it will be necessary to stop and release. You will find as you become accustomed to this process that it will all happen very quickly. Each time the voices come you will become quicker at recognizing what is happening. Once you recognize what is happening you will be able to release and come back to your life today.

During this time and each time you release these old untruths you will find your body feeling lighter. You will become more sure of yourselves. You will find your confidence increasing. New and different things will not seem so far away. Reaching out and taking part in more of what the world has been offering you will seem possible.

Of course always remembering that we are right here with you. As you are working your way through the process of recognizing and releasing, call on us for help. Even if it is just wanting us to hold your hand or stand by your side. We are offering you help in whatever way you may need. You each are loved greatly by everyone here on this side. We are showering your being with love, laughter, and light. We are holding you in our hearts.

Know you only need call my name and I will be there.
In Love, Mother Mary
5/19/11

LETTER 137

Dear Ones,

Today let us talk of Kindness and Reaching Out. I am speaking of stepping out of your circle of friends and reaching out to help other beings on your planet. Your helping may be nothing more than a smile. Your smile projects wondrous feelings of acknowledgement and acceptance to other beings.

Walking on your planet and through your world as if no one else exists, this is damaging to your heart and spirit. Human beings were meant to interact with each other, to support and nurture each other, and to love and care for each other. Human contact is as important to your being as food is to your body.

There once was an old saying on your Mother Earth that an apple a day keeps the doctor away. My saying is a HUG a day keeps the Doctor away. One HUG a day is a bare minimum. Human beings need attention and affection. Words are not enough to fill the heart to over flowing and that is what each of you is in need of. A heart that is overflowing with love and affection is healthy both in body and spirit. Knowing that you are cared for and appreciated will help to fill the empty spaces in your hearts.

Maybe I should speak of what I am going to call a disease that is running rampant on your planet. It is called Empty Heart. Almost all beings of your planet have this disease. There is no prescription that you can go to the drug store and get that will cure it. The only cure is genuine loving human contact. There are some of you who have built walls so high no amount of love and caring will be able to get through or go over the top. The walls are for protection, because of past hurts and traumas. Part of the getting over the old hurts and traumas is letting go of the walls and seeing that there are other beings who wish to love and care about you. It is important to know that you each are responsible for taking down your own walls. Asking for our help to assist you will make it easier to take down the walls. We are right here waiting for you to you call.

The size of your wall doesn't matter it must come down before you can enter the 5D world. In your 3D world, it may have seemed necessary to live with walls around you, but it will not be necessary in the 5D world. REMEMBERING NOW THAT THE 5D WORLD IS ABOUT LOVE. EACH AND EVERY THING THAT HAPPENS AND EXISTS IN THAT WORLD COMES FROM THE HEART CENTER. There will no longer be a need or reason to live in fear and anxiety. All beings are stepping out of that environment and moving into a heart-centered world.

I am asking you today to go out of your way to Reach Out and offer some Kindness to another human being on your Mother Earth. A smile or gentle word will go a long way in lifting the vibration of yourself, other beings, and Mother Earth. REMEMBERING NOW THAT KINDNESS IS CONTAGIOUS AND CAN TRAVEL RAPIDLY THROUGH THE BEINGS OF YOUR PLANET.

As always, we are right here ready to help you in anyway. KNOW THAT I AM SMILING AT YOU AND HOPING THAT YOU WILL PASS IT ALONG. KNOW ALSO THAT I AM LOVING YOU DEARLY AND HOLDING YOU IN MY HEART.

Know you only need call my name and I will be there.
In Love, Mother Mary
5/23/11

LETTER 138

Dear Ones,

What should we talk about today? My favorite subject to talk about is you. What you're doing, how is your journey going, what do you need help with, and do you know how much you are loved? With all of that there must be at least 3 or 4 letters. So, I will pick one and my question to you is "How is your journey going"?

The energies of May have been overwhelming and intense to say the least. You are almost there, at the end of May. Do you know that you have done well or is all that is coming through your mind now about how tired you are and how much you still have to do? Well, today for just a few moments I am going to ask you to just STOP. Right now, I would ask that you just stop. Come and be with me. Take my hand, listen to the words I am speaking in your head.

Yes, you can all hear what I say in your heads. If you are shaking your head and saying no, I can't hear you in my head, then I will say the words out loud to you. I AM PROUD OF YOU AND EVERYONE HERE ON THIS SIDE IS PROUD OF YOU. THESE LAST MONTHS HAVE NOT BEEN EASY. THERE HAS BEEN TURMOIL, CHAOS, CONFUSION, AND A NEVER-ENDING LIST OF THINGS THAT HAD TO BE DONE.

FOR TODAY GIVE YOURSELF PERMISSION TO STOP. Take time to step outside, smell the fresh air, and if you live in a place where the air is not fresh then go to your mind and imagine it so. Give yourself room to breathe and be. NOW MORE THAN ANY OTHER TIME IN YOUR JOURNEY IT IS IMPORTANT TO STOP AND TAKE CARE OF YOURSELVES.

IT IS BEYOND IMPORTANT THAT YOU STOP AND TAKE CARE OF YOURSELF AT THIS TIME. THE JOURNEY IS NOT OVER AND YOU WILL NEED YOUR BODY, MIND, AND SPIRIT REFRESHED AND RESTED TO CONTINUE ON OVER THE NEXT FEW MONTHS.

You each have worked so hard with such determination and courage that we here on this side stand in awe of who you are. Do you each see how you have changed and grown over the last year? Can you see the differences in yourself? Your hearts are opening and letting go of old ways. Your mind and body has let go of old forms of judgment and negativity. Your perceptions and attitudes have lifted and opened, seeing yourselves and others in a different way. Are you taller or are you just standing taller now? Yourself worth and self-confidence has grown and flourished.

You are starting to respect yourself, which allows you to respect others. You are opening your minds to the idea that there are many other kinds of life forms on your planet and the other planets of the universe. Love and respect go hand in hand. Of course, all of this is in preparation for the final steps of crossing the footbridge and becoming part of the 5D world. Yes, the 5D world is right here on earth, but the 5D is how you choose to live on earth. The 5D world is about living on earth as you were always meant to, AS A HEART- CENTERED BEING, ALLOWING YOUR HEART TO BE FULLY OPENED AND FREE AT LAST. You each are working your way to that spot in time when you are truly a heart-centered person.

WE HERE ARE SO PROUD OF ALL YOU HAVE DONE AND ALL YOU ARE DOING. REMEMBERING THAT WE ARE HERE TO HELP YOU IN WHATEVER WAY WE CAN. WE ARE LOVING YOU EACH AND EVERYONE. I LOVE YOU, I LOVE YOU, AND I LOVE YOU. ARE YOU HEARING ME? I LOVE YOU!

Know you only need call my name and I will be there.
In Love, Mother Mary
5/25/11

LETTER 139

Dear Ones,

As I have said before, this month of May has been intense and a little overwhelming for some of you. It is a time of great clearing and cleaning. Your body, minds, and spirits are going through a time of releasing and letting go of old and deeply buried feelings, emotions, and forgotten dreams.

There are many of you who are aware of what is happening and are releasing as you go about your day. Some of you are doing your releasing during your sleeping time. So if you find yourselves waking up in the morning feeling as tired as when you went to bed, know that you are releasing and letting go during your sleep time. For all of you who are doing your releasing during the daytime and night time, just continue to hold strong and know that all will be cleared soon.

During this time of releasing and clearing it is most important that you take care of yourselves. Being gentle and nurturing with yourselves. It would be most wonderful if you could even go so far as to baby yourself just a little. Caring for yourself in whatever way comes to your mind and heart, be it favorite comfort foods, hot baths, massages, or sharing with a friend. All of these things are wonderful and nurturing. I am sure there are others that will come into your mind. Do all of these things for yourselves.

Remembering that all of these old feelings, emotions, and forgotten dreams are weighing your body down and holding you firmly to the old ways of being. Letting go of these things is a big part of your journey into the 5D world. All of the old needs to be released so that you can open your hearts and begin to live your lives as heart-centered beings. If you are carrying old hurts and forgotten dreams in your hearts, then the door to your hearts will stay closed, holding all the old inside. So it is necessary to open the doors and allow the old to flow out. Once your heart is empty of these old things the doors can start to stay more open. Over time the doors will start to open wider and wider.

REMEMBERING NOW THAT WE ARE RIGHT HERE READY TO HELP YOU AS YOU ARE RELEASING AND LETTING GO OF THE OLD. WE KNOW THAT YOU MAY BE THINKING THAT

YOU HAVE LET GO OF EVERYTHING AND THERE IS NOTHING LEFT. KNOW THAT THERE IS NO BEING ON YOUR PLANET AT THIS TIME WHO HAS CLEARED AWAY ALL OF THEIR OLD WAYS. EACH AND EVERY ONE OF YOU IS STILL IN THE PROCESS OF CLEANING AND CLEARING. THERE ARE SOME OF YOU WHO ONLY HAVE A SMALL AMOUNT LEFT, THERE ARE OTHERS WHO HAVE MUCH WORK TO DO, AND OF COURSE, THERE ARE OTHERS WHO HAVE NOT EVEN STARTED TO LET GO OF ANY OF THE OLD. We know that each of you will be letting go of the old in your own unique time and we honor that process in each of you.

KNOW THAT WE ARE LOVING YOU GREATLY AND ADMIRING YOUR DETERMINATION AND COURAGE DURING THESE TIMES. I LOVE YOU, I LOVE YOU, AND I LOVE YOU.

Know you only need call my name and I will be there.
In Love, Mother Mary
5/28/11

LETTER 140

Dear Ones,

Today's letter will be a reminder letter. In other words, I am asking you to go back and revisit other letters or I will be putting the reminders into words in this letter. My first reminder is to ask you to go back and listen to Letter 120. If I had named that Letter it would be called "I Love You, I Love You, and I Love You." During that letter, I ask you to come and spend time with me, just you and me sharing our love for each other.

If you are one of the beings who cannot hear my words on your computer, then I ask you to go to a computer where you can hear my words. It is important that you hear my words, "I Love You, I Love You, and I Love You" being spoken out loud to you. I am wondering if there will ever come a time when everyone on Mother Earth will hear those words and believe it in their hearts. Those words are meant to travel to the very depths of your soul, so that there is no part of you who does not recognize the truth of my words.

My second reminder today is about the voices in your head. I am speaking again of the harmful, unkind, and abusive voices that speak so very loudly inside your head. Are you remembering what I am speaking of? You know the ones I mean. They tell you that you can't do certain things or you're not smart enough and it goes on and on. In my previous letters, we talked about the untruths of those voices and what you need to do to release them.

So when you recognize the voices and what is happening, it will be necessary to stop what you're doing and deal with those voices. First recognize what is happening, secondly speak the truth out loud. Say what is true today. Remembering now that these are the voices of the past, either your own voice or perhaps the voice of your parents or a teacher. So speak your truth out loud, saying what is truth today. As you speak your truth out loud the voices will start to release and you will be able to feel the energy of those words leaving your bodies. It will be necessary to stop and give yourself a moment to process all that has happened if you want to be aware of the energy leaving.

If you find yourself somewhere that you are unable to follow this procedure at the exact moment that the voices are speaking in your mind, then acknowledge inside yourself that the voices are not truth. At a later time when you can take a moment, go back to the voices and follow the procedure of speaking the truth out loud and allowing the voices to release and leave your body. Do not be fooled into thinking because you acknowledged them in your mind that they will be gone. It will always be necessary to speak your truth out loud. Speaking the truth out loud is the key to releasing those voices.

I am thinking perhaps these two reminders are enough for today. For I know that your hearing and believing my words, of "I Love You" is a very big reminder to take in. I also know that taking care of the voices and speaking the truth of who you are today is a wondrous realization for you. As you begin to believe my words and release the old voices in your head you are turning your thoughts to the knowing and believing in yourselves. You are seeing your own worthiness, your own beauty, and great value to yourself and the universe.

Of course, you must know what my parting words will be to you today. I Love You, I Love You, and I Love You.

Know you only need call my name and I will be there.
In Love, Mother Mary
5/31/11

LETTER 141

Dear Ones,

Yes indeed the black cloud has lifted. The energy has lightened. It is time to stop and take a breath, time to feel the warmth of the sun on your face. The energies of May have disbursed and released. Most of the beings of earth can once again take a breath. May was so intense and disturbing that we here find it amazing that you did not all take to your beds for the whole of the month.

You are all filled with such determination and strength that we applaud you. June will indeed be an easier month in many ways. The energy waves coming in this month will be as intense as May, but you will have breaks in between the waves. During the month of May, there were no breaks it was a continuous barrage of energy waves.

So for the next few days there will be a short break before the next waves arrive. Take a break, allow yourselves to relax and reflect back on the month of May. Look at what has occurred and what you have released. Many of your old voices have released and left your being. There were times during the month when old memories came to the surface to be released; memories needing to be looked at in a different way and perhaps people and situations that needed to be forgiven.

Most importantly for many of you there were and still are many issues that you need to forgive yourself for. IT IS MOST IMPORTANT FOR YOU ALL TO KNOW THAT THERE IS NOTHING THAT YOU HAVE NOT BEEN FORGIVEN FOR. YOU EACH ARE HELD IN THE HIGHEST REGARD AND GREAT MOUNTAINS OF LOVE ARE SURROUNDING EACH OF YOU. The only forgiveness needed at this point is your own. I will say to you if we here on this side have forgiven you for all your actions and are loving you dearly for who you are, how can you not do the same?

Are you thinking that you know better than we do? Are you thinking that we don't remember this or that? My answer to you is NO. We do not remember this or that which was done by you. Those times and those situations are gone never to be known or remembered again. All those times are in the past and are of no consequence today. There are no remembrances here of all the yesterdays. We are living in the NOW, in today.

So I say to you wash yourself clean and release the past. WHO YOU ARE TODAY IS WHAT WE ARE LOOKING AT. HOW DO YOU INTEND TO LIVE THIS DAY? TODAY IS YOUR HEART FILLED WITH LOVE AND UNDERSTANDING FOR EVERY OTHER BEING ON YOUR MOTHER EARTH? WHAT ABOUT YOUR MOTHER EARTH, IS YOUR HEART FILLED WITH LOVE AND CARING FOR HER? ARE YOU GOING TO BE STEPPING UP TO CARE FOR YOURSELF, OTHERS AND MOTHER EARTH IN A MORE GENTLE AND LOVING WAY?

WE HERE, ARE CONCERNED WITH TODAY. WE ARE LOVING WHO YOU ARE TODAY. WE SEE NO TOMORROWS OR YESTERDAYS. Remembering now that the 5D world that you are journeying to is all about the NOW, there are no yesterdays or tomorrows there. THIS MONTH OF JUNE WILL BE ALL ABOUT LETTING GO OF THE PAST. SO AS YOU TAKE TIME TO LOOK BACK, ALLOW ALL OF YOUR EMOTIONS TO RELEASE AND BE FINALLY FREE. NOW IS THE TIME TO ALLOW YOURSELVES TO BE FREE. IT IS NO LONGER NECESSARY FOR YOU TO CARRY THESE HEAVY WEIGHTS AROUND WITH YOU. FOR HERE ON OUR SIDE THE PAST NO LONGER EXISTS AND IN THE 5D WORLD, THE PAST NO LONGER EXISTS.

So we ask you to come and join us. Allow your past to release and set yourselves free. FREE TO LIVE IN THE NOW, FREE TO LOVE IN THE NOW, AND FREE TO BE WHO YOU ARE WITHOUT RESTRICTIONS AND SORROWS. KNOW THAT WE ARE LOVING YOU GREATLY AND HOLDING YOU MOST DEARLY IN OUR HEARTS.

Know you only need call my name and I will be there.
In Love, Mother Mary
6/2/11

LETTER 142

Dear Ones,

Today let us talk about JUDGMENTS. Are you still judging and comparing yourself to others? This is a game where there are no winners. The people who you are comparing yourselves to have no idea that there is a game going on, so they are not winning. The only other person playing the game is you. Do you see yourself as winning this game?

There are two ways to play this game. The first is you compare yourself and you always come out less than. You're not as pretty, not as smart, your figure isn't as good, they have better clothes and more money. The list goes on and on. You will never be the winner in this game. You come out feeling less than in every aspect of your lives.

The second way to play this game is to find someone who you think of as less than you. Then you can tell yourself that you are better looking, thinner, smarter, happier, have a better house, handsomer husband or partner, and you have more money. During the game, you make the other person smaller and less than in every way. THERE ARE NO WINNERS IN THIS GAME EITHER.

LOOK AT YOURSELF RIGHT NOW AFTER PLAYING THE GAME. HOW DO YOU FEEL? IS NOT YOUR HEART HURTING AND CRYING OUT? OUTWARDLY, YOU MAY NOT BE SHOWING ANY SIGNS OF YOUR ACUTE DISTRESS. INSIDE YOU ARE SHRIVELED UP AND WANTING TO DISAPPEAR. Are you wondering how you could think of another person in those terms and what about how you are thinking of yourself? Is this the only way you can find to fit into the world?

MY WORDS ABOUT THESE GAMES MAY SEEM HARSH AND THEY WERE MEANT TO BE HARSH. THIS IS A VERY SERIOUS HURTFUL GAME TO PLAY. YES, NO ONE ELSE KNOWS THAT YOU PLAY THIS GAME. BUT, REMEMBER NOW THAT I KNOW YOU PLAY THESE KINDS OF GAMES. MORE IMPORTANTLY YOU KNOW THAT YOU PLAY THESE KINDS OF GAMES.

CAN YOU SEE HOW HARMFUL THESE GAMES ARE? THERE

WILL NEVER BE A TIME WHEN YOU WILL FIND THE TRUTH BY PLAYING THESE GAMES. THE TRUTH WILL ONLY COME TO THE FOREFRONT ONCE YOU STOP PLAYING THESE GAMES.

IT IS BEYOND IMPORTANT FOR EACH OF YOU TO RECOGNIZE AND REMEMBER THAT EACH OF YOU IS SEPARATE AND UNIQUE. There is no way to make a comparison between a diamond and a pearl. They are two separate and unique kinds of gems. There is no way to compare a chocolate cake to a white cake, two very different desserts. It is the same with you human beings, there is no way to compare you with another.

IN YOUR SEARCH TO FIND WHO YOU ARE AND HOW YOU CAN FIT IN THE WORLD, YOU HAVE TRIED DESPERATELY TO MAKE YOURSELVES LIKE OTHERS.

THE TRUTH IS YOU WILL NEVER FIND OUT WHO YOU ARE OR HOW YOU FIT IN THE WORLD BY COMPARING YOURSELF WITH SOMEONE ELSE. YOU WILL ONLY FIT IN BY BEING WHO YOU TRULY ARE. JOY AND HAPPINESS COMES WITH THE ALLOWING OF YOURSELF TO BE WHO YOU TRULY ARE. For you are like no other human. You are separate and unique. THE JOY AND WONDER OF HUMAN BEINGS IS THAT THEY ARE ALL UNIQUE AND DIFFERENT. YOU EACH ARE LIKE PIECES OF A PUZZLE, ALL FITTING TOGETHER TO MAKE THE WHOLE. IN THE PUZZLE NO TWO PIECES CAN BE THE SAME.

WE ARE LOVING YOU, EACH AND EVERYONE. WE ARE LOVING YOUR DIFFERENCES AND THE WONDER OF EACH ONE OF YOU. WE ARE HOPING THAT YOU WILL ALSO START TO LOVE YOUR DIFFERENCES AND APPRECIATE YOUR UNIQUENESS. I LOVE YOU, I LOVE YOU, AND I LOVE YOU.

Know you only need call my name and I will be there.
In Love, Mother Mary
6/4/11

LETTER 143

Dear Ones,

Today let us talk about the times that will be coming to your earth. Let us talk of the 5D world and what that means. I often speak of the 5D world and tell you that it will be a heart-centered world. Each of you in your own mind decides what heart-centered means to you. I want to explain to you what I mean. Our thoughts may be similar and in some cases I believe they are very far apart.

When I say your world will be heart-centered I am meaning that all thoughts, actions, or reactions will be heart directed. Is it almost impossible to imagine that your mind will no longer be in control of your thoughts, actions, and reactions? Let me give you an example of what I am speaking of. You find yourself walking down the street in a busy, big city. You are holding on to your purse or wallet; you are paying close attention to what is happening around you, and finally, you have walls up guarding you. In all of these instances your mind is in control telling you to be very careful. Your mind is telling you that these people on the street, might mug you, steal your money, get in your face, and hurt you. There is pushing and shoving going on and everyone is in a hurry to get here or there. Fear, stress, hate, and unhappiness are running rampant all about you. Your mind is in control of all your thoughts, actions, and reactions.

Where is your heart during all of this? Your heart is shut down, quiet, and perhaps asleep. There is no place in that world for your heart. Now imagine you are on the same busy street. People are walking by smiling, saying good morning, looking you in the eyes and you can tell that they are meaning their words. There is no fear, stress, hate, or unhappiness running rampant in the streets and you do not need to watch your purse or wallet. No one is going to hurt you. All the energy coming towards you from everyone, including Mother Earth is love and caring. You are feeling light and airy almost as if your feet are not touching the ground.

Look at the people around you, look at yourself. Everyone is relaxed, happy. No one is wanting to hurt anyone nor is anyone hurting inside themselves. People are shopping or going to work and no one is hating the thought of shopping or work. They are enjoying their lives and what they do daily in their lives. NO ONE IS WORKING AT JOBS THEY HATE SO THEY CAN DO WHAT THEY LOVE ON THEIR DAYS OFF.

THEY ARE LOVING WHAT THEY ARE DOING EVERY MINUTE OF EVERY DAY.

Is that almost un-imaginable that people are liking their jobs? Jobs are not stressful and boring. People are working at jobs they like and find them fulfilling. I am aware that all of this is almost impossible to believe. How can the world you know today turn into the world I am talking about? All of this will not take place in one day or one year. It is a process that your world is going through right now and has been going through for some time.

This transformation will happen slowly over time. The Wayshowers and Keepers of the Light will be the first to move into your new world. All of their friends, relatives, people they work with, and the people they see on the street will be watching as they move into the new world. The differences in how they live their lives will be so clear and remarkable to all who watch them that others will want what they have. The Wayshowers and Keepers of the Light will spend much time explaining how they got to the 5D world and what others need to do to get where they are.

When I speak of loving you dearly and holding you in my heart, that is the way each of you will be feeling and speaking of all other life forms once you pass into the 5D world. There will be no harsh judgments of yourself or anyone else. You will see everyone with different eyes, the eyes of your heart. You will understand what has happened to others and why they are like they are. No judgments will go with those thoughts only love and support and a knowing that all is as it should be in their world and your world.

Each and every one of you who wish to journey to the 5D world will be able to do that. There will be many of you who choose not to make that journey. REMEMBERING NOW THAT ALL OF YOU HAVE FREE WILL AND THAT IS ALWAYS HONORED AND RESPECTED BY EVERYONE HERE ON OUR SIDE.

THERE IS MUCH MORE TO SAY ABOUT THE 5D WORLD, BUT I WILL SAVE THAT FOR ANOTHER LETTER AND ANOTHER DAY. I WILL SAY AGAIN THAT WE ARE LOVING YOU GREATLY AND HOLDING YOU IN OUR HEARTS. I LOVE YOU, I LOVE YOU, AND I LOVE YOU.

Know you only need call my name and I will be there.
In Love, Mother Mary
6/8/11

LETTER 144

Dear Ones,

Today let us talk about what it means to be a heart-centered being. How does one become a heart-centered being? What do I have to learn and what do I need to read? Let us start with this. Each and every one of you can become a heart-centered being. This is not an easy journey to undertake. The rewards are un-imaginable. You will be learning to live your life as it was meant to be lived.

There is no one book to read or easy quick path to follow. Each being will find the path they need to follow on this journey by going inside themselves. I am sure there are many of you right now who are saying no way, I am not going inside of me. There is too much confusion and chaos inside my head. I WILL SAY TO YOU VERY LOUDLY RIGHT NOW THE ONLY PATH TO BECOMING A HEART-CENTERED BEING IS THE ONE INSIDE OF YOU. REMEMBERING NOW THAT THE 5D WORLD IS A HEART-CENTERED WORLD AND ALL BEINGS WHO LIVE IN THE 5D WORLD ARE HEART-CENTERED.

Those first steps inside yourself may seem a little scary and overwhelming, but you will find that it is a place that you have been waiting to journey to your whole life. This journey to become a heart-centered being will be one of un-teaching yourself much that you have learned from the time of your birth. It will mean letting go of any of the comments that you took in and believed about yourself that were not truth. It will be letting go of any thought that spoke of you not being absolutely perfect in every way. It will be letting go of any thought where you were comparing yourself or being compared to some other being. There can be no comparisons as you are unique and like no one else in the universe.

It is a total and complete understanding that each being in the universe is separate, whole, and perfect, just as they are. Physical form and shape are of no consequence or matter in the heart-centered world. It means recognizing that each and every being is here for a specific reason and purpose, recognizing that each and every being is connected to the whole. Every thought and action vibrates through the whole. Thoughts and actions are like radio waves running through the whole of the universe. If you are thinking in your mind that you are unworthy, then that message is beaming out to the whole and others are hearing the message that they are unworthy also. Your thoughts and everyone else's thoughts are circling around and around touching everyone in the whole. What each person does every minute of every day is of the utmost importance.

You each are affecting each other in every minute. You each are making up a huge circle of the whole. All parts are interconnected and needed for the whole to be complete. Do you see how important each of you are and what an immense part you play in the whole? Many of you will want to say, no, that can't be true. I just don't matter that much. ONCE AGAIN I WILL SPEAK MOST LOUDLY, EACH AND EVERY ONE OF YOU IS IMPORTANT BEYOND YOUR WILDEST IMAGINATION. YOU EACH HAVE A PURPOSE AND REASON FOR BEING HERE.

Your individual journeys will be as separate and unique as each of you are. It is a journey that you will need support and encouragement on as you travel this path. So I will say to you again that we are right here waiting to help you on your journey. We are humbled by your strength and courage as you undertake this journey. Unlearning all that you have learned is no small accomplishment. We know and inside of yourself you know, that you have been waiting to take this journey for sometime. So we say to you come and be with us and we will show you the way. There are many others who are on this path and who have been traveling for sometime and they will help to show you the way also. Know in your hearts that it will be no accident when you meet these beings that are already traveling their paths.

KNOW THAT WE ARE LOVING YOU SO GREATLY AND HOLDING YOU IN OUR HEARTS.

Know you only need call my name and I will be there.
In Love, Mother Mary
6/9/11

LETTER 145

Dear Ones,

Today we are going to talk more about being a heart-centered being. Yesterday we talked about un-learning everything that you have been taught about yourselves that is untrue. We are going to take it one step further today and talk about all of the untruths you have been taught about the world, God and other human beings.

All of this comes under one heading and I will call it Fear. Many of you have been taught to fear God, that his retribution on sinners is harsh and unloving and that not only will harmful actions be punished, but also harmful thoughts will be punished. There has been much talk about going to hell for any harmful actions or thoughts and anything that is included on the long list of things that can and will make you a sinner.

This is what I know of God and I assure you there is nothing to fear from the God I know. GOD IS LOVE AND THAT LOVE ENCOMPASSES EACH AND EVERY LIVING LIFE FORM IN THE UNIVERSE. GOD DOES NOT SIT IN JUDGMENT DECIDING WHO WILL AND WHO WON'T GO TO HELL. GOD DOES NOT EVEN KNOW OF ANY PLACE CALLED HELL OR ANY LONG LIST OF SINS. GOD IS LOVE, ONLY LOVE. EACH AND EVERY LIVING LIFE FORM IN THE UNIVERSE IS PART OF GOD. GOD IS THE WHOLE AND EACH AND EVERY LIVING LIFE FORM IS PART OF THE WHOLE. YOU AND I ARE PART OF THE WHOLE. WE EACH ARE LOVE. LOVE IS ALL THERE IS.

The opposite of LOVE is FEAR. FEAR SEPARATES PEOPLE FROM EACH OTHER AND FROM THE WHOLE. I WILL SAY AGAIN THAT FEAR IS THE OPPOSITE OF LOVE.

Many of you have been taught to fear or to be afraid of other people. You have been taught to fear anything and anyone who is different from you. REMEMBERING NOW THAT FEAR IS THE OPPOSITE OF LOVE.

If you had been taught to love and appreciate people who are different from you what would your world be like today? There would be no WARS; there would be no hate, no violence, no greed, and no need to struggle for power. 90% of the beings of Mother Earth would not be walking around feeling unloved and unlovable.

My heart is filled with great sadness to know that this is true. My heart is filled with sadness to know how much time and energy it will take on your parts to unlearn all these untruths. My heart is filled will sadness to see and know the harm that these untruths have caused all living life forms of the universe.

YOUR WORLD WAS MEANT TO BE ABOUT LOVE. ALL BEINGS WERE MEANT TO BE ABLE TO WALK ABOUT WITH THEIR HEARTS OPEN AND FULL OF LOVE FOR EVERYTHING. NO BEING WAS MEANT TO WALK ABOUT WITH THEIR HEARTS CLOSED DOWN AND THEIR MINDS CLOSED AND FILLED WITH FEAR AND DOUBT. Fear is the opposite of Love.

GOD IS LOVE; YOU ARE LOVE, AND I AM LOVE. LOVE IS ALL THERE IS. WE ARE HERE LOVING YOU EACH AND EVERY MOMENT OF EVERY DAY.

Know you only need call my name and I will be there.
In Love, Mother Mary
6/10/11

LETTER 146

Dear Ones,

Today let us talk of the Eclipse that is occurring on June 15th. This will be a total lunar eclipse and will bring forth transformation. This transformation will be an awakening of your soul as if it is being called to come forward and be all that it was meant to be. It will be a time to shed all the old ways of hiding and being fearful to show who you really are.

Many of you are going to be called to step forward. For some of you, the calling will be very strong and powerful, for others it will seem as a gentle whisper in your ear. I urge you to answer these calls. They will speak of your purpose for being here at this time and the part you are to play in the coming of the 5D world.

Each of you has been working towards becoming a heart–centered being and walking your path into the 5D world. This calling is just the next step in this process. REMEMBERING NOW THAT WE ARE RIGHT HERE READY AND WILLING TO HELP YOU IN ANYWAY. REMEMBER ALSO THAT THIS IS A TIME OF CELEBRATION OF THE PATH THAT YOU ARE FOLLOWING. YOUR STRENGTH AND DETERMINATION HAS ALLOWED YOU TO ARRIVE AT THIS POINT.

If you are one of the beings that does not hear a calling, know that there will be another time for you to experience the calling and the stepping forward. All beings are making this journey in their own time and way. Your purpose in being aware that some beings are going to be called forward will allow you to be of support and encouragement as they step forward into their new roles. Being the person offering support and encouragement is an honored role and one to be respected and cherished. REMEMBERING NOW THAT YOUR TURN WILL COME AND SOMEONE WILL BE THERE TO OFFER YOU SUPPORT AND ENCOURAGEMENT.

YOUR WORLD IS CHANGING VERY RAPIDLY RIGHT NOW AND WILL CONTINUE TO DO SO OVER THE NEXT MONTHS. HAVE YOU NOTICED THAT EACH OF YOU IS CHANGING RAPIDLY? TAKE A LOOK BACK AT WHO YOU WERE ONE MONTH AGO AND WHAT ABOUT FOUR MONTHS AGO. CAN YOU SEE

THE CHANGES AND APPLAUD YOURSELVES FOR WHAT YOU HAVE ACCOMPLISHED?

WE here are hoping that each of you are reaching out and surrounding everyone in the world with love and support. We, here, are hoping that you are remembering to surround yourselves with love and support. REMEMBERING NOW THAT EVERYONE ON YOUR MOTHER EARTH IS ON A JOURNEY AND ARE IN NEED OF GREAT SUPPORT AND LOVE.

WE ARE LOVING YOU GREATLY AND HOLDING YOU IN OUR HEARTS. I LOVE YOU, I LOVE YOU AND I LOVE YOU ALWAYS.

Know you only need call my name and I will be there.
In Love, Mother Mary,
6/14/11

LETTER 147

Hello Dear Ones,

Today let us talk about you. I am wondering how you are all doing? You have had your second eclipse in just over 15 days and you are looking at having another one in about 15 days. Are you ready to run away and hide? The only problem with that is there is no place to hide. What is going on in your city is also going on all over the universe.

So there is no place to run to and no place to hide. There are ways to make this a little gentler and easier on yourselves. The only way to do this is self-care. WE have talked of this so many times in the past. It is truly the only way to lessen the stress of what is happening in your world right now. I am once again going to repeat the same-old things over again. Give yourself some time to think and breathe without running here or there. This can be meditating or simply sitting in a chair and daydreaming for a few moments. There is no need to make a big production out of doing this. Simply stop for 5 minutes or 10 minutes and let yourself be.

Most of you are going so fast right now you can't even keep up with yourselves. It is not surprising, because that is what the energy on your planet is doing right now. So it is not that you are doing anything wrong it is just the way it is on your earth. So it will take deliberate action on your part to stop all of this. I would imagine that most of you are feeling frazzled, wrung out, and utterly overwhelmed by all that is happening.

You need to be aware that there is no way that you can keep up with all that is happening in your world. You will literally have to stop this yourself. It is no different than if someone was standing in front of you and punching you in the head. Would you just stand there and take the punches or would you take action to stop it? My guess is that each one of you would take some action to stop this. So I am telling you it is time to take actions for yourselves and stop running with the energy that is coming to your planet.

I know it is difficult to stop yourselves and pull back. Indeed, you might miss something or things might not get done as fast as you think they should. REMEMBERING NOW THAT ALL YOU NEED DO IS ASK FOR HELP AND WE WILL BE RIGHT THERE. WE WILL HELP

YOU TO PULL BACK AND TAKE CARE OF YOURSELVES. It is ok for things to get done tomorrow or even the next day. What is most important is that you are feeling strong and confident in yourselves again, no longer running around like the whirling dervish is chasing you. When you are functioning in that way things are forgotten, not completed, and not done the way you like best.

SO FOR TODAY CAN YOU JUST STOP FOR 5 MINUTES, 10 MINUTES, OR EVEN 20 MINUTES AND ALLOW YOURSELVES TO JUST BREATHE? WE ARE KNOWING HOW DESPERATELY YOU NEED TO DO THIS FOR YOURSELVES. KNOW THAT WE ARE HONORING YOU AND SENDING YOU LOVE AND SUPPORT EVERY MINUTE OF EVERY DAY.

Know you only need call my name and I will be there.
In Love, Mother Mary
6/17/11

LETTER 148

Dear Ones,

Today let us talk of CHANGE. Both the changes your earth is going through right now and that each of you are also going through right now. During Mother Earth's changes, she is releasing and letting go of the pressure that builds inside of her. This release of pressure causes earthquakes and volcanoes to occur in your world. REMEMBERING NOW THAT THESE TWO OCCURRENCES HAPPEN AS MOTHER EARTH LETS GO OF THE OLD AND TRANSFORMS INTO THE NEW.

Yes, the changes and letting go cause much confusion and chaos for those of you who live on Mother Earth. There has also been much change to the weather that occurs on Mother Earth. Weather patterns have shifted and changed. You are finding that on the parts of Mother Earth where it should be cool it is now starting to be much warmer and the changes go on and on. These changes are causing great disturbances, which is causing tornadoes and hurricanes where none has occurred before.

ALL OF THESE CHANGES ARE CAUSED BY THE ENERGY CHANGES OF THE MOTHER EARTH. REMEMBERING NOW THAT SHE IS A LIVING, BREATHING LIFE FORM. Just as you are changing and letting go of the old, so she is doing the same. Just as her changes are affecting each of you, so your changes are affecting others in your world.

You will notice that as you try to stop the changes that are happening in your lives immense pressure builds inside of you. Many times it can feel as though you have hurricanes, tornadoes, earthquakes, volcanoes inside of you. I AM GOING TO SPEAK VERY LOUDLY RIGHT NOW TO THOSE OF YOU WHO HAVE DECIDED TO HOLD YOUR GROUND AND NOT TO MOVE FORWARD. JUST AS MOTHER EARTH HAS TO LET GO AND RELEASE THE PRESSURE, SO DO YOU.

The struggles and holding on, trying to stay in the same place causes much pain in your body, mind, and spirit. It is as if you are waging a great civil war inside yourself. Your heart is struggling to become all that it was meant to be and your body and mind are wanting to stay in control. It is much like the old dictators of the Middle East who refuse to let go of their control and the great wars that are taking place for them to stay in power. That same war is going on inside many of you. These wars that are being fought in the Middle East and inside of you are so that all can stay as it is. UNDERNEATH ALL OF THAT WANTING TO STAY THE SAME IS FEAR. GREAT HUGE ALL CONSUMING FEAR OF CHANGE AND WHAT IT WILL BRING.

WHAT IF!!!!!!!!!!!!!!!!!! The changes are for the good? What if the changes are leading you to how your life was meant to be lived? WHAT IF? WHAT IF? WHAT IF? WHAT IF? WHAT IF? WHAT IF?

I have a thousand "WHAT IFS?" to give you. If you can let go of the fear for just a moment and consider the possibilities that are awaiting you. IMAGINE THE IMMENSE LOVE THAT YOU CAN EXPERIENCE IF YOU ALLOW YOUR HEART TO BE OPEN AND IN CONTROL OF YOUR LIFE. ALLOWING YOURSELF TO LIVE YOUR LIFE WITHOUT FEAR. THESE DIFFERENCES ARE SO GREAT YOU WILL FEEL AS IF YOU HAVE A WHOLE NEW LIFE AND YOU WILL. There are parts of yourselves that you have never explored. Each of you has so much hidden away inside yourselves that you have never allowed into the light of day. You each are capable of so much more than you have allowed. There is a whole new world and a whole new you living inside of yourselves. IT IS TRULY TIME TO LET GO OF THE FEAR AND ALLOW YOURSELVES TO TRULY LIVE.

We do not expect for you to do this on your own. We are right here waiting and willing to help you make these changes. WE ARE RIGHT HERE READY TO WALK BESIDE YOU OR EVEN CARRY YOU IF THAT IS WHAT YOU NEED. KNOW THAT THERE ARE THOUSANDS OF US HERE ON THIS SIDE WAITING FOR YOUR CALL. EACH AND EVERY ONE OF US IS LOVING AND CARING ABOUT EACH OF YOU. KNOW THAT I LOVE YOU, I LOVE YOU, AND I LOVE YOU.

Know you only need call my name and I will be there.
In Love, Mother Mary
6/19/11

LETTER 149

Dear Ones,

As these first days of summer come into being, let us rejoice at this new season and this time of change and growth. Summer comes to us with warmth, blue sky, thoughts of play, and good times. Summer comes with times of growth and gardens. It is a time of inner-growth and change. The time has come for reaching out and pushing past old barriers.

As each of you reach out and push past what you have known, you will be shedding old ways, customs, and traditions. This is a time of getting ready for what the universe is growing into and becoming. It is a time to recognize your growth and who you are becoming. It is a time of waking up and seeing the truth of your world and what it has become. One of the first steps in allowing the old ways of the world to fall away is to clearly see the truth of what it has become. I am speaking of seeing the whole picture not just part of the picture. This is not a time of agreeing or disagreeing with what the world has become, it is just about seeing the whole truth of what it is.

It is about recognizing the strengths and weakness of the world and yourselves. Are you ready to change that picture? Are you ready to look inside and find the truth of yourself and the world? As each of you brings the truth of yourself into being, you will affect the picture of the world. With your becoming who you are meant to be, then in turn the world will start to become who and what it was meant to be. Each being of this universe is connected and affects each other and the whole of your world.

It is past time to let go of the illusion that what you do and what you say does not matter to other beings or the whole of your world. Every thought, action, and deed affects every other living breathing life form. Are you consciously aware of these actions of others? No, most of you are not, but all actions, thoughts, and deeds changes the energy in the universe. That energy reaches out and touches each of you and in the touching of that energy, you are changed and affected.

SO I SAY TO YOU TODAY, WELCOME TO THIS SUMMER SEASON. WELCOME TO THIS TIME OF RENEWAL, GROWTH, NUR-

TURING, AND HEALING. AS YOU EACH GROW AND HEAL IN THE WARMTH OF THE SUN MAY THE OLD OUTER LAYERS OF UNTRUTHS RELEASE. WITH THE RELEASE COMES ROOM FOR GROWTH AND RENEWAL OF THE PRECIOUS TRUTH OF YOU AND THE UNIVERSE.

Know that we are right here standing with you ready to help you weed your garden or shed your old untruths. We number in the thousands and we are loving each and every one of you. We are hoping that you can feel our love, support, and encouragement flowing into your world.

Know that you only need call my name and I will be there.
In Love, Mother Mary
6/21/11

LETTER 150

Dear Ones,

Today let us talk of Hope, Faith, and Trust. I am not speaking of having those beliefs in others, but in yourselves. Many of you often wonder if you have the courage and strength to continue on with this journey that you have undertaken. In those times of wondering it becomes difficult to find that place inside yourselves where Hope, Faith, and Trust dwells.

You would not be Wayshowers and Keepers of the Light if you did not have a deep abundant knowledge of the Faith, Hope, and Trust that you hold inside yourselves. You each have deep a connection to my world and to the knowing of all that is to happen in your world. You are trusting yourselves and everyone here on my side to help you arrive at the place you are journeying to.

You each have great faith in yourselves and the knowing that resides in your heart, mind, and body. This knowing is what is leading you forward and giving you hope that the humans of earth will be able to make the transition into the new way of living on Mother Earth. There is great Hope that all beings will be able to come together in love and harmony. You carry great hope in your body, mind, and spirit that human beings have not traveled too far into the realms of selfishness, greed, and disconnection from source.

I want each and every one of you to know that the Hope, Faith, and Trust that dwells in each of you is not unfounded. We, here on this side, are knowing that all beings of your Mother Earth will be able to reconnect to source and come back to who they are. We also know that it will take some much longer than others to come back to what your world was meant to be about. REMEMBERING NOW THAT THIS IS A PROCESS AND JOURNEY FOR EVERYONE ON EARTH. ALL BEINGS WILL BE TRAVELING AT THEIR OWN TIME AND SPEED. INDEED THERE ARE SOME WHO WILL CHOOSE NOT TO MAKE THIS JOURNEY. DO NOT BE DISMAYED FOR THE ONES WHO CHOOSE NOT TO MAKE A JOURNEY SIMILAR TO YOURS. REMEMBERING NOW THAT YOURS IS A WORLD OF FREE WILL.

Each and every one of you is traveling at your own speed and that is absolutely perfect in all ways. You each are perfect in every way. Know that you are never traveling alone. We are with you every step of the way. Know also that there are many others watching you as you make your journey and because of you; they will be able to make their journey also. Each and every one of you are leaders and teachers. You may not knowingly be aware of this, but it is so. REMEMBERING NOW THAT EVERYONE IS FOLLOWING SOMEONE AND THERE IS ALWAYS SOMEONE FOLLOWING THEM. That is the way it has always been. Know now that we here on my side are the ones leading the way, as you decide to journey with us, there is always someone behind you deciding to journey with you also.

We thank you for your Faith and Trust in us. Know that we are honoring you and that we have great Faith and Trust in each of you. I Love You, I Love You, and I Love You.

Know you only need call my name and I will be there.
In Love, Mother Mary
6/25/11

LETTER 151

Dear Ones,

Today let us talk about the third eclipse that is going to occur at the end of your week. This eclipse is about the complete letting go of the old energy and ways of being. It is the beginning of a new and different way of being. So as you go through your week preparing yourself for what is to come focus on releasing and allowing yourselves to be open to the possibilities of the universe.

During this week as you go through your days allow your body to release and let go of any old energy that is no longer needed or helpful. Take time during your days to feel the energy releasing and leaving your body.

Let us now go on a journey of releasing and letting go. Take my hand and come with me. TAKE SEVERAL DEEP BREATHS AND JUST CONTINUE BEING RIGHT HERE WITH ME. I AM TAKING YOU TO A SPECIAL VALLEY WHERE WE WILL FIND WATER FALLS, CREEKS, ANIMALS, BEAUTIFUL TREES, AND WILD FLOWERS. CAN YOU SEE HOW BEAUTIFUL THIS PLACE IS? NOTICE HOW IT FEELS HERE IN THE VALLEY. THERE IS A WARMTH AND COMFORT THAT JUST SEEMS TO SURROUND EVERYTHING, INCLUDING YOU. JUST CONTINUE TO BE HERE IN THE VALLEY NOTICING HOW YOU ARE FEELING AND WHAT IS HAPPENING TO YOUR MIND AND BODY.

CONTINUE BREATHING AND TAKING IN ALL THAT THE VALLEY IS OFFERING TO YOU. NOTICE NOW THAT OLD MEMORIES AND THOUGHTS ARE FLOWING INTO YOUR MIND. KNOW THAT THESE MEMORIES AND THOUGHTS ARE COMING FORWARD TO BE RELEASED AND LET GO OF. IT IS TIME TO FIND CLOSURE FOR MANY THINGS THAT HAVE OCCURRED DURING YOUR LIFE. IT IS NO LONGER NECESSARY TO CARRY THESE THINGS INSIDE YOUR BODY, MIND, AND HEART. JUST ALLOW YOURSELF TO STAY RIGHT HERE AND RELEASE ALL THAT YOU ARE READY TO LET GO OF.

WHEN YOU HAVE FINISHED WITH ALL THAT YOU WANT

TO RELEASE WALK OVER TO THE WATER FALL AND ALLOW THIS SPECIAL WATER TO WASH YOU CLEAN INSIDE AND OUT. WASHING EACH CELL AND ORGAN OF YOUR BODIES. STAY THERE IN THE WATER FALL AS LONG AS YOU NEED, UNTIL ALL HAS BEEN WASHED AWAY.

When you are ready return to this day and this letter, giving yourself time now to understand and take in all that has occurred for you in the valley. KNOW THAT THE VALLEY WILL ALWAYS BE THERE AND THAT YOU CAN RETURN AT ANY TIME. DURING THE NEXT DAYS, WEEKS, AND MONTHS YOU WILL FIND THERE ARE MORE THOUGHTS AND MEMORIES THAT WILL BE READY TO BE RELEASED AND LET GO OF. Allow yourselves to return here as many times as you need. REMEMBERING NOW that there is no need to go to the valley by yourself. There are thousands of us here who will be more than honored to travel with you to this valley.

Know that I am loving you greatly and holding you most dearly in my heart. I LOVE YOU, I LOVE YOU, AND I LOVE YOU.

Know you only need call my name and I will be there.
In Love, Mother Mary
6/28/11

LETTER 152

Dear Ones,

Welcome to July. Congratulations are in order, you made in it through your month of June and the three eclipses that occurred during that month. Are all of you still standing and walking around or have you fallen over on the ground so you can take a break from all that is happening?

The energy waves that have been coming to your Mother Earth have been strong enough to knock over an elephant. Each of you has such courage and determination as you keep on walking through the energy waves. You keep working your jobs, taking care of your families and self, being in the world, hitting up against all of the other crazy energy from other beings and you just keep on ticking. We are thinking that all humans must have an energizer bunny inside their beings.

And bless you each for having those energizer bunnies inside of you. We are in awe of what you are accomplishing and how you're choosing to travel this journey. Each of you is walking in grace and spirit. REMEMBERING NOW THAT WE ARE INDEED WALKING WITH YOU EACH AND EVERY STEP OF THE WAY. YOU ARE NEVER ALONE, NOR WILL YOU EVER BE ALONE. YES, WE ARE AWARE THAT THERE ARE MANY TIMES WHEN YOU FEEL ALONE. That is our reason for assuring you once again that you are never alone. You may not be able to see us, hear us, or even feel us there beside you, but we are there always.

We are rejoicing and celebrating that you have made it into the month of July. So let it be a time of celebration and rejoicing for you also. A time of acknowledging all that you have accomplished. There will be many new opportunities coming your way in the months ahead. You will be able to see more clearly that there are other new and different ways for you to be in the world. Of course, it will be up to each of you to choose if you will stay with the old way or will you dare to step out and try the new. It is not to say that you must try every new way that is shown to you. It is OK to step back and try one new way at a time.

If there is something that you choose not to try at this time, then speak out loud asking it to return at a different time. Allow yourselves the space to try these new ways next week or next month. All of this is your choice, you may stay with the old ways or not. I cannot imagine after all the time and work you each have put into this journey that you would choose to turn away and not try the new ways of being. Please remember that this is an individual journey and the new ways of being that will be offered will be very individual. Do not allow yourselves to be sidetracked because someone else is not shown the same new way as you. The wonder of all of this will be your sharing with others the new ways that are coming forward to you. In your sharing, you will give support to the next one to try this new way of being.

It is a wonder how you're sharing of your journey adds support and encouragement to your fellow travelers. This sharing opens hearts and minds to the new ways coming to your world and all that is waiting for you as you journey into the 5D. Know that I am here with you hearing your thoughts and prayers. I am loving you greatly and holding each of you in my heart. I LOVE YOU, I LOVE YOU, AND I LOVE YOU.

Know you only need call my name and I will be there.
In Love, Mother Mary
7/1/11

LETTER 153

Dear Ones,

Let us talk of this Holiday that you are celebrating today. In the United States it is called the 4th of July or Independence Day. It is a celebration of freedom. I am wanting to take it one step further and make it a day of individual freedom for each of you. Freedom from your old ways of being. Freedom from living in a world that is mind directed. Freedom from living in a world where your heart is shut down most of the time.

Beings in your world often live their whole life without realizing that their heart is not functioning as it was meant to function. Their heart has been closed down at an early age or through some trauma, in some cases never to be opened again. Beings are not realizing that with their hearts closed they are not feeling the true measure of love. Love is not felt either in the giving or the receiving. They are missing out on the sweetness of life.

Let us speak of the energy of that love which is never expressed or received. What happens in your energetic field when love is being sent to you, but you cannot take it in? In your mind visualize if you will for just a moment. Love energy is being sent to you. In your mind, you know that it is being sent but you cannot feel it and the energy never enters your body. When the love energy arrives to enter your body it comes up against a solid wall that you have placed there. Can you almost see a sign reading LOVE IS NOT ALLOWED---GO AWAY? That is literally what happens. You have put a protective shield around your body and it is especially thick and heavy around the heart. Are you consciously aware of doing this? The answer to this is NO.

You have never consciously told yourself that you do not want love. In fact the very opposite is true. You are desperate to be loved. Your mind has told you, don't get close to people, don't care about people, nobody cares about you, and most of all never ever trust anyone. Those kinds of words and thoughts put the walls in place. YES, IT IS POSSIBLE TO TAKE DOWN THE WALLS ONCE YOU RECOGNIZE THEY ARE THERE. ALSO RECOGNIZE THAT YOUR WORDS MAY NOT BE EXACTLY THE SAME AS THE ONES I HAVE MENTIONED. LOOK INSIDE

YOURSELVES AND YOU WILL BE ABLE TO SEE IF YOU HAVE PUT YOUR OWN WALLS IN PLACE.

Are there some of you today that are recognizing that you do have a wall up stopping the thing that you most desperately need and want? WE ARE RIGHT HERE BESIDE YOU AND WE CAN HELP YOU REMOVE THOSE ENERGETIC WALLS. RELEASING AND LETTING GO OF THE WALLS IS AN ENORMOUS STEP IN GAINING YOUR PERSONAL FREEDOM. IT IS A HUGE STEP TOWARDS LEARNING TO LIVE YOUR LIFE FROM YOUR HEART AND NOT YOUR MIND.

REMEMBERING NOW THAT YOUR MIND WAS NEVER MEANT TO BE THE DIRECTOR OF YOUR LIFE. IT WAS MEANT TO BE AN ORGANIZED STORAGE FACILITY FOR INFORMATION GATHERED DURING YOUR LIFETIME. As you are finding your way into the 5D world much of what you have learned during your time in the 3D will need to be let go of and released. Allowing your mind to direct your life is one of the things that needs to be let go and released.

Many of you have been working tirelessly towards that goal for some time. More and more beings are joining you each day. So look about you and reach out your hands to the new ones who are just beginning their journeys. OF COURSE, ALWAYS REMEMBERING THAT WE ARE RIGHT HERE WAITING TO HELP YOU IN ANY WAY. WE ARE SO PROUD AND HONORED TO BE OF ASSISTANCE TO YOU. WE ARE LOVING YOU, EACH AND EVERYONE.

Know you only need call my name and I will be there.
In Love, Mother Mary
7/3/11

LETTER 154

Dear Ones,

Now is a good time to stop and take a breath. June is over and your holiday is over. So is there room in your lives right now to stop for just a moment and take a breath. You each have been living in such intense energy, confusion, and chaos for some time. So I will say again now is a good time to stop and take a breath.

With all that has been happening in your physical world and your physical body, I would say that most of you have reached a point of exhaustion. So I will say again, now is a good time to stop and take a breath. If you are thinking, NO, I can't do that right now, maybe next week. Do you not realize that your physical body is only capable of handling so much stress and tension before it becomes ill?

So now it is time to stop and listen. So now it is time to stop and take a breath. Have you forgotten about self-care and how important it is for each of you? What do you need and what do you want? What can we do to help you? Can you now, for just a few moments in time, stop and come with me?

TAKE SEVERAL DEEP BREATHS, CLOSING YOUR EYES, CALLING MY NAME, AND REACHING NOW TO TAKE MY HAND. JUST CONTINUE BREATHING AND BEING HERE WITH ME. ALLOWING NOW FOR YOUR MIND TO EMPTY. ALL WORRIES, TROUBLES, CHAOS, AND CONFUSION ARE FLOWING AWAY FROM YOUR MIND. JUST SEE ALL THOSE THOUGHTS AND WORRIES FLOWING INTO THAT LARGE CONTAINER THERE BESIDE US. CONTINUE BREATHING NOW ALLOWING YOUR MIND TO EMPTY INTO THE CONTAINER. ONCE YOUR MIND IS EMPTY VISUALIZE PUTTING A LID ON THE CONTAINER. EVERYTHING IN THE CONTAINER IS SAFE AND WILL BE WAITING FOR YOU IF THAT IS WHAT YOU CHOOSE.

COME NOW AND TAKE A WALK WITH ME, WE CAN GO TO THE FOREST, THE OCEAN, OR YOUR MOST FAVORITE PLACE IN THE WHOLE OF THE UNIVERSE. YOU DECIDE AND WE WILL GO THERE. JUST BREATHING IN THE FRESH AIR, NOTIC-

ING NOW WHAT IS AROUND YOU AND HOW YOU ARE FEELING. ALLOWING YOUR BODY NOW TO TAKE IN THE CALMNESS AND BEAUTY OF THIS P LACE. CAN WE FIND A PLACE TO SIT AND ENJOY WHAT IS AROUND US?

ARE YOU FEELING CALM AND SMOOTH NOW? HAS YOUR BODY SLOWED DOWN? ARE YOU BREATHING EASIER NOW? LET US JUST SIT HERE AND ENJOY THE BEAUTY AND QUIET OF THIS PLACE.

Now that you are quiet and fully present here with me, there are some questions you have been asking me. Let me TALK with you about all of those questions. Just stay right here with me hearing what I am sharing with you. Take the time now to process what I have shared with you. Once you have finished return to the container and decide what you would like to leave in the container and what you would like to take back with you. REMEMBERING NOW THAT THIS IS YOUR CHOICE. IT IS NOT NECESSARY TO LIVE IN CHAOS, CONFUSION, AND WORRY.

ONCE YOU HAVE MADE YOUR DECISION RETURN TO THIS LETTER AND THIS DAY. Many times in the coming weeks and months you will need to take the time to come back to this letter and this time, we spent together. Giving yourself the time and space to receive the answers you have been looking for. Giving yourself a few moments to leave your world behind and allow yourself to slow down and take a breath.

Of course, there are thousands of us here on this side waiting to walk and talk with you. Know that we are loving you, each and everyone. I am holding you most dearly in my heart.

Know you only need call my name and I will be there.
In Love, Mother Mary
7/6/11

LETTER 155

Dear Ones,

Let us today talk about control and your assumption that you are in control. For many beings of earth, it is an urgent need to believe they are in control of everything in their lives. Some beings only need to control a small section of their lives and then there are others who find it necessary to be in complete control. Those beings that go to the extreme with control are even trying to control the other beings that are part of their lives.

Your thoughts of being in control are a huge fabrication on your part. There is so much in your world that you are totally unable to control. It is an untruth to think that you are really ever in control. Your world is not designed for you, the individual to be in control; it is designed for just the very few who are in charge of the worlds monies to be in control. This control is something designed by a few men of your world many centuries ago, when greed and selfishness first showed its face in your 3D world.

Yes, I am aware these are not comfortable thoughts to put in your minds or for you to think about at all. It is most important for each of you to gain a better understanding of these false hoods associated with control. It is most difficult for many of you to trust those of us here on my side for very few of you can see us or hear us. Your belief in us is based on FAITH. It is based on an inner knowing that there is something more than yourselves.

For those of you who have the inner knowing and faith to believe in us, we want you to know that we are honored and humbled by each of you. In your knowing and faith you are beginning to let go of your control and the false believe in that control. The opposite of control is trust. Trust in yourselves, trust in your fellow beings, and most of all trust in us here on this side.

In your 3D world there has been little room for trust in anyone or anything. Greed and selfishness destroys and eliminates trust. Many beings of your world find themselves either joining in the games of greed and selfishness or turning to isolation and separateness as a way to protect themselves. Neither of those ways are helpful to your personal growth or Mother Earth.

Now is the time on your Mother Earth when greed, selfishness, isolation, and separation have to be eliminated and let go of. This is your time of coming together and joining hearts and hands so that all beings of earth can learn to live in the ways of love and trust. We here are asking you for your complete trust. We are knowing that for many this will seem almost impossible. We say to you that this is not something you will do in one day, one week, one month, or one year. This is the direction that you need to be working towards. It is to be taken in small steps, learning to trust us in small ways and working towards larger ways.

For those of you who are already in the trusting mode, we say to you it is time to step it up a notch. If you are worrying about yesterday or today, then you have forgotten about trusting us. If worry is part of your lifestyle then it is time to let that go. REMEMBERING NOW THAT WORRY IS TRULY A BIG PART OF THE 3D WORLD AND WILL NOT BE TRAVELING WITH YOU INTO THE 5D WORLD.

We are here waiting to talk with you about control, trust, limits, greed, selfishness, and your own personal pathway into the 5D world. REMEMBERING NOW THAT YOU ARE NOT ON THIS JOURNEY BY YOURSELF, NOR HAVE YOU EVER BEEN BY YOURSELF. WE ARE HERE LOVING AND TRUSTING YOU WHETHER OR NOT YOU ARE LOVING AND TRUSTING US. I AM YOU HOLDING DEARLY IN MY HEART AND I AM LOVING YOU WITH ALL MY HEART.

Know you only need call my name and I will be there.
In Love, Mother Mary
7/11/11

LETTER 156

Dear Ones,

Today let us talk about you and the beauty of who you are. Yes, I know that your thoughts of yourselves are not the same as mine. When you look in the mirror and see yourself, you do not see who you truly are. Your face is covered with the masks of the things you have done or not done. There are masks of other peoples expectations of who you should be and your expectations of yourself.

To truly see yourself, you must be willing to let go of all the masks. For the masks are not who you truly are. The truth of your being is hidden behind the masks. The masks are from the past and have no place in your world today and will never have a place in the 5D world. It can be scary to let go of the masks and see the truth of yourself. For most of you, in your minds, you are not thinking in terms of beauty and open-heartedness; you will be thinking just the opposite.

Each and every one of you is reaching towards becoming open-minded, openhearted, courageous, and determined to be more than you believe you are. You are so much more than you believe. I can say a hundred thousand words to you today trying to convince you of the truth of yourselves. I am thinking that at the end of the words that you will not believe me. SO I AM ASKING YOU TODAY WHAT WILL IT TAKE FOR YOU TO BELIEVE ME? WHAT WILL IT TAKE FOR YOU TO SEE THE TRUTH OF WHO YOU ARE? WHAT WORDS OF LOVE AND ENCOURAGEMENT ARE YOU WAITING TO HEAR?

SO TODAY I AM ASKING YOU TO TAKE ME ON A JOURNEY. TAKE MY HAND AND LEAD ME TO YOUR FAVORITE PLACE. TAKE ME WHERE YOU FEEL SAFE. SHOW ME THE WORLD THAT YOU DREAM ABOUT. I WOULD ASK THAT YOU BRING ONE THING WITH US ON THIS JOURNEY. I ASK FOR A LARGE MIRROR THAT WE BOTH MAY LOOK INTO AT THE SAME TIME.

I WANT YOU TO SHOW ME WHO YOU BELIEVE YOU ARE AND WHY YOU ARE WEARING THOSE MASKS. WHAT DO THEY MEAN AND HOW DID THEY GET THERE? DID YOU PUT THEM

THERE OR DID SOMEONE ELSE'S WORDS PUT THEM THERE?

I AM HEARING YOUR WORDS AND UNDERSTANDING WHAT YOU ARE TELLING ME. NOW I WANT YOU TO SEE AND HEAR WHAT YOU HAVE TOLD ME FROM MY EYES AND EARS. It is not the same picture is it? Are you now able to see these things from a different perspective? ARE YOU SEEING YOURSELF DIFFERENTLY NOW? Are you seeing the world differently right now?

LETTING GO OF OLD THOUGHTS AND PERCEPTIONS IS VITAL TO BEING ABLE TO SEE THE TRUTH. THE TRUTH IS WHAT WE ARE LOOKING FOR. NOW I WILL SHARE WITH YOU WHAT I SEE WHEN I LOOK AT YOU. I ASK THAT YOU KEEP YOUR EARS, HEART, AND EYES OPEN SO THAT YOU MAY HEAR MY WORDS. CAN YOU SEE THE TRUTH OF WHAT I AM SHARING WITH YOU?

Take the time now to take in and process all you have learned about yourself today. When you are ready come back to this day and this letter. There was much to let go of today and much to take in. AS YOU LOOK IN THE MIRROR NOW TELL ME WHAT YOU ARE SEEING AND I WILL TELL YOU WHAT I AM SEEING.

I AM AMAZED AT THE BEAUTY OF WHO YOU ARE. YOUR STRENGTH AND COURAGE IS BEYOND BELIEF. YOU HAVE EACH WALKED SO MANY MILES TO ARRIVE AT THIS POINT IN YOUR JOURNEY. I AM HONORED AND HUMBLED TO BE YOUR WITNESS AND HELPER AS YOU CONTINUE ON YOUR JOURNEY. EVERYONE HERE ON THIS SIDE IS HONORED AND GRATEFUL TO BE OF SERVICE TO YOU. YOU EACH HAVE ANSWERED A CALL FROM THE UNIVERSE TO COME FORWARD AND PLAY A PART IN ALL THAT IS TAKING PLACE HERE ON YOUR MOTHER EARTH.

REMEMBERING ALWAYS THAT I AM LOVING YOU AND WALKING RIGHT HERE BESIDE YOU.

Know you only need call my name and I will be there.
In Love, Mother Mary
7/14/11

LETTER 157

Dear Ones,

Today I want to reassure you that everything is exactly as it was meant to be. You are wondering how I could say that when you look at your country, your Mother Earth, and the whole of the universe. Even when you are looking out into the whole of the universe, you are using only that very small amount of information that pertains to you. You have no knowledge of the whole grand picture of everything.

There is no wrong or harm in that. There has been no way for you to collect or know more information than what you do. That is why I am wanting to reassure you that all is going as planned. ALL IS WELL. There are a very few people there on your Mother Earth who have been given information about the coming times of your world. There are many people who are claiming that they have the knowledge of what is to be and how it is to come about.

In the next weeks and months, you will find that many of these people will be falling away, and their voices will not be heard again for they are doing great harm, causing more confusion and chaos for those who are listening to them. It is not their intention to cause confusion or chaos. It is their belief that they are being helpful, but the information they are passing along is for their journey only. There is no need for this chaos and confusion. Is not this process that you each are going through not confusing and chaotic enough without any outside help? So if you are listening to many voices about all that is happening in your world, I will say to you "LISTEN TO YOUR INNER VOICE." Listen to those beings from my side that are working very hard to help and guide you through this process. It is most important for each of you to recognize that you have great stores of knowledge and understanding inside yourselves. You each are wise beyond what you can imagine. Once the voices from outside of you have been silenced then you will be better able to hear your own wisdom and knowledge and much of the confusion and chaos will evaporate.

Of course, I am speaking of TRUSTING yourself over others. You have the most knowing of what is right for you and what it is that you need to do in every moment of everyday. I can hear screams of NO that is not so, how could I know more than "whatever their name might be." I AM TELLING YOU MOST LOUDLY THAT YOU KNOW INSIDE OF YOURSELVES EXACTLY, WHAT YOU NEED TO DO AND HOW YOU NEED TO DO IT.

REMEMBERING THAT EACH OF YOU WAS CALLED AND EACH OF YOU VOLUNTEERED TO BE A PART OF THIS PROCESS. EACH OF YOU WERE GIVEN THE KNOWLEDGE AND THE KNOW HOW TO MAKE THIS JOURNEY. IT IS TIME TO ACCESS THAT KNOWLEDGE. Are you saying right now, how do I do that? You do that by listening to your inner voice and by listening to the helpers from this side that you each have. If you are thinking, you do not have helpers that work with you, then I will say, close your eyes and open your mind and allow yourselves to really see. No, they will not appear as if they were a person from your world. They will appear as an unexpected flash or a speck of light, or a gentle breeze where none should be. With your mind open and accepting of the unknown you will finally be able to see what has been there all the time.

REMEMBERING NOW THAT WE ARE RIGHT HERE. CALL ON US AND WE WILL SHOW EACH OF YOU HOW TO LISTEN TO YOUR INNER VOICE AND HOW TO SEE WHAT YOU HAVE NOT SEEN BEFORE. YOU EACH HAVE THE KNOWLEDGE AND WISDOM TO ACCOMPLISH ALL THAT YOU ARE STRIVING FOR. I AM SAYING TO YOU ONCE AGAIN THAT I LOVE YOU, I LOVE YOU, AND I LOVE YOU.

Know you only need call my name and I will be there.
In Love, Mother Mary
7/16/11

LETTER 158
CHANGES

Dear Ones,

Over the last months, we have often talked of change. Changes in the whole of the world and personal changes to come as you each prepare for the 5D world. For many of the beings of your world change is difficult and much time is spent fighting the change and what it might mean. Fear steps in and all that is to change gets stopped and held away. The fear becomes like a solid wall that you can encase yourself in. YOU ARE STUCK UNABLE TO GO FORWARD OR BACKWARDS.

Resistance causes physical discomfort, emotional pain, and spiritual chaos. Beings end up not knowing which way to turn or go. CONFUSION AND CHAOS REIGN. There is not one being on your planet that has not experienced this in some way during their lifetime or even in the last few days. CHANGE IS IN THE AIR. So if you are reading my letter and your body starts jerking around, butterflies appear in your stomach, and you want to stop reading, then you can know for sure that change is in the air.

IT IS TIME TO LET GO OF YOUR RESISTANCE AND ALLOW YOURSELF THE FREEDOM TO BE. THE UNIVERSE, MOTHER EARTH, AND EVERY LIVING BREATHING LIFE FORM IS WAITING FOR YOU JOIN THEM IN THE FLOW OF ALL THAT IS COMING. NOW IS THE TIME TO JOIN THE PARTY.

Now is the time to tell of a change that is happening with "LETTERS FROM MOTHER MARY." This letter will be the last letter in this form that Barbara and I have been using. There may be special letters that come out on occasion, but there will be no more daily or weekly letters for now. Barbara and I will still be offering personal letters for anyone who would like one.

At this time, I am asking Barbara to take my letters and have them published in a book. The name of the book will be "THE LIVING LETTERS OF MOTHER MARY." The key word here is LIVING. The Letters were never meant to be read for one day and then put away. The Letters are filled with love for each and ever being of the universe. They are alive, moving, and flowing with energy from my world to yours.

The Letters were always meant to go into book form. So that is what I am asking Barbara to do at this time. Does she know how to do this? NO, she does not have a clue, but just as she did not know about blogs back in the beginning, she will learn. I would ask if there is anyone who is reading my letters who has knowledge or tips about this to pass them along to her. There will be costs incurred with publishing this book that Barbara will not be able to handle on her own, so anyone who wants to help in that way, please pass that along to her also.

In the days, weeks, and months ahead know that The Letters will be here on the blog. The Letters are all archived so that you can go each day and pick out a new one at random and find loving answers to your questions. As you pick your random letter, you will be surprised at how that particular letter fits exactly for what you need to see and hear that day.

I AM SPEAKING MOST LOUDLY TO EACH OF YOU RIGHT NOW. I AM NOT GOING AWAY. I WILL ALWAYS BE RIGHT HERE WITH EACH AND EVERY ONE OF YOU. I AM STILL LOVING EACH AND EVERY ONE OF YOU GREATLY. INDEED, YOU ARE LIVING IN MY HEART AND WILL ALWAYS LIVE IN MY HEART. THERE ARE THOUSANDS OF HELPERS HERE STANDING BESIDE ME AND WE ARE ALL WAITING TO HELP YOU IN ANY WAY WE CAN.

I WANT TO STRESS AGAIN THAT I AM NOT GOING AWAY. ALL YOU NEED TO DO IS CALL MY NAME AND I WILL BE THERE. GO TO MY LETTERS AND YOU WILL FEEL ME. REMEMBERING NOW THAT THE LETTERS ARE ALIVE, MOVING, AND FLOWING WITH ENERGY FROM ME. I LOVE YOU, I LOVE YOU, AND I LOVE YOU.

Know you only need call my name and I will be there.
In Love, Mother Mary
7/20/11

LETTER 159
"LIVE ON KICKSTARTER"

Dear Ones,

I have missed speaking to you and now we once again get to be in touch. I have never really been gone of course; all you had to do was call my name. I have been watching and sending you each love and support over the last two months. Yes, I know that these past two months have been very strong and intense.

Your lives have speeded up until you can hardly remember where you have been or what you had for breakfast this morning and it is just now lunchtime. I wish that I could tell you that all will be slowing down. The truth is it will stay at this speed for sometime. I know there are times when you think you can hardly keep going. My words to you are to just keep breathing, doing conscious breathing. Conscious breathing is a process of just focusing on your breath and slowly breathing in and out. Continue this process for about one minute you will find your world has once again righted itself. All will seem slower and more contained.

I want to let you know that today my book project has gone live on Kickstarter. This is what Barbara is calling it "Live on Kickstarter." Her words make me giggle and I think I will be doing a song and dance on their stage. There is no song and dance but I will be talking to you through Barbara. This was the first time I talked through her to a group of people. Meaning all of you. As I say in the video, it will not be the last. Please visit my project on Kickstarter and help me to get my book published. Here is the link so that you can find your way there.

Kickstarter is a website that allows people to post their projects of creativity in their efforts to raise funds to make their dreams come true. Visitors come to the website and donate money to help that happen. For donating to a project the backers, as they are called, will receive rewards for doing so. Come and see what kind of goodies you can get for being a backer, besides my deepest thanks and humble gratitude.

Please know and remember that I am always right here with you and that there are thousands of others here with me waiting to help each of you.

YOU ARE SO GREATLY LOVED AND CHERISHED. I LOVE YOU, I LOVE YOU, AND I LOVE YOU.

Know you only need call my name and I will be there.
In Love, Mother Mary
9/29/11

THE FOLLOWING PAGES ARE FROM MOTHER MARY'S KICKSTARTER PROJECT.

A Book Called "The Living Letters of Mother Mary."
A Writing & Publishing project in Seaside, OR by Barbara Beach.
The video from Mother Mary's project is now available on You Tube.

MOTHER MARY'S PROJECT

The Living Letters of Mother Mary

Dear Ones,

Let me tell you about my project. Over the past twelve months, I have channeled 159 letters to Barbara. These letters are tools for each of you to use in making your way through all the changes that are happening in your world. You will find many words of comfort, hope, love, support, and encouragement in these letters.

As you are all aware in some level of your thinking, your world is changing very rapidly. Is it not overwhelming and confusing trying to figure out what to do and which way to go?

This is the reason for my project. I want the book published and in your hands. The book will be a daily guide for each of you. In your morning quiet or afternoon craziness simply pick up the book and flip through the pages until it feels right to stop. As you read my letter open your hearts and minds to take in all that I am offering you. I LOVE YOU, I LOVE YOU, AND I LOVE YOU.

Know you only need call my name and I will be there.
In Love, Mother Mary
9/29/11

MOTHER MARY'S PROJECT

OUR NEXT STEP

The Letters have been channeled and put to paper. The publisher has been found. The cover of the book has appeared. Barbara and I have one thing left to do. We need to raise the funds to pay the publisher and have the book printed. We need your help to do this. So right now today I am asking you to step forward and help us take this book to print. Mill City Press is our publisher of choice. For publishing, printing, and marketing we will need to pay them $5,300.00. Amazon merchant fees of 3 to 5%, rewards, video, Kickstarter, and use of artwork comes to $3,000.00. Kickstarter team earns 5% of whatever is pledged, well earned! Thank you for allowing this project on your website. So when it is all added up, we will need $8,300.00 to fund this project and get this book published. PLEASE GIVE US YOUR SUPPORT AND ALLOW US TO ADD YOUR NAME TO THE APPRECIATION AND GRATITUDE PAGE OF MY BOOK. THANK YOU, THANK YOU, AND THANK YOU FOR YOUR SUPPORT.

HOW IT ALL GOT STARTED
According to Barbara:

In September of 2010, I scheduled a reading with Peggy Black and Her Team from www.morningmessages.com. During my reading Mother Mary came through Peggy and asked if I would be willing to be her Scribe. She asked that her writings be called "Letters From Mother Mary." Out loud I was saying yes, I would do that and inside, I was saying no way. On October 1st of 2010 I sat down at my computer and said out loud "all right Mother Mary, I will do The Letters but I don't have a clue how to do this."

All of a sudden, words were coming into my head and I knew they were not mine. I started typing and the first letter was born. While typing the letter "I was saying ok, I will do this, but I am not showing it to anyone." Within a few days, I found myself showing the letter to a friend, then two more friends, and then a whole group of friends. Then I went to emailing her letters to a group of friends. Those same friends started emailing The

Letters to their friends. After about a month of emailing her letters out, she asked me to put her letters on the Internet. I was thinking website and wondering where the money would come from to do this.

Friends started telling me about doing a blog. I had never heard of a blog before, let alone trying to figure out how to set one up and get her letters posted. To make a long story a little shorter, I did indeed figure out about blogging and how to get her letters up and posted. By February of 2011 we not only were posting her letters to the blog; I was also making a recording of each letter so viewers could hear the words or read the words.

We continued that way until near the end of July of this year when Mother Mary asked me to take The Letters and publish a book. Well, that is a whole other adventure and this brings you up to date and now you know why we are here on Kickstarter with Mother Mary's project. Let me add some final words...I am proud and honored to be her Scribe. I am so grateful she allowed me time to work through all the fear that this whole adventure brought up for me. Please offer us your support by becoming a backer of her project.

Thank you so much.
Barbara Beach, Scribe

THE FINAL WORDS OF MY BOOK.

I am loving you and holding you most dearly in my heart.
I Love You, I Love You, and I Love you.

In Love, Mother Mary

ABOUT THE SCRIBE

Barbara is a native Oregonian, born and raised in the Portland area. Ten years ago, she fulfilled one of her dreams and moved to the North Oregon Coast. Barbara's love of the ocean comes from happy memories of being at the beach with her Mom and her sister Wanda during her childhood. She lives there now with her dog Mollie and her cat Smokey Bear lovingly known as Smokey Bad Boy.

Barbara is a non-denominational minister who enjoys performing wedding ceremonies in the open-air standing near the ocean. She is also a Reiki Master and has been involved in energy healing for the last thirty years. Barbara has been channeling for many years, but only upon request from close friends or family. She came out of the closet when Mother Mary knocked on the door and asked her to step out and be her scribe.

Mother Mary and Barbara are offering personal letters or channeled readings to everyone. Please email Barbara with any questions or to make an appointment (barbara@thelivingllettersofmothermary.com). We would love to hear from you.